ork Library

C

D0065887

DATE DUE

AMERICAN

POLITICAL

PLAYS

American
Political
Plays

AN ANTHOLOGY

Edited by Allan Havis

UNIVERSITY OF

ILLINOIS PRESS

Urbana and Chicago

Library of Congress
Cataloging-in-Publication Data

American political plays :
an anthology / edited by Allan Havis.
p.   cm.
Includes bibliographical references (p.   )
and index.
ISBN 0-252-02694-2 (cloth : acid-free paper)
ISBN 0-252-07000-3 (paper : acid-free paper)
1. Political plays, American. I. Havis, Allan.
PS627.P65A44   2001
812'.54080358—dc21   2001001488

To Richard Gilman

and in memory of

William Foeller,

dear friend and

collaborator

Contents

Acknowledgments

Thanks are extended to Julia Fulton, Ellen Schiff, Laura Henry, OyamO, Susan Yankowitz, Aishah Rahman, William Hoffman, Christopher Gould, Jody McAuliffe, Kathy Sova, Richard L. Wentworth, Theresa L. Sears, Michelle Volanski, the Theatre Communication Group, and Broadway Play Publishing. Grateful acknowledgment is also made of a generous research grant from the University of California at San Diego.

Introduction

The maddening endeavor to select highly unusual and significant key plays to represent an American decade's political portrait was facilitated by the discovery of this collection of sly, remarkable scripts that deserve wider recognition in the theater and the classroom. Let it be stated at once that there is no single national topic or issue that neatly frames this anthology. Rather, this volume typifies an eclectic web of social thought and imagination that are uniquely American. Some of these plays explore critical urban, racial, and sexual questions, while others focus on American international problems of privilege, moral freedom, military postures, and xenophobia. Clearly, the 1990s was a defining decade of unquestionable American economic power set against the amazing collapse of the Iron Curtain and the implosion of the former Soviet Union. It was a decade of memorable social and symbolic shifts as major corporations, universities, and state governments began to allow health benefits to nonmarried partners of either sex. For America and the industrialized world, the 1990s was loudly the decade of the personal computer, the Internet, and the ticking bomb called Y2K. It was also the decade of curious biotech hopes and fears as a sheep named Daisy was cloned successfully just across the Atlantic Ocean while an entrepreneur-pornographer named Ron Harris caught world headlines with his daring, fashion models' "auction egg" Internet site. It was the decade of Bill and Hillary and Monica, of Viagra and Bob Dole, of ubiquitous tabloid television, and of a dying National Endowment for the Arts. It was the decade when Blockbuster Video became more influential than both the Public Broadcasting Service and any remaining serious theater on Broadway. Just the kind of decade that Bill Clinton and others could declare "a bridge to America's promising twenty-first century."

To shed proper light on the matter, we must think back to the mid-1980s, when so many prominent funding agencies and playwriting awards encouraged regional theaters to gamble on new writing for their main stage or smaller second-stage arenas: the Rockefeller Fellowship, the Foundation of Dramatists Guild/CBS Award, NEA fellowships, the Kennedy Center/American Express New Play Fund, HBO's Playwright USA Award, and so on. Regrettably, these grants and awards frequently reflected the political and idiosyncratic tastes of those who held the purse strings. Given the rapidly shrinking foundation dollars and far fewer risky, second-stage venues, most nonprofit theaters reduced their box office losses by scheduling material that was least likely to offend their subscribers. "Least offensive" translated into "nonpolitical," which is often the case. Moreover, only a handful of newspaper and magazine critics tossed off an obituary to political drama. Perhaps the problem is best expressed in terms of 1980s Reagonomics: namely, nonprofit theaters had to sell enough tickets to survive. Neither the private sector nor any government agency was willing to wipe away the red ink—in stark contrast to the visible government largesse of so many European countries and cities when it comes to performing arts groups and individual artists.

Needless to say, money and popularity serve as fundamental factors to the dilemma. If one can accept the fact that political plays are harder to sell to the public, then why write or produce political plays? And regardless of commercial viability, what exactly is an American political play? Is the definition something horribly elusive or one that holds certain objective properties? Does such an American play illustrate the positioning of public power and privilege against the prevailing status quo? Does it succumb to a classic Hegelian truth that the conflict between personal freedom and community rights best illustrates a politically dramatic event on stage? One of Hegel's famous examples was Antigone's bold defiance against the city-state of Thebes and her ruling uncle Creon to bury her brother. For Hegel, Sophocles' *Antigone* proved to be an extremely political and vexing story.

Political theater enables us to see our moral choices, our mixed aspirations, and our difficult upsets. America's dramatic rite of passage after World War II singularly marked our maturing, problematic stature and new place among leading nations. Acquiring superpower status thoroughly erased our age of innocence and—perhaps more damaging—our young country's insurance policy for bad behavior on the world stage. Conversely, our profound trauma during and after the Vietnam War heralded a new chapter of confusion, culpability, and contrition. In the midst of the civil rights and antiwar movements, a vibrant generation of Protest Art arose that helped to dethrone Lyndon Johnson. Ironically and despite their energetic efforts, the same rebellious factions witnessed a resurrected Richard Nixon in 1968, followed by Watergate and growing cynical journalism from the Fourth Estate.

As the 1990s concluded, one wanted to say, "These are days of heady editorial issues." Or shout, "These are days of hysterical public debate!" Truly, what are we supposed to make of Bill Clinton's "Don't ask, don't tell" reform for the armed forces? Is it a cruel blending of Lewis Carroll and Franz Kafka? What are we supposed to make of the twenty-year explosion of issues-related "talk radio" and Don Imus? Perhaps our most popular performing arts and media mirror our coarse, daily struggles while burying a more genuine and profound hue and cry? Indeed, respected network television national news programs more and more resemble the embarrassing tabloid broadcasts of "Inside Edition," "Hard Copy," and "Entertainment Tonight."

Ideally, each generation's burning literary canon awakens us to our societal burdens, our unmistakable prejudices, and our uncomfortable human paradoxes. But as another American century has come to a decisive close, can we say that we know ourselves to the bone? Do we yet know who we really are? Are we different from the myths of America? Who are we to the world? Does the world know us better than we know ourselves? I suspect that the plays included in this anthology will answer some of these questions.

There are impressive landmarks during the last sixty years of American political playwriting that give ample perspective to the works selected for this anthology. In lieu of a stage history, let me mention a few illustrious productions that come to mind. Plainly, Clifford Odets's *Waiting for Lefty* (1935) created an unforgettable, theatrical flash point on the heels of America's Great Depression. What a thrilling notion: a rather simple, undisguised one-act play that magically stirred up the working man's (and woman's) ire and widespread economic unrest during a crucial moment of trade unionism. Equally powerful in the late 1940s were the Arthur Miller plays *All My Sons* (1947) and *Death of a Salesman* (1949). Some critics would say that Miller's strongest political statement culminated with *The Crucible* (1953), a fiery play written in direct response to the shameful McCarthy era.

In the decade that followed, the landmark musical *Hair* (1967) celebrated the unbridled sexual revolution and drug-happy hippie life while attacking the Vietnam War. In that same outrageous decade far from Broadway, the Becks' radical Living Theatre ignited both Europe and the United States with its touring, chaotic, near-pornographic *Paradise Now* (1968)—a blustery concoction of antiwar and hedonistic furies. War-protest plays continued into the 1970s with such offerings as David Rabe's raging *Sticks and Bones* (1973).

The first AIDS plays came along a dozen years later: William Hoffman's sentimental *As Is* (1985) and Larry Kramer's polemic *The Normal Heart* (1985). The popular appeal of the two-term Reagan presidency and the revival of American conservatism may have helped to spark the potent political dramas of Maria Irene Fornes (*Conduct for Life*, 1985), Emily Mann (*Execution of Justice*, 1986), Wallace Shawn (*Aunt Dan and Lemon*, 1986), George Wolfe (*The Colored Museum*, 1986), Richard Nelson (*Principia Scriptoriae*, 1986), Wendy Wasserstein (*Heidi Chronicles*, 1988), and David Henry Hwang (*M. Butterfly*, 1989). Toward the end of the 1980s we were blessed with Tony Kushner's towering six-hour *Angels in America*, first seen in the modest

Eureka Theatre in San Francisco before it landed on Broadway a few years later via London's National Theatre.

It would be unthinkable to trace the course of political theater from the late 1960s to the present without mentioning the leading experimental groups that deemphasized the playwright to some degree: Joseph Chaikin's Open Theatre, Peter Schumann's Bread and Puppet Theatre, Richard Scheckner's Performance Group, Andre Gregory's Manhattan Project, Mabou Mines, the San Francisco Mime Troupe, and the Wooster Group.

Harold Clurman, the renowned founder of the 1930s activist Group Theatre, once declared that all outstanding plays are political, be they the private domestic sagas of Eugene O'Neill (*Long Day's Journey into Night*, 1940) and Tennessee Williams (*Glass Menagerie*, 1945) or the more declarative works of Elmer L. Rice (*Adding Machine*, 1923) and Herman Wouk (*The Caine Mutiny Court Martial*, 1953). But is it the audience's obligation to provide the larger social context when nothing within the narrative is politically overt? Certainly, Clurman's declaration begs the question of themes both explicit and implicit. Furthermore, his Group Theatre in part was an unabashed attempt to foster social and political change. But if the play's tale is quietly implicit of political thought, does the author's message have the commensurate power and controversy of more brash dramas? Was there a considerable risk personally or economically in staging the text? Finally, can an autobiographical dramatist ask blankly, Is my life someone's propaganda?

The seven plays included in this anthology are culturally, stylistically, and geographically diverse, yet all of them are, I believe, overtly political. Taken together, they manage to touch on the forceful and salient issues of the 1990s, including the Gulf War, racial and sexual relations, crises unique to big cities, immigration and multiculturalism, art and censorship, revisionist history, academic freedom, and the transformation of the American presidency. The playwrights' distinct, incisive voices are empowered by provocation and personally held beliefs. Their plays offer the reader a splendid, honest study of a rich society in search of itself.

In several public interviews, Suzan-Lori Parks, the author of *The American Play* (1993), has expressed her fascination for unchained musical forms in her elliptical creative process. Her improvisational jazz style allows her to depart from traditional dramatic structures, especially in the outrageous, idiosyncratic play included here. Parks sets her play in a great hole in the middle of nowhere, an exact replica of The Great Hole of History, and thereby subverts all notions of epic drama and historical pantheons. *The America Play* gives its audience an ersatz Lincoln in blackface who occupies a demented carnival attraction and a repetitive event not dissimilar to the archival Zapruder 8mm film playing endlessly on JFK's assassination. Such treatment neatly inverts the offensive minstrel show that features whites as blacks.

Parks's play is more an American meditation on a pivotal moment in time and race relations than a conventional story unfolding. In her Beckett-like world, spoken language (along with historical matter) is extremely slippery, inaccurate beyond measure and eternally flawed. *The America Play*'s short first act reconstructs John Wilkes Booth's infamous attack on a towering president; in its second act, the Lincoln impersonator's son and mother share a vast wasteland punctuated by a plain coffin. If this sardonic play had been written at the end of the 1960s, its dramatic statement might have struck the audience as a literal mourning for the Kennedys and Martin Luther King. Today, however, its puns and distillations maintain a healthy distance from any one event.

Velina Hasu Houston's *Kokoro* (1994) captures the stark predicament of a Japanese woman and mother caught between two impossible worlds. Rather in the manner of a Greek tragedy and Japanese Noh drama, one of the play's revelations concerns the horrible beauty and consequence of absolute personal choices. These are two women of opposite sensibilities: the immigrant Yasako Yamashita, who suffers immensely for her deeds, and her sophisticated, American, court-appointed attorney Angela Rossetti. Although there is a superficial parallel to the sensational 1994 Susan Smith infanticide case, Houston's play focuses on Yasako's subtle virtue and the spirituality of her sacrifice. From *Medea* to *Sophie's Choice*, the shadow mystery of a flawed motherhood defies easy analysis. One might want a happier ending for Yasako in light of her purity and abundant emotional underpinning. However, the political logic that governs the play's action has a less-hopeful inevitability. With the sentencing from California's Superior Court, we witness a more devastating punishment. *Kokoro* uses succinct words and precise silences to orchestrate a set of delicate compositions, the total effect of which is quite chilling.

Naomi Wallace's *In the Heart of America* (1994) grew naturally out of her poem "Kentucky Soldier in the Saudi Desert on the Eve of War." This enigmatic Gulf War tale jumps back and forth in time and locale, but its animus remains constant and knowable. The drama goes well beyond the familiar critique of a senseless war—"blood for oil"—by centering on Remzi, a Palestinian American from Atlanta who is caught up in George Bush Sr.'s New World Order. The irony is most apparent. As an Arab, Remzi is denigrated in the United States, yet he is expected to serve his country and kill Arabs in Iraq. With brutal clarity and wit, Wallace investigates the dire links between racism and homophobia inside a long-standing American institution. Was Operation Desert Storm a beneficial remedy for our paralyzing Vietnam Syndrome? The euphoric victory was all too brief, as Saddam Hussein outlasted his American adversary. The sympathetic realignment found within the play is one of the novel angles to Wallace's political perspective. Remzi's central relationship to a fellow American carries barbed, intimate flourishes of acceptance and denial. If Craver is the true survivor, what exactly in his moral residue?

When *Marisol* (1992) premiered at Louisville's Actors Theatre/Humana Festival, critics stood up and took notice of José Rivera's uncompromising, lyrical rendering of a wartorn New York. Etched in the disturbing ink of poetic paranoia, *Marisol* gives us an apocalyptic cityscape seen through the cross-hairs of battling angels and struggling innocents. In sharp contrast to Kushner's world of flying angels, Rivera's world offers a survivalist's sense of humor and exaggerated broad strokes of magical realism as it conveys the dark fairytale life of a young Latin woman named Marisol. Act 1 sets the groundwork for an uninhabitable urban neighborhood, only to lead to act 2's terrifying mise-en-scène. Indeed, there can never be enough locks on Marisol's front door to keep out the uninvited. Neither cautious optimism nor total despair decides the narrative's grand finale, but it is clear that Rivera maintains very critical, unbending views of an American society that cannot function honorably and of an American society that refuses to protect its oldest metropolis from a death sentence.

In *The Gift* (1996), I tackle the issue of academic freedom on college and university campuses. It may be debated well into the twenty-first century that academic freedom in the United States was brutally (or laughably) held hostage throughout the 1990s. One approach to that debate, for me, is to examine the blurring of academic freedom with compromising university politics. Rather than lining up on two sides of an ideological gymnasium, canny intellectuals require something greater than chic, polar reductions. *The Gift* offers several individuals maneuvering for high status and power at the expense of open and private ethics. I would be hard-pressed to declare any one character a hero or a villain, for the ensemble wrestles with an overwhelming moral ambiguity. For some on campus, as in life, survival is the highest good and vanquishing an enemy is the sweetest reward. As a comedy of ideas and inspired kitsch, *The Gift* pays wry homage to Dr. Seuss, Jacques Derrida, and liberal philanthropy. Along the way, it also tries to address how an estranged parent can return to a discarded child.

Russell Lees's *Nixon's Nixon* (1996) is, ostensibly, a comedy of failed careers. The irresistibly infamous, foul-mouthed Richard Nixon, the only American president to resign from office, cast a major shadow on the last third of the twentieth century and has proven to be a durable dramatic fixture, perhaps surprising even the greatest of his critics. Oliver Stone's *Nixon* projected a strained Shakespearean grandeur onto the silver screen, and the solemn, avant-garde opera *Nixon in China* by John Adams brought unexpected, empathic tones to the legend. Yet for sheer economy of expression and quick candor, there is nothing more cogent than *Nixon's Nixon*. Like the Adams opera, Lees's adroit script celebrates the fascinating, tortured Nixon/Kissinger relationship without sending it up for cabaret laughter. *Nixon's Nixon*, clocked on the eve of resignation, has exquisite and distilled fragments of Nixonspeak and his political cancer. The haunting Nixonian pathos in this two-character play fills each scene quite deceptively and provides a necessary denouement to our Vietnam horror.

By way of introduction to Mac Wellman's antic Washington farce, the indiscreetly titled *7 Blowjobs* (1991), it is helpful to recall the Swiftian congressional reaction to the scandalous Mapplethorpe and Serrano art exhibition of 1988 and the horrific vivisection of the National Endowment for the Arts at the hands of Senator Jesse "Mr. Tobacco" Helms and others. What followed in 1991 was strange, to say the least: a congressional resolution that released the much-maligned NEA from Helms's restrictive obscenity clause, whose purpose was to protect America's religious holiness and excrescence of decadence. Newspapers around the country titled the compromise "Corn for Porn" because western states had traded increased grazing rights for NEA liberties. What a splendid coda: years of ferocious fighting on both sides quickly ended over sensitive cattle needs. The inclusion of Wellman's wicked send-up rounds out this anthology with delightful brio and prankster sophistry worthy of Aristophanes.

Perhaps during the next ten years these plays will take on new, unexpected meaning and shed more light on the preceding millennium's close; perhaps they will mellow in the light cast by younger, more topical plays and become passionate time capsules of the issues that confronted the late twentieth century. In either case these playwrights will encourage re-reading and reward new interpretation. Like the best political writing, their voices challenge us to examine our own personal contract with society and the individual's place in the world. They remind us that the best debates always end, as the curtain falls, with the most haunting questions left among ourselves.

The
America
Play

SUZAN-LORI PARKS

In the beginning, all the world was America.

—*John Locke*

The America Play was commissioned and developed by the Theatre for a New Audience in New York City and workshopped in 1993 at the Arena Stage and Dallas Theatre Center. The world premiere on January 13, 1994, was coproduced by the Yale Repertory Theatre and the New York Shakespeare Festival in association with the Theatre for a New Audience, directed by Liz Diamond.

Cast of Characters

The Foundling Father, as Abraham Lincoln

A variety of visitors, played by the two actors who assume the roles in the passages from Our American Cousin *in act 2*

Lucy

Brazil

Two actors

Setting

A great hole. In the middle of nowhere. The hole is an exact replica of The Great Hole of History.

Production Note

Brackets in the text indicate optional cuts for production.

ACT 1: LINCOLN ACT

(*A great hole. In the middle of nowhere. The hole is an exact replica of The Great Hole of History.*)

The Foundling Father: "To stop too fearful and too faint to go."[1]

(*Rest*)

"He digged the hole and the whole held him."

(*Rest*)

"I cannot dig, to beg I am ashamed."[2]

(*Rest*)

"He went to the theater but home went she."[3]

(*Rest*)

Goatee. Goatee. What he sported when he died. Its not my favorite.

(*Rest*)

"He digged the hole and the whole held him." Huh.

(*Rest*)

There was once a man who was told that he bore a strong resemblance to Abraham Lincoln. He was tall and thinly built just like the Great Man. His legs were the longer part just like the Great Mans legs. His hands and feet were large as the Great Mans were large. The Lesser Known had several beards which he carried around in a box. The

---

1. An example of chiasmus, by Oliver Goldsmith, is cited in *Webster's Ninth New Collegiate Dictionary* (Springfield, Mass.: Merriam-Webster, 1983), s.v. "chiasmus." See also notes 2 and 3.

2. H. W. Fowler, *A Dictionary of Modern English Usage* (New York: Oxford University Press, 1983), s.v. "chiasmus."

3. *The New American Heritage Dictionary of the English Language* (Boston: Houghton Mifflin Co., 1981), s.v. "chiasmus."

beards were his although he himself had not grown them on his face but since he'd secretly bought the hairs from his barber and arranged their beard shapes and since the procurement and upkeep of his beards took so much work he figured that the beards were completely his. Were as authentic as he was, so to speak. His beard box was of cherry wood and lined with purple velvet. He had the initials "A.L." tooled in gold on the lid.

(*Rest*)

While the Great Mans livelihood kept him in Big Town the Lesser Knowns work kept him in Small Town. The Great Man by trade was a President. The Lesser Known was a Digger by trade. From a family of Diggers. Digged graves. He was known in Small Town to dig his graves quickly and neatly. This brought him a steady business.

(*Rest*)

A wink to Mr. Lincolns pasteboard cutout. (*Winks at Lincoln's pasteboard cutout*)

(*Rest*)

It would be helpful to our story if when the Great Man died in death he were to meet the Lesser Known. It would be helpful to our story if, say, the Lesser Known were summoned to Big Town by the Great Mans wife: "*Emergency* oh, *Emergency*, please put the Great Man in the ground"[4] (they say the Great Mans wife was given to hysterics: one young son dead others sickly: even the Great Man couldnt save them: a war on then off and surrendered to: "Play Dixie I always liked that song":[5] the brother against the brother: a new nation all conceived and ready to be hatched: the Great Man takes to guffawing guffawing at thin jokes in bad plays: "You sockdologizing old man-trap!"[6] haw haw haw because he wants so very badly to laugh at something and one moment guffawing and the next moment the Great Man is gunned down. In his rocker. "Useless Useless."[7] And there were bills to pay.) "*Emergency,* oh *Emergency* please put the Great Man in the ground."

(*Rest*)

---

4. Possibly the words of Mary Todd Lincoln after the death of her husband.

5. At the end of the Civil War, President Lincoln told his troops to play "Dixie," the song of the South, in tribute to the Confederacy.

6. A very funny line from the play *Our American Cousin*. As the audience roared with laughter, Booth entered Lincoln's box and shot him dead.

7. The last words of President Lincoln's assassin, John Wilkes Booth.

It is said that the Great Mans wife did call out and it is said that the Lesser Known would [sneak away from his digging and stand behind a tree where he couldnt be seen or get up and] leave his wife and child after the blessing had been said and [the meat carved during the distribution of the vegetables it is said that he would leave his wife and his child and] standing in the kitchen or sometimes out in the yard [behind the right angles of the house] stand out there where he couldnt be seen standing with his ear cocked. "*Emergency*, oh *Emergency*, please put the Great Man in the ground."

(*Rest*)

It would help if she had called out and if he had been summoned been given a ticket all bought and paid for and boarded a train in his look-alike black frock coat bought on time and already exhausted. Ridiculous. If he had been summoned. [Been summoned between the meat and the vegetables and boarded a train to Big Town where he would line up and gawk at the Great Mans corpse along with the rest of them.] But none of this was meant to be.

(*Rest*)

A nod to the bust of Mr. Lincoln. (*Nods to the bust of Lincoln*) But none of this was meant to be. For the Great Man had been murdered long before the Lesser Known had been born. Howuhboutthat. [So that any calling that had been done he couldnt hear, any summoning he had hoped for he couldnt answer but somehow not even unheard and unanswered because he hadnt even been there] although you should note that he talked about the murder and the mourning that followed as if he'd been called away on business at the time and because of the business had missed it. Living regretting he hadnt arrived sooner. Being told from birth practically that he and the Great Man were dead ringers, more or less, and knowing that he, if he had been in the slightest vicinity back then, would have had at least a chance at the great honor of digging the Great Mans grave.

(*Rest*)

This beard I wear for the holidays. I got shoes to match. Rarely wear em together. Its a little *much*.

(*Rest*)

[His son named in a fit of meanspirit after the bad joke about fancy nuts and old mens toes his son looked like a nobody. Not Mr. Lincoln or the father or the mother either for that matter although the father had assumed the superiority of his own blood and hadnt really expected the mother to exert any influence.]

(*Rest*)

Sunday. Always slow on Sunday. I'll get thuh shoes. Youll see. A wink to Mr. Lincolns pasteboard cutout. (*Winks at Lincoln's cutout*)

(*Rest*)

Everyone who has ever walked the earth has a shape around which their entire lives and their posterity shapes itself. The Great Man had his log cabin into which he was born, the distance between the cabin and Big Town multiplied by the half-life, the staying power of his words and image, being the true measurement of the Great Mans stature. The Lesser Known had a favorite hole. A chasm, really. Not a hole he had digged but one he'd visited. Long before the son was born. When he and his Lucy were newly wedded. Lucy kept secrets for the dead. And they figured what with his digging and her Confidence work they could build a mourning business. The son would be a weeper. Such a long time uhgo. So long uhgo. When he and his Lucy were newly wedded and looking for some postnuptial excitement: A Big Hole. A theme park. With historical parades. The size of the hole itself was enough to impress any Digger but it was the Historicity of the place the order and beauty of the pageants which marched by them the Greats on parade in front of them. From the sidelines he'd be calling "Ohwayohwhyohwayoh" and "Hello" and waving and saluting. The Hole and its Historicity and the part he played in it all gave a shape to the life and posterity of the Lesser Known that he could never shake.

(*Rest*)

Here they are. I wont put them on. I'll just hold them up. See. Too much. Told ya. [Much much later when the Lesser Known had made a name for himself he began to record his own movements. He hoped he'd be of interest to posterity. As in the Great Mans footsteps.]

(*Rest*)

Traveling home again from the honeymoon at the Big Hole riding the train with his wife beside him the Reconstructed Historicities he has witnessed continue to march before him in his minds eye as they had at the Hole. Cannon wicks were lit and the rockets did blare and the enemy was slain and lay stretched out and smoldering for dead and rose up again to take their bows. On the way home again the histories paraded again on past him although it wasnt on past him at all it wasnt something he could expect but again like Lincolns life not "on past" but *past. Behind him.* Like an echo in his head.

(*Rest*)

When he got home again he began to hear the summoning. At first they thought it only an echo. Memories sometimes stuck like that and he and his Lucy had both seen visions. But after a while it only called to him. And it became louder not softer but louder louder as if he were moving toward it.

(*Rest*)

This is my fancy beard. Yellow. Mr. Lincolns hair was dark so I dont wear it much. If you deviate too much they wont get their pleasure. Thats my experience. Some inconsistencies are perpetuatable because theyre good for business. But not the yellow beard. Its just my fancy. Ev-ery once and a while. Of course, his hair was dark.

(*Rest*)

The Lesser Known left his wife and child and went out West finally. [Between the meat and the vegetables. A monumentous journey. Enduring all the elements. Without a friend in the world. And the beasts of the forest took him in. He got there and he got his plot he staked his claim he tried his hand at his own Big Hole.] As it had been back East everywhere out West he went people remarked on his likeness to Lincoln. How, in a limited sort of way, taking into account of course his natural God-given limitations, how he was identical to the Great Man in gait and manner how his legs were long and torso short. The Lesser Known had by this time taken to wearing a false wart on his cheek in remembrance of the Great Mans wart. When the Westerners noted his wart they pronounced the two men in virtual twinship.

(*Rest*)

Goatee. Huh. Goatee.

(*Rest*)

"He digged the Hole and the Whole held him."

(*Rest*)

"I cannot dig, to beg I am ashamed."

(*Rest*)

The Lesser Known had under his belt a few of the Great Mans words and after a day of digging, in the evenings, would stand in his hole reciting. But the Lesser Known was a curiosity at best. None of those who spoke of his virtual twinship with greatness would actually pay money to watch him be that greatness. One day he tacked up posters inviting them to come and throw old food at him while he spoke. This was a moderate success. People began to save their old food "for Mr. Lincoln" they said. He took to traveling playing small towns. Made money. And when someone remarked that he played Lincoln so well that he ought to be shot, it was as if the Great Mans footsteps had been suddenly revealed:

(*Rest*)

The Lesser Known returned to his hole and, instead of speeching, his act would now consist of a single chair, a rocker, in a dark box. The public was invited to pay a penny, choose from the selection of provided pistols, enter the darkened box and "Shoot Mr. Lincoln." The Lesser Known became famous overnight.

(*A Man, as John Wilkes Booth, enters. He takes a gun and "stands in position": at the left side of The Foundling Father, as Abraham Lincoln, pointing the gun at The Foundling Father's head.*)

A Man: Ready.

The Foundling Father: Haw Haw Haw Haw

(*Rest*)

HAW HAW HAW HAW

(*Booth shoots. Lincoln "slumps in his chair." Booth jumps.*)

A Man (*Theatrically*): "Thus to the tyrants!"[8]

(*Rest*)

Hhhh. (*Exits*)

The Foundling Father: Most of them do that, thuh "Thus to the tyrants!"— what they say the killer said. "Thus to the tyrants!" The killer was also heard to say, "The South is avenged!"[9] Sometimes they yell that.

---

8. Or "Sic semper tyrannis," purportedly Booth's words after he slew Lincoln and leapt from the presidential box to the stage of Ford's Theatre in Washington, D.C., on April 14, 1865, not only killing the President but also interrupting a performance of *Our American Cousin*, starring Miss Laura Keene.

9. Allegedly Booth's words.

(*A Man, the same man as before, enters again, again as John Wilkes Booth. He takes a gun and "stands in position": at the left side of The Foundling Father, as Abraham Lincoln, pointing the gun at The Foundling Father's head.*)

A Man: Ready.

The Foundling Father: Haw Haw Haw Haw

(*Rest*)

HAW HAW HAW HAW

(*Booth shoots. Lincoln "slumps in his chair." Booth jumps.*)

A Man (*Theatrically*): "The South is avenged!"

(*Rest*)

Hhhh.

(*Rest*)

Thank you.

The Foundling Father: Pleasures mine.

A Man: Till next week.

The Foundling Father: Till next week.

(*A Man exits.*)

The Foundling Father: Comes once a week that one. Always chooses the Derringer although we've got several styles he always chooses the Derringer. Always "The tyrants" and then "The South avenged." The ones who choose the Derringer are the ones for History. He's one for History. As It Used To Be. Never wavers. No frills. By the book. Nothing excessive.

(*Rest*)

A nod to Mr. Lincolns bust. (*Nods to Lincoln's bust*)

(*Rest*)

I'll wear this one. He sported this style in the early war years. Years of uncertainty. When he didnt know if the war was right when it could be said he didnt always know which side he was on not because he was a stupid man but because it was sometimes not two different sides at all but one great side surging toward something beyond either Northern or Southern. A beard of uncertainty. The Lesser Known meanwhile living his life long after all this had happened and not knowing much about it until he was much older [(as a boy "The Civil War" was an afterschool game and his folks didnt mention the Great Mans murder for fear of frightening him)] knew only that he was a dead ringer in a family of Diggers and that he wanted to grow and have others think of him and remove their hats and touch their hearts and look up into the heavens and say something about the freeing of the slaves. That is, he wanted to make a great impression as he understood Mr. Lincoln to have made.

(Rest)

And so in his youth the Lesser Known familiarized himself with all aspects of the Great Mans existence. What interested the Lesser Known most was the murder and what was most captivating about the murder was the twenty feet—

(A Woman, as Booth, enters.)

A Woman: Excuse me.

The Foundling Father: Not at all.

(A Woman, as Booth, "stands in position.")

The Foundling Father: Haw Haw Haw Haw

(Rest)

HAW HAW HAW HAW

(Booth shoots. Lincoln "slumps in his chair." Booth jumps.)

A Woman: "Strike the tent."[10] (Exits)

The Foundling Father: What interested the Lesser Known most about the Great Mans murder was the twenty feet which separated the presidents box from the stage. In the presidents box sat the president his wife and their two friends. On the stage that night was *Our American Cousin* starring Miss Laura Keene. The plot of this play is of little consequence to our story. Suffice it to say that it was thinly comedic and somewhere in the third act a man holds a gun to his head—something about despair—

(Rest)

---

10. The last words of General Robert E. Lee, commander of the Confederate Army.

Ladies and Gentlemen: *Our American Cousin—*

(*B Woman, as Booth enters. She "stands in position."*)

B Woman: Go ahead.

The Foundling Father: Haw Haw Haw Haw

(*Rest*)

HAW HAW HAW HAW

(*Booth shoots. Lincoln "slumps in his chair." Booth jumps.*)

B Woman (*Rest*): LIES!

(*Rest*)

LIIIIIIIIIIIIIIIIIIIIIIIIIIIES!

(*Rest*)

LIIIIIIIIIIIIIIIIIIIIARRRRRRRRRRRRRRRRS!

(*Rest*)

Lies.

(*Rest. Exits. Re-enters. Steps downstage. Rest.*)

LIES!

(*Rest*)

LIIIIIIIIIIIIIIIIIIIIIIIIIIIIES!

(*Rest*)

LIIIIIIIIIIIIIIIIIIIIIARRRRRRRRRRRRRRRRS!

(*Rest*)

Lies.

(*Rest. Exits.*)

The Foundling Father (*Rest*): I think I'll wear the yellow beard. Variety. Works like uh tonic.

(*Rest*)

Some inaccuracies are good for business. Take the stovepipe hat! Never really worn indoors but people dont like their Lincoln hatless.

(*Rest*)

Mr. Lincoln my apologies. (*Nods to the bust and winks to the cutout*)

(*Rest*)

[Blonde. Not bad if you like a stretch. Hmmm. Let us pretend for a moment that our beloved Mr. Lincoln was a blonde. "The sun on his fair hair looked like the sun itself."[11] —. Now. What interested our Mr. Lesser Known most was those feet between where the Great *Blonde* Man sat, in his rocker, the stage, the time it took the murderer to cross that expanse, and how the murderer crossed it. He jumped. Broke his leg in the jumping. It was said that the Great Mans wife then began to scream. (She was given to hysterics several years afterward in fact declared insane did you know she ran around Big Town poor desperate for money trying to sell her clothing? On that sad night she begged her servant: "Bring in Taddy, Father will speak to Taddy."[12] But Father died instead unconscious. And she went mad from grief. Off her rocker. Mad Mary claims she hears her dead men. Summoning. The older son, Robert, he locked her up: "*Emergency*, oh, *Emergency* please put the Great Man in the ground.")

(*Enter B Man, as Booth. He "stands in position."*)

The Foundling Father: Haw Haw Haw Haw

(*Rest*)

HAW HAW HAW HAW

(*Booth shoots. Lincoln "slumps in his chair." Booth jumps.*)

B Man: "Now he belongs to the ages."[13]

(*Rest*)

Blonde?

The Foundling Father: (I only talk with the regulars.)

B Man: He wasnt blonde. (*Exits*)

The Foundling Father: A slight deafness in this ear other than that there are no side effects.

(*Rest*)

---

11. From "The Sun," an unpublished composition by The Foundling Father.
12. Mary Todd Lincoln, who wanted her dying husband to speak to their son Tad, might have said this that night.
13. The words of Secretary of War Edwin Stanton as Lincoln died.

Hhh. Clean-shaven for a while. The face needs air. Clean-shaven as in his youth. When he met his Mary. —. Hhh. Blonde.

(*Rest*)

Six feet under is a long way to go. Imagine. When the Lesser Known left to find his way out West he figured he had dug over seven hundred and twenty-three graves. Seven hundred and twenty-three. Excluding his Big Hole. Excluding the hundreds of shallow holes he later digs the hundreds of shallow holes he'll use to bury his faux-historical knickknacks when he finally quits this business. Not including those. Seven hundred and twenty-three graves.

(*C Man and C Woman enter.*)

C Man: You allow two at once?

The Foundling Father

(*Rest*)

C Woman: We're just married. You know: newlyweds. We hope you dont mind. Us both at once.

The Foundling Father

(*Rest*)

C Man: We're just married.

C Woman: Newlyweds.

The Foundling Father

(*Rest*)

(*They "stand in position." Both hold one gun.*)

C Man and **C Woman:** Shoot.

The Foundling Father: Haw Haw Haw Haw

(*Rest*)

HAW HAW HAW HAW

(*Rest*)

(*Rest*)

HAW HAW HAW HAW

(*They shoot. Lincoln "slumps in his chair." They jump.*)

C Man: Go on.

C Woman (*Theatrically*): "Theyve killed the president!"[14]

(*Rest. They exit.*)

The Foundling Father: Theyll have children and theyll bring their children here. A slight deafness in this ear other than that there are no side effects. Little ringing in the ears. Slight deafness. I cant complain.

(*Rest*)

The passage of time. The crossing of space. [The Lesser Known recorded his every movement.] He'd hoped he'd be of interest in his posterity. [Once again riding in the Great Mans footsteps.] A nod to the presidents bust.

(*Nod*)

(*Rest*)

The Great Man lived in the past that is was an inhabitant of time immemorial and the Lesser Known out West alive a resident of the present. And the Great Mans deeds had transpired during the life of the Great Man somewhere in past-land that is somewhere "back there" and all this while the Lesser Known digging his holes bearing the burden of his resemblance all the while trying somehow to equal the Great Man in stature, word and deed going forward with his lesser life trying somehow to follow in the Great Mans footsteps footsteps that were of course behind him. The Lesser Known trying somehow to catch up to the Great Man all this while and maybe running too fast in the wrong direction. Which is to say that maybe the Great Man had to catch him. Hhhh. Ridiculous.

(*Rest*)

Full fringe. The way he appears on the money.

(*Rest*)

A wink to Mr. Lincolns pasteboard cutout. A nod to Mr. Lincolns bust.

(*Rest. Time passes. Rest.*)

When someone remarked that he played Lincoln so well that he ought to be shot it was as if the Great Mans footsteps had been suddenly revealed: instead of making speeches his act would now consist of a single chair, a rocker, in a dark box. The public was cordially invited

---

14. The words of Mary Todd Lincoln, just after her husband was shot.

to pay a penny, choose from a selection of provided pistols enter the darkened box and "Shoot Mr. Lincoln." The Lesser Known became famous overnight.

(A Man, as John Wilkes Booth, enters. He takes a gun and "stands in position": at the left side of The Foundling Father, as Abraham Lincoln, pointing the gun at The Foundling Father's head.)

The Foundling Father: Mmm. Like clockwork.

A Man: Ready.

The Foundling Father: Haw Haw Haw Haw

(Rest)

HAW HAW HAW HAW

(Booth shoots. Lincoln "slumps in his chair." Booth jumps.)

A Man *(Theatrically)*: "Thus to the tyrants!"

(Rest)

Hhhh.

Lincoln

Booth

Lincoln

Booth

Lincoln

Booth

Lincoln

Booth

Lincoln

(Booth jumps.)

A Man *(Theatrically)*: "The South is avenged!"

(Rest)

Hhhh.

(Rest)

Thank you.

The Foundling Father: Pleasures mine.

A Man: Next week then. (*Exits*)

The Foundling Father: Little ringing in the ears. Slight deafness.

(*Rest*)

Little ringing in the ears.

(*Rest*)

A wink to the Great Mans cutout. A nod to the Great Mans bust. Once again striding in the Great Mans footsteps. Riding on in. Riding to the rescue the way they do. They both had such long legs. Such big feet. And the Greater Man had such a lead although of course somehow still "back there." If the Lesser Known had slowed down stopped moving completely gone in reverse died maybe the Greater Man could have caught up. Woulda had a chance. Woulda sneaked up behind him the Greater Man would have sneaked up behind the Lesser Known unbeknownst and wrestled him to the ground. Stabbed him in the back. In revenge. "Thus to the tyrants!" Shot him maybe. The Lesser Known forgets who he is and just crumples. His bones cannot be found. The Greater Man continues on.

(*Rest*)

"*Emergency,* oh *Emergency,* please put the Great Man in the ground."

(*Rest*)

Only a little ringing in the ears. Thats all. Slight deafness.

(*Rest*)

(*He puts on the blonde beard.*)

Huh. Whatdoyou say I wear the blonde.

(*Rest*)

(*A gunshot echoes. Softly. And echoes.*)

ACT 2: THE HALL OF WONDERS

(*A gunshot echoes. Loudly. And echoes.*

They are in a great hole. In the middle of nowhere. The hole is an exact replica of The Great Hole of History.

A gunshot echoes. Loudly. And echoes. Lucy with ear trumpet circulates. Brazil digs.)

SCENE 1: BIG BANG

Lucy: Hear that?

Brazil: Zit him?

Lucy: No.

Brazil: Oh.

(A gunshot echoes. Loudly. And echoes.)

Lucy: Hear?

Brazil: Zit him?!

Lucy: Nope. Ssuhecho.

Brazil: Ssuhecho.

Lucy: Uh echo uh huhn. Of gunplay. Once upon uh time somebody had uh little gunplay and now thuh gun goes on playing: KER-BANG! KERBANG-Kerbang-kerbang-(kerbang)-((kerbang)).

Brazil: Thuh echoes.

(Rest)

Lucy: Youre stopped.

Brazil: Mmlistenin.

Lucy: Dig on, Brazil. Cant stop diggin till you dig up somethin. Your Daddy was uh Digger.

Brazil: Uh huhnnn.

Lucy

Brazil

(A gunshot echoes. Loudly. And echoes. Rest. A gunshot echoes. Loudly. And echoes. Rest.)

[**Lucy:** Itssalways been important in my line to distinguish. Tuh know thuh difference. Not like your Fathuh. Your Fathuh became confused. His lonely death and lack of proper burial is our embarrassment. Go on: dig. Now me I need tuh know thuh real thing from thuh echo. Thuh truth from thuh hearsay.

(*Rest*)

Bram Price for example. His dear ones and relations told me his dying words but Bram Price hisself of course told me something quite different.

Brazil: I wept forim.

Lucy: Whispered his true secrets to me and to me uhlone.

Brazil: Then he died.

Lucy: Then he died.

(*Rest*)

Thuh things he told me I will never tell. Mr. Bram Price. Huh.

(*Rest*)

Dig on.

Brazil

Lucy

Brazil

Lucy: Little Bram Price Junior.

Brazil: Thuh fat one?

Lucy: Burned my eardrums. Just like his Dad did.

Brazil: I wailed forim.

Lucy: Ten days dead wept over and buried and that boy comes back. Not him though. His echo. Sits down tuh dinner and eats up everybodys food just like he did when he was livin.

(*Rest*)

(*Rest*)

Little Bram Junior. Burned my eardrums. Miz Penny Price his mother. Thuh things she told me I will never tell.

(*Rest*)

You remember her.

Brazil: Wore red velvet in August.

Lucy: When her two Brams passed she sold herself, son.

Brazil: O.

Lucy: Also lost her mind. —. She finally went. Like your Fathuh went, perhaps. Foul play.

Brazil: I gnashed for her.

Lucy: You did.

Brazil: Couldnt choose between wailin or gnashin. Weepin sobbin or moanin. Went for gnashing. More to it. Gnashed for her and hers like I have never gnashed. I woulda tore at my coat but thats extra. Chipped uh tooth. One in thuh front.

Lucy: You did your job son.

Brazil: I did my job.

Lucy: Confidence. Huh. Thuh things she told me I will never tell. Miz Penny Price. Miz Penny Price.

(*Rest*)

Youre stopped.

Brazil: Mmlistenin.

Lucy: Dig on, Brazil.

Brazil

Lucy

Brazil: We arent from these parts.

Lucy: No. We're not.

Brazil: Daddy iduhnt either.

Lucy: Your Daddy iduhnt either.

(*Rest*)

Dig on, son. —. Cant stop diggin till you dig up somethin. You dig that something up you brush that something off you give that something uh designated place. Its own place. Along with thuh other discoveries. In thuh Hall of Wonders. Uh place in the Hall of Wonders right uhlong with thuh rest of thuh Wonders hear?

Brazil: Uh huhn.

(*Rest*)

Lucy: Bram Price Senior, son. Bram Price Senior was not thuh man he claimed tuh be. Huh. Nope. Was not thuh man he claimed tuh be atall. You ever see him in his stocking feet? Or barefoot? Course not. I guessed before he told me. He told me then he died. He told me and I havent told no one. I'm uh good Confidence. As Confidences go. Huh. One of thuh best. As Confidence, mmonly contracted tuh keep quiet twelve years. After twelve years nobody cares. For nineteen years I have kept his secret. In my bosom.

(Rest)

He wore lifts in his shoes, son.

Brazil: Lifts?

Lucy: Lifts. Made him seem taller than he was.

Brazil: Bram Price Senior?

Lucy: Bram Price Senior wore lifts in his shoes yes he did, Brazil. I tell you just as he told me with his last breaths on his dying bed: "Lifts." Thats all he said. Then he died. I put thuh puzzle pieces in place. I put thuh puzzle pieces in place. Couldnt tell no one though. Not even your Pa. "Lifts." I never told no one son. For nineteen years I have kept Brams secret in my bosom. Youre thuh first tuh know. Hhh! Dig on. Dig on.

Brazil: Dig on.

Lucy

Brazil

Lucy

(A gunshot echoes. Loudly. And echoes.)

BRAZIL *(Rest)*: Ff Pa was here weud find his bones.

Lucy: Not always.

Brazil: Thereud be his bones and thereud be thuh Wonders surrounding his bones.

Lucy: Ive heard of different.

Brazil: Thereud be thuh Wonders surrounding his bones and thereud be his Whispers.

Lucy: Maybe.

Brazil: Ffhe sspast like they say he'd of parlayed to uh Confidence his last words and dying wishes. His secrets and his dreams.

Lucy: Thats how we pass back East. They could pass different out here.

Brazil: We got Daddys ways Daddyssgot ours. When there's no Confidence available we just dribble thuh words out. In uh whisper.

Lucy: Sometimes.

Brazil: Thuh Confidencell gather up thuh whispers when she arrives.

Lucy: Youre uh prize, Brazil. Uh prize.]

Brazil

Lucy

Brazil

Lucy

Brazil: You hear him then? His whispers?

Lucy: Not exactly.

Brazil: He wuduhnt here then.

Lucy: He was here.

Brazil: Ffyou dont hear his whispers he wuduhnt here.

Lucy: Whispers dont always come up right away. Takes time sometimes. Whispers could travel different out West than they do back East. Maybe slower. Maybe. Whispers are secrets and often shy. We aint seen your Pa in thirty years. That could be part of it. We also could be experiencing some sort of interference. Or some sort of technical difficulty. Ssard tuh tell.

(*Rest*)

So much to live for.

Brazil: So much to live for.

Lucy: Look on thuh bright side.

Brazil: Look on thuh bright side. Look on thuh bright side. Loook onnnnn thuhhhh briiiiiiiight siiiiiiiiide!!!!

Lucy: DIIIIIIIIIIIG!

Brazil: Dig.

Lucy

Brazil

Lucy: Helloooo! —. Hellooooo!

Brazil

Lucy

Brazil: We're from out East. We're not from these parts.

(*Rest*)

My foe-father, her husband, my Daddy, her mate, her man, my Pa come out here. Out West.

(*Rest*)

Come out here all uhlone. Cleared thuh path tamed thuh wilderness dug this whole Hole with his own two hands and et cetera.

(*Rest*)

Left his family behind. Back East. His Lucy and his child. He waved "Goodbye." Left us tuh carry on. I was only five.

(*Rest*)

My Daddy was uh Digger. She's whatcha call uh Confidence. I did thuh weepin and thuh moanin.

(*Rest*)

His lonely death and lack of proper burial is our embarrassment.

(*Rest*)

Diggin was his livelihood but fakin was his callin. Ssonly natural heud come out here and combine thuh two. Back East he was always diggin. He was uh natural. Could dig uh hole for uh body that passed like no one else. Digged em quick and they looked good too. This Hole here— this large one—sshis biggest venture to date. So says hearsay.

(*Rest*)

Uh exact replica of thuh Great Hole of History!

Lucy: Sshhhhhht.

Brazil (*Rest*): Thuh original ssback East. He and Lucy they honey-mooned there. At thuh original Great Hole. Its uh popular spot. He and Her would sit on thuh lip and watch everybody who was ever anybody parade on by. Daily parades! Just like thuh Tee Vee. Mr. George Washington, for example, thuh Fathuh of our Country hisself, would rise up from thuh dead and walk uhround and cross thuh Delaware and say stuff!! Right before their very eyes!!!!

Lucy: Son?

Brazil: Huh?

Lucy: That iduhnt how it went.

Brazil: Oh.

Lucy: Thuh Mr. Washington me and your Daddy seen was uh lookuh-like of thuh Mr. Washington of history-fame, son.

Brazil: Oh.

Lucy: Thuh original Mr. Washingtonssbeen long dead.

Brazil: O.

Lucy: That Hole back East was uh theme park son. Keep your story to scale.

Brazil: K.

(*Rest*)

Him and Her would sit by thuh lip uhlong with thuh others all in uh row cameras clickin and theyud look down into that Hole and see—ooooo—you name it. Ever-y-day you could look down that Hole and see—ooooo you name it. Amerigo Vespucci hisself made regular appearances. Marcus Garvey. Ferdinand and Isabella. Mary Queen of thuh Scots! Tarzan King of thuh Apes! Washington Jefferson Harding and Millard Fillmore. Mistufer Columbus even. Oh they saw all thuh greats. Parading daily in thuh Great Hole of History.

(*Rest*)

My Fathuh did thuh living and thuh dead. Small-town and big-time. Mr. Lincoln was of course his favorite.

(*Rest*)

Not only Mr. Lincoln but Mr. Lincolns last show. His last deeds. His last laughs.

(*Rest*)

Being uh Digger of some renown Daddy comes out here tuh build uh like attraction. So says hearsay. Figures there's people out here who'll enjoy amusements such as them amusements He and Her enjoyed. We're all citizens of one country afterall.

(*Rest*)

Mmrestin.

(*A gunshot echoes. Loudly. And echoes.*)

Brazil: Woooo! (*Drops dead*)

Lucy: Youre fakin Mr. Brazil.

Brazil: Uh uhnnn.

Lucy: Tryin tuh get you some benefits.

Brazil: Uh uhnnnnnnnn.

Lucy: I know me uh faker when I see one. Your Father was uh faker. Huh. One of thuh best. There wuduhnt nobody your Fathuh couldnt do. Did thuh living and thuh dead. Small-town and big-time. Made-up and historical. Fakin was your Daddys callin but diggin was his livelihood. Oh, back East he was always diggin. Was uh natural. Could dig uh hole for uh body that passed like no one else. Digged em quick and they looked good too. You dont remember of course you dont.

Brazil: I was only five.

Lucy: You were only five. When your Fathuh spoke he'd quote thuh Greats. Mister George Washington. Thuh Misters Roosevelt. Mister Millard Fillmore. Huh. All thuh greats. You dont remember of course you dont.

Brazil: I was only five—

Lucy: —only five. Mr. Lincoln was of course your Fathuhs favorite. Wuz. Huh. Wuz. Huh. Heresay says he's past. Your Daddy. Digged this hole then he died. So says hearsay.

(*Rest*)

Dig, Brazil.

Brazil: My paw—

Lucy: Ssonly natural that heud come out here tuh dig out one of his own. He loved that Great Hole so. He'd stand at thuh lip of that Great Hole: "OHWAYOHWHYOHWAYOH!"

Brazil: "OHWAYOHWHYOHWAYOH!"

Lucy: "OHWAYOHWHYOHWAYOH!" You know: hole talk. Ohwayohwhyohwayoh, just tuh get their attention, then: "Hellooo!" He'd shout down to em. Theyd call back "Hellllooooo!" and wave. He loved that Great Hole so. Came out here. Digged this lookuhlike.

Brazil: Then he died?

Lucy: Then he died. Your Daddy died right here. Huh. Oh, he was uh faker. Uh greaaaaat biiiiig faker too. He was your Fathuh. Thats thuh connection. You take after him.

Brazil: I do?

Lucy: Sure. Put your paw back where it belongs. Go on-back on its stump. —. Poke it on out of your sleeve son. There you go. I'll draw uh X for you. See? Heresuh X. Huh. Dig here.

(*Rest*)

DIG!

Brazil

Lucy

Brazil

Lucy: Woah! Woah!

Brazil: Whatchaheard?!

Lucy: No tellin, son. Cant say.

(*Brazil digs. Lucy circulates.*)

Brazil (*Rest. Rest.*): On thuh day he claimed to be the 100th anniversary of the founding of our country the Father took the Son out into the yard. The Father threw himself down in front of the Son and bit into the dirt with his teeth. His eyes leaked. "This is how youll make your mark, Son" the Father said. The Son was only two then. "This is the Wail," the Father said. "There's money init," the Father said. The Son was only two then. Quiet. On what he claimed was the 101st anniversary the Father showed the Son "the Weep" "the Sob" and "the Moan." How to stand just so what to do with the hands and feet (to capitalize on what we in the business call "the Mourning Moment"). Formal stances the Fatherd picked up at the History Hole. The Son studied night and day. By candlelight. No one could best him. The money came pouring in. On the 102nd anniversary[15] the Son was five and the Father taught him "the Gnash." The day after that the Father left for out West. To seek his fortune. In the middle of dinnertime. The Son was eating his peas.

Lucy

Brazil

Lucy

Brazil

Lucy: Hellooooo! Hellooooo!

(*Rest*)

Brazil

Lucy

Brazil: HO! (*Unearths something*)

Lucy: Whatcha got?

Brazil: Uh Wonder!

Lucy: Uh Wonder!

Brazil: Uh Wonder: Ho!

Lucy: Dust it off and put it over with thuh rest of thuh Wonders.

Brazil: Uh bust.

Lucy: Whose?

Brazil: Says "A. Lincoln." A. Lincolns bust. —. Abraham Lincolns bust!!!

Lucy: Howuhboutthat!

(*Rest*)

Woah! Woah!

Brazil: Whatchaheard?

Lucy: Uh—. Cant say.

---

15. Hearsay.

Brazil: Whatchaheard?!!

Lucy: SSShhhhhhhhhhhhhhhhhhht!

(*Rest*)

Dig!

SCENE 2: ECHO

The Foundling Father: Ladies and Gentlemen: *Our American Cousin*, act 3, scene 5.

Mr. Trenchard: Have you found it?

Miss Keene: I find no trace of it. (*Discovering*) What is this?!

Mr. Trenchard: This is the place where father kept all the old deeds.

Miss Keene: Oh my poor muddled brain! What can this mean?!

Mr. Trenchard (*With difficulty*): I cannot survive the downfall of my house but choose instead to end my life with a pistol to my head!

(*Applause*)

The Foundling Father: OHWAYOHWHYOHWAYOH!

(*Rest*)

Hellloooooooo!

(*Rest*)

Hellloooooooo!

(*Rest. Waves.*)

SCENE 3: ARCHEOLOGY

Brazil: You hear im?

Lucy: Echo of thuh first sort: thuh sound. (E.g. thuh gunplay.)

(*Rest*)

Echo of thuh second sort: thuh words. Type A: thuh words from thuh dead. Category: Unrelated.

(*Rest*)

Echo of thuh second sort, Type B: words less fortunate: thuh Disem-
bodied Voice. Also known as "Thuh Whispers." Category: Related.
Like your Fathuhs.

(*Rest*)

Echo of thuh third sort: thuh body itself.

(*Rest*)

Brazil: You hear im.

Lucy: Cant say. Cant say, son.

Brazil: My faux-father. Thuh one who comed out here before us. Thuh
one who left us behind. Tuh come out here all uhlone. Tuh do his bit.
All them who comed before us-my Daddy. He's one of them.

Lucy

(*Rest*)

[**Brazil:** He's one of them. All of them who comed before us-my Daddy.

(*Rest*)

I'd say thuh creation of thuh world must uh been just like thuh
clearing off of this plot. Just like him diggin his Hole. I'd say. Must uh
been just as dug up. And unfair.

(*Rest*)

Peoples (or thuh what-was), just had tuh hit thuh road. In thuh
beginning there was one of those voids here and then "bang" and then
voilà! And here we is.

(*Rest*)

But where did those voids that was here before we was here go off to?
Hmmm. In thuh beginning there were some of them voids here and
then: KERBANG-KERBLAMMO! And now it all belongs tuh us.

Lucy

(*Rest*)]

Brazil: This Hole is our inheritance of sorts. My Daddy died and left it
to me and Her. And when She goes, She's gonna give it all to me!!

Lucy: Dig, son.

Brazil: I'd rather dust and polish. (*Puts something on*)

Lucy: Dust and polish then. —. You dont got tuh put on that tuh do it.

Brazil: It helps. Uh Hehm. *Uh Hehm.* WELCOME WELCOME WELCOME TUH THUH HALL OF—

Lucy: Sssht.

Brazil

Lucy

Brazil: (welcome welcome welcome to thuh hall of wonnndersss: To our right A Jewel Box made of cherry wood, lined in velvet, letters "A.L." carved in gold on thuh lid: the jewels have long escaped. Over here one of Mr. Washingtons bones, right pointer so they say; here is his likeness and here: his wooden teeth. Yes, uh top and bottom pair of nibblers: nibblers, lookin for uh meal. Nibblin. I iduhnt your lunch. Quit nibblin. Quit that nibblin you. Quit that nibblin you nibblers you nibblin nibblers you.)

Lucy: Keep it tuh scale.

Brazil: (Over here our newest Wonder: uh bust of Mr. Lincoln carved of marble lookin like he looked in life. Right heress thuh bit from thuh mouth of thuh mount on which some great Someone rode tuh thuh rescue. This is all thats left. Uh glass tradin bead—one of thuh first. Here are thuh lick-ed boots. Here, uh dried scrap of whales blubber. Uh petrified scrap of uh great blubberer, servin to remind us that once this land was covered with sea. And blubberers were Kings. In this area here are several documents: peace pacts, writs, bills of sale, treaties, notices, handbills and circulars, freein papers, summonses, declarations of war, addresses, title deeds, obits, long lists of dids. And thuh medals: for bravery and honesty; for trustworthiness and for standing straight; for standing tall; for standing still. For advancing and retreating. For makin do. For skills in whittlin, for skills in painting and drawing, for uh knowledge of sewin, of handicrafts and building things, for leather tannin, blacksmithery, lacemakin, horseback riding, swimmin, croquet and badminton. Community Service. For cookin and for cleanin. For bowin and scrapin. Uh medal for fakin? Huh. This could uh been his. Zsis his? This is his! This is his!!!

Lucy: Keep it tuh scale, Brazil.

Brazil: This could be his!

Lucy: May well be.

Brazil (*Rest*): Whaddyahear?

Lucy: Bits and pieces.

Brazil: This could be his.

Lucy: Could well be.

Brazil (*Rest. Rest.*): waaaaaahhhhhhhhHHHHHHHHHHHHHH!
HUH HEE HUH HEE HUH HEE HUH.

Lucy: There there, Brazil. Dont weep.

Brazil: WAHHHHHHHHHHH!-imissim-WAHHHHHHHHHHHHH!

Lucy: It is an honor to be of his line. He cleared this plot for us. He was
uh Digger.

Brazil: Huh huh huh. Uh Digger.

Lucy: Mr. Lincoln was his favorite.

Brazil: I was only five.

Lucy: He dug this whole Hole.

Brazil: Sssnuch. This whole Hole.

Lucy: This whole Hole.

(*Rest*)

Brazil

Lucy

Brazil

Lucy

Brazil

Lucy:
>   I couldnt never deny him nothin.
>   I gived intuh him on everything.
>   Thuh moon. Thuh stars.
>   Thuh bees knees. Thuh cats pyjamas.

(*Rest*)

Brazil

Lucy

Brazil: Anything?

Lucy: Stories too horrible tuh mention.

Brazil: His stories?

Lucy: Nope.

(*Rest*)

Brazil: Mama Lucy?

Lucy: Whut.

Brazil: —Imissim—.

Lucy: Hhh. (Dig.)

SCENE 4: ECHO

The Foundling Father: Ladies and Gentlemen: *Our American Cousin*, act 3, scene 2.

Mr. Trenchard: You crave affection, you do. Now I've no fortune, but I'm biling over with affections, which I'm ready to pour out to all of you, like apple sass over roast pork.

Augusta: Sir, your American talk do woo me.

The Foundling Father (*as Mrs. Mount*): Mr. Trenchard, you will please recollect you are addressing my daughter and in my presence.

Mr. Trenchard: Yes, I'm offering her my heart and hand just as she wants them, with nothing in 'em.

The Foundling Father (*as Mrs. Mount*): Augusta dear, to your room.

Augusta: Yes, Ma, the nasty beast.

The Foundling Father (*as Mrs. Mount*): I am aware, Mr. Trenchard, that you are not used to the manners of good society, and that, alone, will excuse the impertinence of which you have been guilty.

Mr. Trenchard: Don't know the manners of good society, eh? Wal, I guess I know enough to turn you inside out, old gal—you sockdologizing old man-trap.

(*Laughter. Applause.*)

The Foundling Father: Thanks. Thanks so much. Snyder has always been a very special very favorite town uh mine. Thank you thank you so very much. Loverly loverly evening loverly tuh be here loverly tuh be here with you with all of you thank you very much.

(*Rest*)

Uh Hehm. I *only* do thuh greats.

(*Rest*)

A crowd pleaser: Four score and seven years ago our fathers brought forth upon this continent a new nation conceived in Liberty and dedicated to the proposition that all men are created equal!

(*Applause*)

Observe!: Indiana? Indianapolis. Louisiana? Baton Rouge. Concord? New Hampshire. Pierre? South Dakota. Honolulu? Hawaii. Springfield? Illinois. Frankfort? Kentucky. Lincoln? Nebraska. Ha! Lickety split!

(*Applause*)

And now, the centerpiece of the evening!!

(*Rest*)

Uh Hehm. The Death of Lincoln! —. The watching of the play, the laughter, the smiles of Lincoln and Mary Todd, the slipping of Booth into the presidential box unseen, the freeing of the slaves, the pulling of the trigger, the bullets piercing above the left ear, the bullets entrance into the great head, the bullets lodging behind the great right eye, the slumping of Lincoln, the leaping onto the stage of Booth, the screaming of Todd, the screaming of Todd, the screaming of Keene, the leaping onto the stage of Booth; the screaming of Todd, the screaming of Keene, the shouting of Booth "Thus to the tyrants!," the death of Lincoln!—And the silence of the nation.

(*Rest*)

Yes. —. The year was way back when. The place: our nations capitol. Four score, back in the olden days, and Mr. Lincolns great head. The the-a-ter was "Fords." The wife "Mary Todd." Thuh freeing of the slaves and thuh great black hole that thuh fatal bullet bored. And how that great head was bleedin. Thuh body stretched crossways acrosst thuh bed. Thuh last words. Thuh last breaths. And how thuh nation mourned.

(*Applause*)

SCENE 5: SPADEWORK

Lucy: Thats uh hard nut tuh crack uh hard nut tuh crack indeed.

Brazil: Alaska—?

Lucy: Thats uh hard nut tuh crack. Thats uh hard nut tuh crack indeed. —. Huh. Juneau.

Brazil: Good!

Lucy: Go uhgain.

Brazil: —. Texas?

Lucy: —. Austin. Wyoming?

Brazil: —. —. Cheyenne. Florida?

Lucy: Tallahassee.

(*Rest*)

Ohio.

Brazil: Oh. Uh. Well: Columbus. Louisiana?

Lucy: Baton Rouge. Arkansas.

Brazil: Little Rock. Jackson.

Lucy: Mississippi. Spell it.

Brazil: M-i-s-s-i-s-s-i-p-p-i!

Lucy: Huh. Youre good. Montgomery.

Brazil: Alabama.

Lucy: Topeka.

Brazil: Kansas?

Lucy: Kansas.

Brazil: Boise, Idaho?

Lucy: Boise, Idaho.

Brazil: Huh. Nebraska.

Lucy: Nebraska. Lincoln.

(*Rest*)

Thuh year was way back when. Thuh place: our nations capitol.

(*Rest*)

Your Fathuh couldnt get that story out of his head: Mr. Lincolns great head. And thuh hole thuh fatal bullet bored. How that great head was bleedin. Thuh body stretched crossways acrosst thuh bed. Thuh last words. Thuh last breaths. And how thuh nation mourned. Huh. Changed your Fathuhs life.

(*Rest*)

Couldnt get that story out of his head. Whuduhnt my favorite page from thuh book of Mr. Lincolns life, me myself now I prefer thuh part where he gets married to Mary Todd and she begins to lose her mind (and then of course where he frees all thuh slaves) but shoot, he couldnt get that story out of his head. Hhh. Changed his life.

(*Rest*)

Brazil: (wahhhhhhhh—)

Lucy: There there, Brazil.

Brazil: (wahhhhhh—)

Lucy: Dont weep. Got somethin for ya.

Brazil: (o)?

Lucy: Spade. —. Dont scrunch up your face like that, son. Go on. Take it.

Brazil: Spade?

Lucy: Spade. He woulda wanted you tuh have it.

Brazil: Daddys diggin spade? Ssnnuch.

Lucy: I swannee you look more and more and more and more like him ever-y day.

Brazil: His chin?

Lucy: You got his chin.

Brazil: His lips?

Lucy: You got his lips.

Brazil: His teeths?

Lucy: Top and bottom. In his youth. He had some. Just like yours. His frock coat. Was just like that. He had hisself uh stovepipe hat which you lack. His medals—yours are for weepin his of course were for diggin.

Brazil: And I got his spade.

Lucy: And now you got his spade.

Brazil: We could say I'm his spittin image.

Lucy: We could say that.

Brazil: We could say I just may follow in thuh footsteps of my foe-father.

Lucy: We could say that.

Brazil: Look on thuh bright side!

Lucy: Look on thuh bright side!

Brazil: So much tuh live for!

Lucy: So much tuh live for! Sweet land of—! Sweet land of—?

Brazil: Of liberty!

Lucy: Of liberty! Thats it thats it and *"Woah!"* Lets say I hear his words!

Brazil: And you could say?

Lucy: And I could say.

Brazil: Lets say you hear his words!

Lucy: Woah!

Brazil: Whatwouldhesay?!

Lucy: He'd say: "Hello." He'd say. —. "Hope you like your spade."

Brazil: Tell him I do.

Lucy: He'd say: "My how youve grown!" He'd say: "Hows your weepin?" He'd say:—Ha! He's running through his states and capitals! Licketysplit!

Brazil: Howuhboutthat!

Lucy: He'd say: "Uh house divided cannot stand!" He'd say: "Four score and seven years uhgoh." Say: "Of thuh people by thuh people and for thuh people." Say: "Malice toward none and charity toward all." Say: "Cheat some of thuh people some of thuh time." He'd say: (and this is only to be spoken between you and me and him—)

Brazil: K.

Lucy: Lean in. Ssfor our ears and our ears uhlone.

Lucy

Brazil

Lucy

Brazil

Brazil: O.

Lucy: Howuhboutthat. And here he comes. Striding on in striding on in and he surveys thuh situation. And he nods tuh what we found cause he knows his Wonders. And he smiles. And he tells us of his doins all these years. And he does his Mr. Lincoln for us. Uh great page from thuh great mans great life! And you n me llsmile, cause then we'll know, more or less, exactly where he is.

(*Rest*)

Brazil: Lucy? Where is he?

Lucy: Lincoln?

Brazil: Papa.

Lucy: Close by, I guess. Huh. Dig.

(*Brazil digs. Times passes.*)

Youre uh Digger. Youre uh Digger. Your Daddy was uh Digger and so are you.

Brazil: Ho!

Lucy: I couldnt never deny him nothin.

Brazil: Wonder: Ho! Wonder: Ho!

Lucy: I gived intuh him on everything.

Brazil: Ssuhtrumpet.

Lucy: Gived intuh him on everything.

Brazil: Ssuhtrumpet, Lucy.

Lucy: Howboutthat.

Brazil: Try it out.

Lucy: How uh-bout that.

Brazil: Anythin?

Lucy: Cant say, son. Cant say.

(*Rest*)

> I couldnt never deny him nothin.
> I gived intuh him on everything.
> Thuh moon. Thuh stars.

Brazil: Ho!

Lucy: Thuh bees knees. Thuh cats pyjamas.

Brazil: Wonder: Ho! Wonder: Ho!

(*Rest*)

Howuhboutthat: Uh bag of pennies. Money, Lucy.

Lucy: Howuhboutthat.

(*Rest*)

> Thuh bees knees.
> Thuh cats pyjamas.
> Thuh best cuts of meat.
> My baby teeth.

Brazil: Wonder: Ho! Wonder: HO!

Lucy:
> Thuh apron from uhround my waist.
> Thuh hair from off my head.

Brazil: Huh. Yellow fur.

Lucy: My mores and my folkways.

Brazil: Oh. Uh beard. Howuhboutthat.

(*Rest*)

Lucy: WOAH. WOAH!

Brazil: Whatchaheard?

Lucy

(*Rest*)

(*Rest*)

Brazil: Whatchaheard?!

Lucy: You dont wanna know.

Brazil

Lucy

Brazil

Lucy

Brazil: Wonder: Ho! Wonder: HO! WONDER: HO!

Lucy:
>   Thuh apron from uhround my waist.
>   Thuh hair from off my head.

Brazil: Huh: uh Tee-Vee.

Lucy: Huh.

Brazil: I'll hold ontooit for uh minit.

(*Rest*)

Lucy:
>   Thuh apron from uhround my waist.
>   Thuh hair from off my head.
>   My mores and my folkways.
>   My rock and my foundation.

Brazil

Lucy

Brazil

Lucy: My re-memberies—you know—thuh stuff out of my head.

(*The TV comes on. The Foundling Father's face appears.*)

Brazil: (ho! ho! wonder: ho!)

Lucy:
>   My spare buttons in their envelopes.
>   Thuh leftovers from all my unmade meals.

Thuh letter R.
Thuh key of G.

Brazil: (ho! ho! wonder: ho!)

Lucy:
All my good jokes. All my jokes that fell flat.
Thuh way I walked, cause you liked it so much.
All my winnin dance steps.
My teeth when yours runned out.
My smile.

Brazil: (ho! ho! wonder: ho!)

Lucy: Sssssht.

(*Rest*)

Well. Its him.

SCENE 6: ECHO

(*A gunshot echoes. Loudly. And echoes.*)

SCENE 7: THE GREAT BEYOND

(*Lucy and Brazil watch the TV: a replay of "The Lincoln Act." The Foundling Father has returned. His coffin awaits him.*)

Lucy: Howuhboutthat!

Brazil: They just gunned him down uhgain.

Lucy: Howuhboutthat.

Brazil: He's dead but not really.

Lucy: Howuhboutthat.

Brazil: Only fakin. Only fakin. See? Hesupuhgain.

Lucy: What-izzysayin?

Brazil: Sound duhnt work.

Lucy: Zat right.

(*Rest*)

The Foundling Father: I believe this is the place where I do the Gettysburg Address, I believe.

Brazil

The Foundling Father

Lucy

Brazil: Woah!

Lucy: Howuhboutthat.

Brazil: Huh. Well.

(*Rest*)

Huh. Zit him?

Lucy: Its him.

Brazil: He's dead?

Lucy: He's dead.

Brazil: Howuhboutthat.

(*Rest*)

Shit.

Lucy

Brazil

Lucy

Brazil: Mail the in-vites?

Lucy: I did.

Brazil: Think theyll come?

Lucy: I do. There are hundreds upon thousands who knew of your Daddy, glorified his reputation, and would like to pay their respects.

The Foundling Father: Howuhboutthat.

Brazil: Howuhboutthat!

Lucy: Turn that off, son.

(*Rest*)

You gonna get in yr coffin now or later?

The Foundling Father: I'd like tuh wait uhwhile.

Lucy: Youd like tuh wait uhwhile.

Brazil: Mmgonna gnash for you. You know: teeth in thuh dirt, hands like this, then jump up rip my clothes up, you know, you know go all out.

The Foundling Father: Howuhboutthat. Open casket or closed?

Lucy: —. Closed.

(*Rest*)

Turn that off, son.

Brazil: K.

The Foundling Father: Hug me.

Brazil: Not yet.

The Foundling Father: You?

Lucy: Gimmieuhminute.

(*A gunshot echoes. Loudly. And echoes.*)

Lucy: That gunplay. Wierdiduhntit. Comes. And goze.

(*They ready his coffin. He inspects it.*)

At thuh Great Hole where we honeymooned—son, at thuh Original Great Hole, you could see thuh whole world without goin too far. You could look intuh that Hole and see your entire life pass before you. Not your own life but someones life from history, you know, [someone who'd done somethin of note, got theirselves known somehow, uh President or] somebody who killed somebody important, uh face on uh postal stamp, you know, someone from History. *Like* you, but *not* you. You know: *Known.*

The Foundling Father: "*Emergency,* oh, *Emergency,* please put the Great Man in the ground."

Lucy: Go on. Get in. Try it out. Ssnot so bad. See? Sstight, but private. Bought on time but we'll manage. And you got enough height for your hat.

(*Rest*)

The Foundling Father: Hug me.

Lucy: Not yet.

The Foundling Father: You?

Brazil: Gimmieuhminute.

(*Rest*)

Lucy: He loved that Great Hole so. Came out here. Digged this lookuhlike.

Brazil: Then he died?

Lucy: Then he died.

The Foundling Father

Brazil

Lucy

The Foundling Father

Brazil

Lucy

The Foundling Father: A monumentous occasion. I'd like to say a few words from the grave. Maybe a little conversation: Such a long story. Uhhem. I quit the business. And buried all my things. I dropped anchor: Bottomless. Your turn.

Lucy

Brazil

The Foundling Father

Lucy (*Rest*): Do your Lincoln for im.

The Foundling Father: Yeah?

Lucy: He was only five.

The Foundling Father: Only five. *Uh Hehm.* So very loverly to be here so very very loverly to be here the town of—Wonderville has always been a special favorite of mine always has been a very very special favorite of mine. Now, I only do thuh greats. Uh hehm: I was born in a log cabin of humble parentage. But I picked up uh few things. Uh Hehm: Four score and seven years ago our fathers—ah you know thuh rest. Lets see now. Yes. Uh house divided cannot stand! You can fool some of thuh people some of thuh time! Of thuh people by thuh people and

for thuh people! Malice toward none and charity toward all! Ha! The
Death of Lincoln! (Highlights): Haw Haw Haw Haw

(*Rest*)

HAW HAW HAW HAW

(*A gunshot echoes. Loudly. And echoes. The Foundling Father
"slumps in his chair."*)

The Foundling Father

Lucy

Brazil

Lucy

The Foundling Father

Brazil: [Izzy dead?

Lucy: Mmlistenin.

Brazil: Anything?

Lucy: Nothin.

Brazil (*Rest*): As a child it was her luck tuh be in thuh same room with
her Uncle when he died. Her family wanted to know what he had said.
What his last words had been. Theyre hadnt been any. Only screaming.
Or, you know, breath. Didnt have uh shape to it. Her family thought
she was holding on to thuh words. For safekeeping. And they pro-
claimed thuh girl uh Confidence. At the age of eight. Sworn tuh
secrecy. She picked up thuh tricks of thuh trade as she went uhlong.]

(*Rest*)

Should I gnash now?

Lucy: Better save it for thuh guests. I guess.

(*Rest*)

Well. Dust and polish, son. I'll circulate.

Brazil: Welcome Welcome Welcome to thuh hall. Of. Wonders.

(*Rest*)

To our right A Jewel Box of cherry wood, lined in velvet, letters "A.L."
carved in gold on thuh lid. Over here one of Mr. Washingtons bones
and here: his wooden teeth. Over here: uh bust of Mr. Lincoln carved

of marble lookin like he looked in life. —More or less. And thuh medals: for bravery and honesty; for trustworthiness and for standing straight; for standing tall; for standing still. For advancing and retreating. For makin do. For skills in whittlin, for skills in painting and drawing, for uh knowledge of sewin, of handicrafts and building things, for leather tannin, blacksmithery, lacemakin, horseback riding, swimmin, croquet and badminton. Community Service. For cookin and for cleanin. For bowin and scrapin. Uh medal for fakin.

(Rest)

To my right: our newest Wonder: One of thuh greats Hisself! Note: thuh body sitting propped upright in our great Hole. Note the large mouth opened wide. Note the top hat and frock coat, just like the greats. Note the death wound: thuh great black hole—thuh great black hole in thuh great head. —And how this great head is bleedin. —Note: thuh last words. —And thuh last breaths. —And how thuh nation mourns—

(Takes his leave)

END OF PLAY

Kokoro ("True Heart")

VELINA HASU HOUSTON

Kokoro—heart . . . mind . . . spirit;
the heart of the matter . . .

Kokoro received its world premiere at the
Theatre of Yugen, San Francisco, in June
1994. It also received a limited special
presentation at the Japan Society, New
York, in May 1994. In 1995 it was produced
in New York at The 28th Street Theatre by
Frances Hill and Margaret Mancinelli-
Cahill, directed by Tina Chen.

Cast of Characters

*Yasako Yamashita, a Japanese
woman, early 30s*

*Hiro Yamashita, Yasako's
husband, a Japanese man, 39*

*Shizuko Mizoguchi, a Japanese
woman, early 30s*

Fuyo, a spirit, Yasako's mother

Angela Rossetti, an attorney

Evelyn Lauderdale, a neighbor

Setting

*San Diego, California, Japan, and
Netherworlds, 1985*

Author's Note

The amalgam of heart and mind brings a different dimension to that ethereal, inexplicable entity that we call love. It is one of discernment that transcends the veneer of language and the hasty fulfillment of love via institution and material objects. When culture—in the sense of behaviors and beliefs inherent to ethnicity, transmitted to succeeding generations—is brought to this kind of love, ethnic idiosyncrasies can have a shattering effect. This is especially true when one culture's idiosyncrasies are judged in the sociopolitical arena of another—in the case of many of my plays, a Japanese feminine culture in a patriarchal European American context.

Oyako shinju *(parent-child suicide) is relatively unthinkable in America, although my research (interviews of Japanese in Japan and America, analyses of media stories and books, family history) has indicated several incidences of it, not only committed by Asian immigrant women, but also by (non-Asian) American women.*

This play seeks to explore why one particular woman—Yasako, a fictional character—is led to oyako shinju *and how the American society in which she lives grapples with her decision. Yasako is my creation, but she embodies the spirit, courage, intelligence, loneliness, and confusion of many Japanese female immigrants whom I have been privileged to know on intimate bases. Yasako's love for her child is one informed with cultural desire and deep obligation. It is a bond that she is not willing to break, not even in death.*

I attempt to explore not only Yasako's point of view (arguably an old-fashioned one even by Japanese standards) but also contemporary Japanese and American points of view. Absolute truth, however, is an illusion. Ultimately, Yasako's actions are not "Japanese" but individual choice (as are the interpretations we make of it).

PROLOGUE

(*Ocean sounds fade in and crescendo. In the darkness, Yasako enters as lights fade in low, whirling, shaping a world around her. There is a scrim as backdrop and ocean waves dress the floor. Yasako comes forward using slow, methodical movements.*)

Yasako: A tiny rock is cast out to sea by the great Sun Goddess Amaterasu and it grows into an island, strong and unwavering, beautiful and bright. I am a root in this soil. I grow best here, all blossoms, all fruits, always. (*Beat*) But, one day, the gardener comes and I am transplanted. The winds, the rain, the gnawing forces of erosion transform the blossoms, scattering them into the river of time.

(*She removes a silky American flag from her kimono sleeve and billows it about her as the figure of Fuyo appears as a shadow lit behind the scrim. Fuyo enters. A spirit, the back of her kimono trails behind her in shredded strands. Her face is snowy white; her hair is wild, long, gray-streaked. She glides beneath a gossamer shroud. The lights on her are shadowy, while the lights on Yasako are a bit brighter.*)

Yasako: Good-bye, Mother.

(*Fuyo shakes her head.*)

Yasako: But I am his wife.

(*Fuyo looks downward in sadness.*)

Yasako: And your daughter becomes a mother.

(*Fuyo beckons to Yasako.*)

Yasako: Do not fear for my child in America, Mother. Her soul is tied with mine. She will never walk alone.

(*Fuyo encircles her daughter as Yasako weaves in and around her.*)

Fuyo: Se o hayami iwa ni sekaruru . . .

Yasako: Our lives like the river's foam split asunder by boulders . . .

Fuyo: . . . takigawa no warete mo sue ni awanto zo omou.

Yasako: In the end,

Fuyo:	**Yasako:**
. . . kono yo de . . .	. . . in this world . . .

Fuyo and **Yasako:** . . . or some other . . .

Yasako: . . . we will find each other again.

(Yasako removes her kimono, startling Fuyo. She gives it to Fuyo. Fuyo kneels to fold it as Yasako kneels to fold the flag. Yasako presents the flag to her mother and bows.)

Yasako: Doozo, Okaasan. *(Beat)* Wife, mother, and now orphan, I go. *(Beat)* Sayoonara.

(Yasako bows again. Fuyo wipes away imaginary tears and runs offstage. Yasako rises as the sound of a seven-year-old girl's laughter tinkles, blending with a news bite that marks the era as 1984, i.e., the re-election of Ronald Reagan. The sounds bridge into act 1.)

ACT 1

SCENE 1

(The Yamashita home, into which Yasako enters as the lights brighten. A hot summer day. Intermittently, sounds of the ocean are heard in the distance. Yasako folds a young girl's dress. She sits and leafs through a journal.)

Yasako: August third. Seven to eight: make breakfast. Eight to nine: wash Kuniko's clothing. Nine to ten: piano. My world. America is outside, a place to visit when I take Kuniko to school. My husband buys the groceries, pays the bills. Once I had to take Kuniko to the doctor. That was hard. *(Puts the book away, calls out)* Kuniko! Kuniko-chan! Come my child. Time for music! *(Imagines a girl running in)* Kuniko! You forgot to take your shoes off! What bad manners you've learned! Sit, sit. Kuniko! Keep your dress on! Nice girls do not sing in their panties! Let's sing Japanese songs today. *(Plays a few notes on the tabletop)* "Haru ga kita, haru ga kita, doko ni kita. Yama ni kita, sato ni kita, no ni mo kita."

(Abruptly, the voice of the seven-year-old Kuniko emanates seemingly from all around Yasako as she looks around in delight.)

Kuniko's Voice *(Sings)*: "Down the river, oh down the river, oh down the river we go-o-o; down the river, oh down the river, oh down the Ohio! The river is up and the channel is deep, the wind is steady and strong. Oh won't we have a jolly good time as we go sailing along!"

(Amid this singing, Yasako stands and the lights diminish to a spotlight on her as she looks out at the audience. She begins to talk over the singing.)

Yasako: In Japan, your grandmother and I lived by the inland sea. But now there is Coronado and the big Pacific Ocean. Papa found this nice apartment so I can hear the waves. I close my eyes and pretend it is the sea shore in Japan. *(Beat)* Kuniko-chan. Did you know there is a world beneath the sea? With mermaids and sapphire fish, coral and sea stars. The mermaids have serious business: they guide lost souls to the next world. *(Beat)* . . . a soul is . . . everything a person feels or dreams, an essence that cannot be touched unless you use your heart, your true heart. Kokoro. Mind, heart, spirit. *(Beat)* You have a soul, too, Kuniko. A seven-year-old soul that has been around the universe many times. And it will never be lost because I will find you easily, wherever there are Japanese peaches. You eat so many that you smell as golden blush and alive as their sweet flesh.

(Bursts of laughter in Kuniko's voice are heard in voiceover as the spotlight fades and the lights go up. Yasako resigns herself to this silliness that she finds endearing.)

Yasako *(Looks at watch and checks journal)*: Okay, silly monkey. Time for homework so you can grow up and go to college like Mommy. Read for an hour, then math. Then we will have lunch and think about O-bon Festival.

Kuniko's Voice: Mommy, when I grow up can I still live with you?

Yasako *(Overlapping)*: Well, I think—

Kuniko's Voice *(Continuous)*: Mommy, why can't I ever have friends sleep over like all the American kids?

Yasako *(Overlapping)*: "Sleep over"?

Kuniko's Voice: *(Continuous)*: Mommy? You ever heard of a group called The Beatles?

Yasako (*Smiles*): Yes! One of them married a Japanese. But he died. You can say hello to his spirit at O-bon Festival. And Obaachan's spirit. And my father's, too. Festival of the Dead, Kuniko; a happy time to visit with our ancestors and then light lanterns to guide them back to their worlds.

(*Hiro Yamashita appears. Lights fade and a spotlight goes up on him and Yasako. Both look out at the audience.*)

Hiro: Good, Yasako. Clothes smell better for my little girl when you wash them by hand.

Yasako: Kuniko? If I was a kangaroo, I would ride you in my pocket forever.

Hiro: Stop carrying that child! She's too old to be carried!

Yasako: Kuniko, come. It is time for tea. I made o-manju.

Hiro: I bought you the recipe book. Page 243, how to make apple pie.

Yasako: Hiro, teach me how to write checks, how to use the ATM.

Hiro: Last week, lady was robbed at an ATM.

Yasako: Hiro, teach me how to talk to her teachers.

Hiro: What's so difficult about talking to a teacher? I could talk to President Reagan, if I had to.

Yasako: One to two: wash floors. Two to three: dusting the furniture.

Hiro: Yasako, make some friends.

Yasako: I do not know what to say to American women.

Hiro: Go borrow a cup of sugar or something. (*Beat*) Here. I bought you a new dress. With a little style. Try it on.

(*The sound of a child running into a lamp and falling is heard. Yasako screams suddenly and Hiro jumps.*)

Yasako: Ara, Kuniko! Papa, she fell and hit her head on the lamp!

Hiro: It's just a flesh wound, Yasako. Calm down.

Yasako: She cut herself twice on that stupid lamp. Poor Kuniko-chan. Get rid of the lamp, Papa.

Hiro: Come here, Kuniko-chan. Papa will make it better. Look at her! She hugs like people in American movie. I love it. Give Papa a great big television kiss, Kuniko.

Yasako: Mommy tries to kiss, Kuniko, but it feels so strange. Do you remember how my mother taught you how to bow? (*Bows*) Bow like this. Very good, Kuniko! (*Beat*) Kuniko-chan, are you ready? Time for O-bon Festival. Put on your yukata.

(*O-bon music begins.*)

Yasako: We will dance under the lanterns and the moon, and welcome back my mother's spirit.

(*Fuyo appears upstage moving gracefully in O-bon odori—festival dance. O-bon paper lanterns gleam from behind the scrim. Yasako joins her, beckoning to Kuniko and then to the reluctant Hiro as a kuro-ko—a black-draped figure of traditional Japanese theater who provides onstage assistance—puts yukata on them. As the dance ends, a bored Hiro ceases first and then Yasako. Fuyo continues to weave around them, still dancing.*)

Hiro (*Dismissing culture*): Bon Festival's just old-country folktale stuff. An excuse to eat and drink. Your mother's not here. She's ashes and dust.

(*Fuyo stamps her foot toward Hiro to protest this remark.*)

Yasako: She is here, listening to all of this; and, when you go to Heaven, she will not make o-manju for you. (*Reacting*) Kuniko! No! Do not shake the urn!

(*Fuyo reacts as if being shaken and gently tumbles to the ground.*)

Yasako: Yes, my mother is in the urn. Yes, she is coming to visit you, but in spirit, not like a genie out of the bottle. Oh, Kuniko, bad girl. You spilled Obaachan's remains all over the floor!

Hiro (*Laughs*): Let's get out the vacuum cleaner.

(*Fuyo reacts.*)

Hiro: Just kidding! Oh, Yasako, all that old Japanese stuff. Nobody cares about Bon Festival or kimono anymore. Not even in Japan.

(*Hiro removes the yukata and drops it to the floor. Fuyo looks at it with sadness, picks it up, and exits.*)

Yasako: Okay, Kuniko, get ready for bed.

(*The presence of "Kuniko" exits.*)

Yasako: I care. My mother raised me to care. (*Beat*) Don't you want Kuniko to learn about Japanese culture?

Hiro: Don't you want her to get along in American culture?

Yasako: We won't live here forever.

Hiro: Let her be different. A California original.

Yasako: A place does not change who she is.

Hiro: It does! Even the cherry trees here are bigger and taller. (*He sits in the chair and soaks his feet in the basin of water as she hands him a towel.*) Why waste your time making homemade o-manju? Just buy it down at Fugetsu-do. My customers at my restaurant never eat it. It just gets hard like rocks. Waitress almost put out my eye when she threw one at me.

Yasako: What? A waitress threw o-manju at you?

Hiro: Yeah. She could pitch professional baseball.

Yasako: You must fire her or ask her to resign. After all, what shame she must feel.

Hiro (*Laughs*): Hardly. Not that one

Yasako: But so bold.

Hiro: She says we should put American food on the menu. Strawberry ice cream.

Yasako: But then it wouldn't be a Japanese restaurant anymore.

Hiro: I mean just change the decoration a little bit, put a small American flag on the counter to make the white people happy.

Yasako (*She dries his feet. Then, no longer interested, she stops.*): We should have moved back to Japan by now.

Hiro: Don't start that again.

Yasako: It has been six years, Hiro. I thought we were going back before Kuniko started school.

Hiro: Good schools here.

Yasako: I want her in Japanese schools.

Hiro: There're Japanese schools right here.

Yasako: One day a week on Saturdays? I want her in real Japanese school.

Hiro: Yes. Of course. (*Touches her hair*) Such beautiful hair. Pull it back, off your face.

(*She pulls it away from her face.*)

Hiro: Well, I'd better get to work. Don't wait up for me. (*Beat*) I might have to sleep there if it gets too late.

Yasako: Oh, don't do that again. You're so grumpy the next day.

Hiro: I need to look at the books. Besides, I don't want to wake you up so late.

Yasako: You are asleep in the morning when Kuniko gets up and gone to work by the time she comes home from school. You work too hard.

Hiro: We're lucky to have such good business, Yasako. You should see the restaurant. So many customers.

Yasako: Hiro, if we went home, you could go back into my family's electric company.

Hiro: Yasako, please.

Yasako: Just promise one day we will go back.

Hiro: Don't worry. Japan isn't going anywhere. And we have a lot to do here.

Yasako: I'm sorry. You're right. I should be helping you at the restaurant instead of worrying about Japan.

Hiro: You stay home, take care of Kuniko. That's your job. That's how you help me.

Yasako: But you said there are so many customers.

Hiro: Come here and kiss me, Yasako.

Yasako: Hiro! Sometimes you sound so American.

Hiro: Good. American men are smart then. Kiss me. (*Yasako looks sad; he kisses her cheek gently.*) I put some tuna in the refrigerator. It's very fresh. Just for you.

Yasako: Thank you.

(*He suddenly comes into the house with shoes on—which she stares at in shock—and then lifts her up in the air, planting a big kiss on her. She's pleased, but embarrassed.*)

Yasako: Hiro!

Hiro: To hell with culture, Yasako. When in Rome, do as the Romans do, right?

Yasako: This is San Diego.

Hiro: Oh, Yasako, it's just a figure of speech.

Yasako: It's a cliché.

Hiro (*Touches her hair*): My mother told me never marry a girl who was smarter than me or who loved me at first sight.

(*Offstage, the sound of Kuniko calling her mother in Japanese— "Okaasan! Kite yo!"—is heard. Yasako reacts.*)

Hiro: Go on. (*Begins to exit*)

Yasako: Hiro? I'm sorry.

Hiro: About what?

Yasako: If I had friends like in Japan, women to have tea with, it would be different.

(*The girl's voice calls from offstage again: "Mama!"*)

Hiro: Better hurry. Go on, my dear wife.

Yasako: Hurry home, Papa.

(*He exits. Lights cross-fade to a downstage spotlight in which Yasako kneels.*)

Yasako: Here, Kuniko. Drink tea. Ban-cha for good dreams. (*Beat*) No matter what, Kuniko, Mommy will keep you by her side, okay? In Japan, we say mother and child are one until you are a big girl who can live outside of my shadow. Go back to sleep now. Sleep. Good girl.

(*Lights cross-fade to another spotlight in which stands Evelyn Lauderdale, a faintly exotic-looking, warm, tomboyish woman. She whistles for a pet.*)

Evelyn: Panther? Here, Panther. Here, kitty, kitty.

(*Yasako enters and hands her the "cat."*)

Evelyn: You found my cat! Bad cat! Gallivanting all around the neighborhood after sundown! Thank you so much, Mrs. Yamashita.

Yasako: Glad to help.

Evelyn: Usually, Kuniko rescues her. It's nice that you found her this time. Gives us a chance to talk.

Yasako: Well, I do not want to bother you. I will be going now.

Evelyn: No, no. It's no bother at all. Ever since you moved in last year, Kuniko's been a bundle of sunshine for me. She's my friend and so you are, too. Okay?

Yasako: Of course. Thank you. (*Mimics handing her another item*) Here. A present. Peaches, my daughter's favorite fruit.

Evelyn: Thank you. To be honest, Kuniko leaves one peach a day on my porch. I made a peach cobbler once and she ate two pieces.

Yasako: "Cobbler"? (*Bows*) I am sorry for the trouble.

Evelyn: Are you kidding? I love it. She's a great kid.

Yasako: Thank you.

Evelyn: Would you like to come in? Please. Let's have the peaches together.

Yasako: Actually . . . I came to ask a favor.

Evelyn: Anything. I owe you and Kuniko for saving my cat. I'd lay bets she only has two lives left. What can I do for you?

Yasako (*Afraid to ask*): Well, I, uh . . . (*Evelyn encourages her with a smile*) I, uh, uh . . . I thought I might borrow a cup of sugar.

Evelyn (*Not what she expected*): Sugar? Of course. What are you baking?

Yasako: Baking? I, uh, well, actually, my favor is a little bigger than that.

Evelyn: Please. Go ahead.

Yasako: Well, my husband needs me at our restaurant. Just for a short while. Could you stay with my daughter for me? She never wakes up so there shouldn't be any problem.

Evelyn: Don't you worry about a thing, Mrs. Yamashita. I'm happy to help out. Let me get my things. I hope everything's okay.

Yasako: It's fine. My husband was hinting this evening that he needs help. Things are very busy. Californians really like Japanese food.

Evelyn: And Japanese like American food, too.

Yasako: Not me.

(*They move to the Yamashita home as lights cross-fade. Yasako hands her a long list.*)

Yasako: These are important numbers. Her pediatrician, her allergist, the restaurant, poison control center. But you know you call 1-9-9 first.

Evelyn (*Kindly*): 9-1-1.

Yasako: Yes, of course.

Evelyn (*Gently guides her away*): Don't worry, Mrs. Yamashita.

Yasako: One more thing.

Evelyn: Yes?

Yasako: The bus.

Evelyn: The bus?

Yasako: Yes. Could you teach me how to take it?

(*Evelyn smiles and nods. They exit as lights cross-fade.*)

SCENE 2

(*A small, trendy, elegant Japanese restaurant represented by a table with chairs, linen tablecloth, and flower; contemporary Japanese music in the background. Yasako sits at a table perusing a menu. Enter Shizuko Mizoguchi, elegant, contemporary, striking. She carries a pad and pen. Her clothing reflects the restaurant's decor.*)

Shizuko: Good evening. Are you ready to order?

Yasako: Age dashi-dofu and unagi no kabayaki, please.

Shizuko (*Smiles broadly*): You made the right choice. The eel is very good. The owner buys his seafood fresh every morning at the fish market.

Yasako (*Looking at her curiously*): Are you Japanese? You have no accent at all.

Shizuko: Yes, I'm Japanese. How long have you been in the States?

Yasako: Since 1978.

Shizuko: Wow. Six years. You seem like the type who'd rather live in Japan. (*Smiles genuinely*) Am I right?

Yasako (*Liking her*): Yes. I married my brother-in-law's cousin and he wanted to live in America. For a while.

Shizuko: I see. Well, you'll do okay. Don't worry. Can I get you something to drink?

Yasako: Hot tea, please.

Shizuko: Sure. Let me put your order in. Great dress.

Yasako: Thank you. My husband gave it to me as a gift. Can you find him for me?

Shizuko: Who?

Yasako: My husband.

Shizuko: Are you supposed to meet him here?

Yasako: Not exactly, but—

Shizuko: What does he look like?

Yasako (*Shy pride*): Well, he's, uh . . . well, you know. Mr. Yamashita.

Shizuko: Mr. Yamashita? Hiro Yamashita? You're . . . Mrs. Yamashita?

Yasako: Yes. And you are?

Shizuko: Shizuko Mizoguchi. Have you heard of me?

Yasako: No. Should I have heard about you?

Shizuko: I'm the one who threw o-manju at your husband.

Yasako (*Surprised*): Oh. I expected someone older and . . . tougher.

Shizuko: Tough? Is that what he said? He means assertive. What do you think?

Yasako: Think? About what?

Shizuko: About me throwing o-manju at your husband.

Yasako: It made me wonder if, well, you know, you were—

Shizuko: Crazy? Yeah. Crazy to still be hanging around here after three years.

Yasako: Well, please be careful. Mr. Yamashita is a patient man, but you must not throw things at your boss.

Shizuko: Yeah. My boss. Thanks for the advice, sister.

Hiro (*Comes running out and stops short at the sight of the two women*): Yasako. Hello. What are you doing here?

Shizuko: She's a customer, just like everybody else in your life, boss.

Yasako: Hello, Papa. I took the bus here!

Hiro: Miss Mizoguchi, please bring my wife some tea.

Yasako: Yes, some tea would be nice, Papa.

Shizuko: I have three paying customers to serve.

Hiro: I said bring her some tea. Do it.

Shizuko (*Simply*): Yes, Papa. Anything Papa say. (*Shizuko saunters off to get tea.*)

Hiro (*Turns to Yasako*): Who's watching Kuniko?

Yasako: Miss Lauderdale.

Hiro: Miss Lauderdale? Who is Miss Lauderdale?

Yasako: Our neighbor. Kuniko's friend.

Hiro: Oh, yes, yes. When did you learn how to take the bus?

Yasako: Tonight. Miss Lauderdale explained it. (*Beat*) I came to help you.

Hiro: No, Yasako. Everything's under control here.

Yasako: Really? Then maybe we can go out. For a walk or—

(*Shizuko saunters back in with tea, places it before Yasako.*)

Hiro: Yasako, I brought you fresh tuna at home. Go home, eat, enjoy.

Shizuko: Never enough for me to take home, but enough for sister here, huh?

Hiro: Go back to work, Miss Mizoguchi.

(*But Shizuko lingers.*)

Yasako: Papa, take a break. Come walk on the beach with me.

Hiro: You always want to walk on the beach. I don't like sand in my shoes or the smell of dead fish.

Yasako: Papa, just tonight. There is a full moon and the beach is so beautiful tonight.

Hiro: You drink your tea and go home, all right?

Shizuko: Oh go walk on the goddamned beach with her.

Hiro: You have customers, Miss Mizoguchi, remember? Get back to them before they leave you. (*To Yasako*) Maybe we'll walk on the beach tomorrow, okay?

Yasako: Okay, Papa.

Shizuko: No it isn't okay. Japanese women gotta learn that. When it isn't okay, don't say it is.

Yasako: You do not talk to my husband like this.

Shizuko (*Surprised at Yasako's tone*): I'm not talking to him. I'm talking to you.

Hiro: Miss Mizoguchi.

Shizuko (*To Yasako*): That was my tea. There's no more left to go around. But I want you to have it.

(*Exits*)

Yasako: Why do you let her talk like that?

Hiro: Miss Mizoguchi . . . is a very good waitress. All the customers like her, okay? Now you drink your tea. I'll have dinner packed for you to take home. And we will talk of going to the beach tomorrow, okay?

(*He starts to go, but Yasako summons the courage to speak.*)

Yasako: No, Papa. It is not okay.

Hiro: Yasako . . .

Yasako: It is not okay.

Hiro (*Exasperated*): Do what you want then. I have work to do.

(*He exits. Yasako isn't at all sure what to do next. But Shizuko's return helps her decide. She stands quickly to go.*)

Shizuko: Sit down. (*But Yaskao still tries to go.*) I said sit down. (*She guides Yasako back into her seat and sits next to her.*) You asked for the tea. Drink it.

Yasako: My daughter may wake up and ask for me. (*Yasako tries to leave. Shizuko forces her to keep her seat.*)

Shizuko: Know what I've got waiting for me at home? A VCR, a color TV, a history worth less than toilet paper. But you, nomi-san, you've had the good life, haven't you? Good and clean. (*Yasako just stares at her. Shizuko laughs.*) My bathroom's all cluttered with lipsticks and lotions and eye shadows. But yours is tidy, isn't it? Although you could use a little lipstick. No offense, but you look like you don't have a mouth. And a woman needs it to speak her mind.

Yasako: I'd better be going now.

Shizuko: I've survived America, Mrs. Yamashita. I'm a pioneer. I'm not afraid of the dark. Are you? I think you are. I can tell by the tilt of your chin when you look at me.

Yasako: What do you want from me?

Shizuko: Let me guess: you were raised in the provinces with servants, old-fashioned mama who still wears kimono, women's college, married down, refused to be naturalized, never leave the house, thirty-three. (*Beat*) I was naturalized, married to an American before. Big trouble, but he taught me how to walk six steps in front of him without shuffling. He was looking for Madame Butterfly; he turned out to be Mr. Moth and he's still chasing the golden light. Aren't they all. That's why I have a Japanese lover now. And nothing they say about Japanese men is true. You know: inflexible, no poetry, small penis. Not true. (*Yasako moves to leave again, but Shizuko detains her.*) By the way, thanks for the lamp.

Yasako: Lamp?

Shizuko: Hiro gave me a lamp you didn't want. He says you sell all the furniture in the house because you don't want your daughter to fall and get hurt. You know, you can't protect her from the whole world. The world just comes, breathing hard. You gotta breathe back. Like Hiro. He breathes back. (*Shizuko rises to leave. This time, Yasako wants her to stay. Shizuko relaxes in her seat.*)

Yasako: What do you mean "he breathes back"?

Shizuko: On my . . . neck.

Yasako: . . . y-your neck?

Shizuko: This long, beautiful thing under my chin.

Yasako: Are you suggesting that—

Shizuko: Yes, Mrs. Yamashita. You win the grand prize.

(*Jarred, Yasako drops her teacup. Shizuko picks it up and plays with it in the palm of her hand.*)

Yasako (*Trembling*): How long?

Shizuko (*Lights a cigarette*): Too long.

Yasako: He is my husband.

Shizuko: That and a bowl of rice might get you through tomorrow. (*Beat*) And don't think I'm skating on silk. He's a piece of work for me, too.

Yasako: B-but do you . . . love him?

Shizuko: Wow, that's a pretty bold question for a nice Japanese girl to ask. I hold him all night long, Mrs. Yamashita. I dream with him, eat cheeseburgers and strawberry ice cream in bed with him, let him wear his shoes in the house.

Yasako: Why are you doing this? These are all lies.

Shizuko: Are you sure? Can you take that chance? (*Shizuko hands Yasako a letter. Yasako doesn't want to take it.*) I've been saving this for a long time. Take it. I said take it. (*She forces the letter into Yasako's hand. Yasako drops it.*) Read it. (*She gives Yasako a business card. Yasako holds it like it has a disease.*) Here's my card: my number and address. When you're ready to talk, come see me. (*Yasako looks at the card, tears it in half, and drops it at her feet where the letter lies.*) Fine. Tear it up. Pretend what is isn't, just like most Japanese do. Go on smiling and, when you get tired of smiling, ask your husband where I live. It's our apartment and he's there at least three times a week.

Yasako: Apartment?

Shizuko: In Japan, the tea is always hot. Go home and you won't have to worry about cold tea ever again. Or try coffee some time. (*Places the teacup in front of Yasako*) Good night, Mrs. Yamashita. Don't drop any more teacups. Where I come from in Shizuoka, they say it's bad luck.

(*Yasako stares quietly at Shizuko, who stares back with discomfort. Shizuko picks up the two pieces of the business card and tucks them into a pocket in Yasako's purse. Yasako turns and walks away. Lights cross-fade to another spotlight in which Yasako bows deeply to Evelyn.*)

Yasako: Thank you so much.

Evelyn: Please, don't mention it. She's sleeping restlessly. You might want to check on her.

(*Yasako nods as Evelyn exits. Yasako kneels as if hovering over her child. Fuyo appears and anxiously looks from Yasako to the unseen Kuniko.*)

Yasako (*Reacts to a waking child*): Go back to sleep, Kuniko. Mommy will sleep right here next to you on the futon.

(*Hiro enters the light.*)

Yasako: What are you doing here?

Hiro: I live here. Good night, Kuniko. Come, Yasako.

Yasako: Where are we going?

Hiro: To bed.

Yasako: I am in bed.

Hiro: My customers would laugh me right out of my restaurant if I told them that my wife prefers to sleep with our daughter.

(*Because he is talking too loud and she fears him waking up the child, she shoos him away from Kuniko and into the main area of the Yamashita home.*)

Yasako: Americans laugh at taking shoes off in the house, too. So what? The three of us should be sleeping together in the same room, just like we did in Japan.

Hiro: We did that because there was so little room in that house.

Yasako: My mother said we do it to protect our souls.

Hiro: To hell with your mother and our souls.

(*Fuyo's spirit reacts.*)

Hiro: Real life, Yasako. Real life. It just isn't right for me to sleep with Kuniko, especially as she gets older.

Yasako: Why not?

Hiro: Because Americans would think something else was going on. They don't understand about the Japanese way. They don't understand that our presence protects Kuniko, or even that we leave the room when it is time for us to be together as man and wife.

Yasako: We are Japanese. If this country is so free, why do we have to give up being who we are to live here? Some things I can change, like learning to shake hands instead of bowing or going to the bathroom differently than I did in Japan. But you are asking me to change the unchangeable.

Hiro: Yasako, here we can wake up late, sing in the street without being thought a lunatic, challenge the system, speak our minds.

Yasako: No. You have that freedom.

Hiro: You have it, too. If you want it. Just like all the other Japanese.

Yasako: Like the ones who work in your restaurant?

Hiro: Come to bed.

Yasako: For a long time now, I come to bed and you act like you don't want to touch me, but you want me to be there. For what? To keep you warm? Go to bed by yourself.

(*Angered, he leaves abruptly.*)

Yasako: Hiro? Where are you going?

Hiro: Back to the restaurant.

Yasako: You just came from the restaurant.

Hiro: If I can't sleep, I'll work. (*An order*) Now go to bed.

Yasako (*Calmly, a test*): Say hello to Miss Mizoguchi for me.

Hiro (*Agitated*): What? What are you saying?

Yasako: What are you saying?

Hiro: What the hell are you talking about?

Yasako: I simply ask you to say hello to a waitress and it makes you very . . . agitated.

Hiro: You're being ridiculous.

(*Frustrated and angry, Hiro storms out. The distraught Yasako comes face to face with Fuyo, whose hands caress her from an inch away, never touching. But Yasako refuses the touch and exits. Fuyo moves urgently through the house as if exorcising evil, the tension she feels demonstrated in the taut pulling and wringing of her kimono sleeves and the wiping away of her own tears, her hands an inch away from her face. She exits as Yasako re-enters and lights widen. A letter flutters down from above. Yasako catches it, opens it, and reads it. She sits down, Japanese style. From upstage center Shizuko steps up behind her. Both women look out to the audience during the entire scene. The letter is held up in Yasako'ss hands.*)

Yasako and **Shizuko:** "Dear Mrs. Yamashita . . . "

Shizuko: I left Japan behind and you carry it with you like a dead weight.

Yasako: "I feel sorry for you,"

Yasako and **Shizuko:** But I have to think of myself, too.

Shizuko: I have been faithful to your husband for three years, waiting for him to fulfill his promises.

Yasako: "My patience is wearing thin. You can imagine what this is like since you have only known about me for a few weeks and already you have lost patience."

Shizuko: Mrs. Yamashita, give him a divorce and return to Japan.

Yasako: "Let him go before he lets you go. It's easier that way."

Shizuko: What other choice is there because of this shame Hiro has brought into your life. Into our lives.

Yasako: "Please forgive me. I didn't go looking for all this trouble."

Shizuko: Trouble came to me and I was too lonely to say no. And now I love him.

Yasako and **Shizuko:** I have no choice but to prepare a future with him.

Shizuko: You will do okay back in Matsuyama.

Yasako: "Return to the place where you belong."

Yasako and **Shizuko:** Don't do anything foolish.

Shizuko: America's no place for those who can't take what they want without saying I'm sorry.

Yasako: "Sincerely yours,"

Shizuko: Shizuko Mizoguchi.

(*Blackout as sounds of children playing in a park fade in. Spotlight on Yasako. She writes in the journal. Kuniko's laughter is heard and, Yasako waves at the unseen child.*)

Yasako: Kuniko, be careful! Don't fall in the mud! Don't go so fast on the monkey bars! Oh, Kuniko, silly little monkey. (*Reacts as if Kuniko is rushing toward her*) Oh, Kuniko, no, no! Don't jump on Mommy! You'll get mud all over . . . (*Stops as she smiles in defeat and wipes imaginary mud from her clothing*) Kuniko-chan. So cute.

(*The spotlight widens to accommodate Shizuko as she enters. Yasako stands protectively around the unseen child and tries to keep her as far away as possible from Shizuko.*)

Yasako (*To "child"*): Kuniko-chan, go play please. Go play on the swings. Mommy will watch you. Good girl. (*Turns to stare at Shizuko*) What do you want?

Shizuko (*Picks up Yasako's journal and leafs through it*): Do you write down everything you do? (*Yasako just stares at her.*) Good idea. Too bad we can't control our men in the same way. Of course, in this situation, it's our man. Just one. Maybe we should just cut him in half. Which half do you want? (*Yasako grabs her book out of Shizuko's hands.*) Did you read my letter?

Yasako: Stop following me, Miss Mizoguchi.

Shizuko: Good, you did read it. When are you leaving?

Yasako: Maybe you better go back to work and mind your own business.

Shizuko: Time's running out for me, Mrs. Yamashita. Read the letter again.

Yasako: I have been married to Hiro for eight years.

Shizuko: . . . and I have been fucking him for three years.

Yasako: You are vulgar.

Shizuko: It's a vulgar world, Mrs. Yamashita. (*Beat*) When something is over, it's over. He will come to live with me. Do you want that kind of shame for you and your daughter?

Yasako: Who are you to talk about shame?

Shizuko: Listen, sister, you're no better than me. We're both trying to cut it in this frontier. The difference is I can and you never will. (*Beat*) He wants to get it over by New Year's.

Yasako: You are lying.

Shizuko: Wait and see. Suddenly, he's going to offer you a trip to Japan. As a Christmas present.

Yasako: Miss Mizoguchi, how is it that you feel free here and I am the cat trapped in a pillowcase?

Shizuko (*The question surprises Shizuko. There is a look of compassion on her face for Yasako.*): Because you don't ask to be more than a cat.

Yasako: What do you ask to be?

Shizuko: Godzilla.

Yasako: My father's mistress was discreet.

Shizuko: I'm not interested in being that stupid.

Yasako: Is it so stupid?

Shizuko: Hiro loves me, Mrs. Yamashita. In a different kind of way than he loves you. And my kind of love is the kind he needs right now.

(*Yasako tries to focus on her child.*)

Shizuko: You think I'm evil, don't you? A jealous devil breaking up your family. Well, I'm not. If you want to blame someone, you have to blame Hiro, too.

Yasako: My husband is not the type to have an affair.

Shizuko: Right. He's the type to have a relationship. Which is exactly what he's having—with me. And now we all have to deal with it.

Yasako: Why do we have to deal with it? Why can't you just go away?

Shizuko: For the same reasons you can't.

Yasako (*Reacts as if Kuniko has run up to her. The child's presence silences the women and forces them to be calm.*): Hi Kuniko-chan. Are you finished? Say good-bye to the . . . nice lady. Papa's . . . friend.

Shizuko: Hi, little girl. I'm Shizuko.

(*Yasako quickly cuts between Shizuko and the imaginary Kuniko to protect her child from this "evil."*)

Yasako (*A warning to back off*): Good evening, Miss Mizoguchi.

Shizuko: Good evening.

(*Shizuko exits. The sound of Kuniko giggling is heard. Yasako turns suddenly in fear.*)

Yasako: Kuniko, no! Don't climb up there. It's too high. No, Kuniko! Come down! (*Witnesses Kuniko's s fall, which is heard as a thump followed with cries*) Kuniko! (*Runs forward and bends over Kuniko*) Are you all right? Oh, Kuniko, poor thing. Your arm. I think it is broken. Come, Kuniko-chan. Mommy will take you to the hospital. (*Yasako picks up the unseen Kuniko. She stares straight ahead.*) Uh, hello. I am Yasako Yamashita. My daughter has a broken arm, I think. (*Beat*) Fill out papers? Get in line again? But how can you make her wait out here with all these strangers when she is in pain? (*Takes the* *papers*) Don't you understand? We have to go back to Japan. You have to fix her, make her just like she was, make everything just like it was.

(*Yasako gathers her child and runs out. Lights cross-fade to another spotlight, which Yasako enters.*)

Yasako: Hello. I would like to buy a book for my daughter. She is a second grader, but she reads eighth-grade level. (*Surprised that she is not understood*) I am speaking English! (*Enunciates s l o w l y, deeply frustrated*) I would like to buy a book for my daughter. Eighth-grade level. (*Taken aback*) Excuse me, sir, but I was here first. Sir! Do you hear me? I was here first!

(*Lights cross-fade to another spotlight, which Yasako enters. She's a powder keg.*)

Yasako: This is Mrs. Yamashita. (*Spells out*) Y-a-m-a-s-h-i-t-a. (*Spells out again, more slowly*) Y-a-m-a-s-h-i-t-a. Yasako. Yasako. No. Yamashita is my last name. Yamashita.

(*Lights cross-fade to another spotlight, which Yasako enters.*)

Yasako: He would not take his hands off Kuniko's face? And you did not scold this . . . this bully? No wonder Kuniko pushed him! Miss Nancy, usually I nod and smile at everything you people say and do. I keep my anger inside and quietly walk away. But don't you under-stand? Kuniko does not want the hands of a child on her face. That boy's hands could have been in dirt, his nose, his pants. (*To audience*) That is what I want to say to this stupid teacher who probably takes a bath only twice a week. (*Pain, sadness, shame*) But I just nod my head, smile, and quietly walk away. And Kuniko looks at me like I am not a hero. She says to me, "Mommy, in Japan could you be Super-Mom?"

(*Lights cross-fade.*)

SCENE 3

(*Twilight. A nervous Yasako paces. A letter and her journal are on the floor. A laundry basket full of folded clothes, a small suitcase, and a small basin of water are present. She looks in her journal, writes, puts it down, paces again.*)

Yasako (*Creating a poem*): "The sea is . . . the sea is a bridge of light, leading back into the warmth of honor, away from its scant reflections in this life, the mere images of honor, those masks of paint and clay."

(*Restless, she throws down the journal. She takes several crumpled checks out of her pocket, kneels, and carefully smoothes them. She places them by the suitcase. Enter Hiro.*)

Hiro: Here you are again. Pacing at three A.M. Are you sure you're okay?

Yasako: You should know that Kuniko broke her arm. She fell off the monkey bars.

Hiro: What happened?

Yasako: I was not watching her closely enough.

Hiro: A mother can't afford to be distracted, Yasako.

Yasako: I am sorry. I won't ever let her get hurt again. (*Beat*) Sit. Let me wash your feet.

Hiro: Go to sleep, Yasako. What's bothering you every single night, walking the floors like a ghost? (*Beat*) It's Japan, right? We'll go back to visit, okay?

Yasako: We will?

Hiro (*Casually*): Yeah. Maybe for Christmas.

Yasako (*Devastated*): Christmas? Not Christmas.

Hiro: Yes. A nice present for you. Five months away. Plenty of time to plan.

(*She nervously pulls at her hair. A tuft comes out.*)

Hiro: What—what's the matter with your hair?

Yasako: . . . everything is falling apart. So much noise.

Hiro: Yasako. Please. Sit down. Let me see your hair. Let me see.

(*She pulls at her hair again and more comes out.*)

Hiro (*Restraining her*): Stop that!

(*She yanks away with a force that surprises him. She grabs the suitcase.*)

Yasako (*Thrusting suitcase at him*): Here.

Hiro: What is this?

Yasako: Your necessary things. (*Quick beat*) Go. Please.

Hiro: Come here. Let me hold you.

Yasako: I said to go.

Hiro: Yasako, I am not having an affair, okay? I am just trying to manage some problems at the restaurant. Can't you understand?

Yasako: What I understand is that we have no honor.

Hiro: Who gives a damn about honor?

(*She reaches for the checks.*)

Hiro: What are you doing?

Yasako: The laundry. (*She shakes them at him, tosses them at his feet.*) Why all the checks to Miss Mizoguchi? What are you buying from her?

Hiro: Nothing.

Yasako: I packed three trousers, four shirts, and seven underwear. I can mail you the rest.

Hiro (*Kicks the suitcase*): Why don't you go? You're the one who can't cut it here.

Yasako: You have made sure of that.

Hiro: You think it'll be any easier if you run home to Matsuyama? No. Not for you. Not as a divorced woman who lived in America too long. Besides, Kuniko doesn't want to live in Japan.

Yasako (*Shocked, angry*): You're trying to take my daughter away from me.

Hiro: It wouldn't have been any different in Japan, Yasako. You know that. Even your brother has a mistress. My father had one, too.

Yasako: Why can't you be different?

Hiro: Why can't you be different?

Yasako: Different from what? A Japanese woman? An American woman? Different from what?

Hiro: You are my wife, Yasako.

Yasako: That and a bowl of rice might get me through tomorrow.

Hiro: Don't talk like that.

Yasako: Or maybe just through the next five minutes.

Hiro: Stop, Yasako.

Yasako: Fire her.

Hiro: What?

Yasako: If I am your wife, fire her.

Hiro: Surely you aren't suggesting you would divorce me.

Yasako: Half of American marriages end up that way.

Hiro: If we were in Japan, you would accept this, live with it honorably.

Yasako: Don't you remember? Honor is what we flush down the toilet. There is no honor in this house, unless you've been to the bathroom lately.

Hiro: Stop talking like that. American women would never act like this. They'd take it in stride.

Yasako: And then kill you in your sleep.

Hiro: Yasako!

Yasako: Poison your drink or—

Hiro: Stop it!

Yasako: Or wait until you were in the deepest sleep and then cut off your penis.

Hiro: Yasako, please! Here. Take some money. Go out tomorrow. To the beach, shopping, buy Kuniko some more books. Something. (*He tries to hand her bills. She takes them, looks at them for a moment, and then lets them flutter to the floor as she stares at him.*) Okay then, get your American divorce. Will that make you happy? Go to Las Vegas and get a twenty-four-hour one. (*He kicks the money on the floor toward her. They stare at each other, at a standoff.*) Business is good now, too good. It has made me busy . . . and crazy. Try to get it through your head that it doesn't mean anything and—

Yasako: Are you going to fire her or not? (*Stares at him intensely*)

Hiro (*Stares back for a few moments and then looks away; sighs with exasperation*): That will solve all your problems?

Yasako: Yes.

Hiro (*Further exasperation*): Okay. Okay then. (*Hiro sits. She gets the basin of water and sits beside him.*)

Yasako: The water may be cold. But I will wash your feet—

Hiro: Don't.

(*She persists.*)

Hiro: I said to stop it. (*Pushes her away*)

Yasako: Papa.

Hiro: Don't be so ridiculous! Can't you see how ridiculous you are? Don't be so nice to me!

(*He storms out. A letter flutters down from above. She stares at it, reluctant to read it, and then picks it up as lights tighten to a spotlight. She begins to read it.*)

Yasako: "Dear Mrs. Yamashita . . . "

(*Shizuko enters and stands on the periphery of the light.*)

Shizuko: Dear Mrs. Yamashita.

Yasako: "Hiro has told me that you are not feeling well."

Shizuko: You have a small bald spot on your head where you have picked your hair, your nerves electric, your hands shaking.

Yasako: "This makes me sad, especially because he speaks of it when he's sleeping in my bed."

Shizuko: I know you have discarded your journal.

Yasako: "As if there is nothing left to record."

Shizuko: We Japanese are funny, aren't we? Each struggling to be the one who ends up with the most honor, but the fight gets so ugly that it's all blown to smithereens and nobody ends up with anything. (*Beat*) Yasako?

Yasako (*Looks up and locks eyes with Shizuko for a moment.*) Yes?

Shizuko (*Embarrassed, frightened*): . . . I am . . . pregnant with your husband's child.

Yasako: Oh no. No.

Shizuko: It will be a boy. Born in January. It's true. I wish it wasn't.

Yasako: No.

Shizuko: I haven't had the courage to tell Hiro.

Yasako: "Thank you for listening. Sincerely yours, . . . "

Shizuko: Shizuko Mizoguchi.

Yasako: "P.S."

Shizuko: Please take care of yourself.

(*Yasako tears up the letter. Lights dim.*)

SCENE 4

(*A spotlight. Evelyn enters. Yasako, disheveled and distraught, comes up behind her, startling her.*)

Evelyn: Oh, it's you, Mrs. Yamashita. Good morning. How are you today?

Yasako (*Eerily calm*): Everything is fine.

Evelyn: Would you like to come in and have a cup of tea?

(*Yasako shakes her head and moves away, as if she's going to leave. Sensing this, Evelyn takes her by the arm.*)

Evelyn: Are you sure everything's fine?

Yasako (*Suddenly desperate, urgent*): Miss Lauderdale, I want to go back to Japan.

Evelyn: For good?

Yasako: Today. I need to go today.

Evelyn: Today?

Yasako: Yes.

Evelyn: Today. Uh, okay. (*Trying to buy time*) Uh, does your husband know about this?

Yasako: I need to borrow money, Miss Lauderdale. For two tickets.

Evelyn: This is very sudden, Mrs. Yamashita. I'm concerned that you—

Yasako: Please. I have family there. I can work and send your money back in a few months.

Evelyn: I'm not worried about the money. You just don't seem like yourself. Maybe you and your husband need to talk about this some more. Maybe I can help in some small—

Yasako: Never mind.

Evelyn: No, I mean it. Come inside. Let me make you a cup of tea. We'll talk about this. Come on.

Yasako: How can I expect you to understand.

(*Hurt, Evelyn exits as Fuyo's spirit enters. Yasako turns toward her home only to face Fuyo's gaze. That gaze holds an answer for Yasako—the one person who can understand. Lights cross-fade.*)

SCENE 5

(*The Yamashita home. Fuyo sits at Yasako's side. The sounds of the ocean are heard.*)

Yasako (*Sad, plaintive*): "Haru ga kita, haru ga kita. Doko ni kita . . ." (*Suddenly she looks up and forces a smile, wiping away her tears.*) Kuniko-chan! Good morning, little one.

(*Fuyo's eyes follow the "child" as she emerges.*)

Yasako: Yes, yes, we will go to the beach. Be a good girl and brush your hair. (*To Fuyo*) Is it time to go?

(*Fuyo nods.*)

Yasako: What if Kuniko stayed here?

(*Fuyo stares at her. Yasako knows the answer. An impatient Hiro enters, puts on a tie. Fuyo, apprehensive toward him, moves to side stage.*)

Hiro: Where are you going?

Yasako: To walk along the shore, play in the sand.

Hiro: Don't go swimming. Bacteria. Just walk.

Yasako: She wants to collect sea shells. (*Beat*) Do you . . . do you want to walk with me? With us?

Hiro (*Evasive*): Not today.

Yasako: I see.

(*He prepares to leave and Yasako suddenly tries to stop him.*)

Yasako: Hiro!

Hiro: What?

Yasako: Stay today. Come to the beach with us.

Hiro: I have work to do, Yasako. Just work. Another day.

Yasako: Just today. Stay home.

Hiro: I can't. Besides, you know I hate the beach. You go, enjoy yourself. Papa loves you Kuniko-chan. Bye-bye.

(*Hiro exits. Fuyo nods her head three times and claps her hands silently once. Ocean sounds intensify as Fuyo beckons to Yasako to follow, her arms moving like waves as lights darken.*)

Yasako: We are going on a long journey, ne, Kuniko-chan. To . . . home. Hold my hand.

(*Ocean sounds crescendo. Downstage, two kuro-ko enter with long streamers of ocean-colored silk that they propel repeatedly from fans. Lights reflect the ocean on the scrim. Yasako faces the audience, the "sea." Fuyo encircles Yasako and becomes part of the kuro-ko's wavelike movement.*)

Yasako: Can you see the mermaids waiting? Bow to the mystical sea, Kuniko. Our souls float, our bodies dance.

(*Yasako and a voiceover of Kuniko and Fuyo chant the earlier poem in unison as Yasako gently pushes the "child" forward.*)

Fuyo, Yasako, and **Voiceover:** Se o hayami iwa ni sekaruru takigawa no warete mo sue ni awanto zo omou. . . . kono yo de . . . ai masho.

(*Crashing waves intensify, lights whirl, drums beat. Yasako sinks beneath the silky, turbulent waters, disappearing in the waves as lights fade to black.*)

ACT 2

SCENE 6

(*Spotlight center stage on Yasako in plain prison garb, her eyes closed. Fuyo moves around her in a frenzy as a taiko drum beats. Kuniko's laughter surrounds her, mixed with ocean sounds. Fuyo kisses her an inch away from her forehead and then runs out. Yasako sits up and looks around in fear and confusion. And then footsteps are heard, and the sound of a cell door clanging shut. The lights suddenly go to full*) *and glaringly bright, revealing Angela Rossetti standing next to Yasako.)*

Angela *(Extends a hand)*: Hello. I'm Angela Rossetti, your attorney. I need to ask you a few questions? *(Silence from Yasako)* Are you okay? Can I get you anything? *(More silence. Giving up on the pleasantries, Angela gets to work.)* Do you remember where you went with your daughter yesterday, Mrs. Yamashita? *(Pronounces it "yama-SHEET-tah")*

Yasako *(Distrust, fear)*: . . . I-I-I woke up and I was in the hospital and . . . and there was a g-g-guard and I asked him where Kuniko was and . . .

Angela: Tell me what happened at the beach.

(Yasako remembers and starts to cry. Angela approaches, pats her gently on the shoulder.)

Angela: You do know that she is . . .

Yasako:	**Angela:**
Gone.	Dead.

Yasako: And you can go now, too. Just tell me when I can go back to the beach.

Angela: I'm afraid you won't be going anywhere for a while, Mrs. Yamashita. *(Beat)* First-degree murder. That's what the State of California plans to charge you with. *(Yasako registers shock.)* The court has appointed me to represent you, and I plan to do so to the best of my ability.

Yasako: Murder?

Angela: I plan to fight for a lesser conviction of voluntary manslaughter. *(Beat)* Problem is, Americans don't take too kindly to people killing children, and it'll be Americans staring out at you from the jury. And probably not the kind who eat steamed white rice with their meals. This is a conservative town full of retired navy guys whose buddies were killed in World War II. *(Beat)* So we've got a fight on our hands.

Yasako: You had no right to stop us!

Angela: Calm down. I didn't. It was two hotel guests. They thought you were drowning. And now your child is dead and you're alive. Though, to be honest, there are a few people in city hall who wish you weren't.

Yasako: Is that what you wish?

Angela: My wishes are irrelevant.

Yasako: I did not kill my child.

Angela: Let's put it this way, when I take my five-year-old daughter to the beach, we walk along the sand, not into the Pacific Ocean.

(*Yasako is taken aback by this outburst. Angela wishes she hadn't let it show. She tries to compose herself; she does a good job of it. She comforts Yasako.*)

Angela: But, of course, this isn't about me. It's about you. And I'm sorry that I acted like a mother first. Sometimes it just swallows up everything else you are.

Yasako: Yes, I know. But it is supposed to. That's why you have to let me catch up with Kuniko.

Angela: She's gone, Mrs. Yamashita. Her body is in the morgue and you don't want to go there. We're trying to locate your husband.

Yasako: No. He must not come here.

Angela (*Concerned*): What happened, Mrs. Yamashita?

Yasako: Promise me you won't let him bother me.

Angela: I'll try. (*Quick beat*) Now I know this is difficult, but I need you to explain to me what happened as best as you can.

Yasako: We were . . . traveling.

Angela: Traveling?

Yasako: In a vessel that you cannot begin to understand.

Angela: A vessel. Uh huh. (*Exasperated, Angela addresses an offstage persona.*) Could somebody bring us some coffee, please?

Yasako (*Urgently*): I need tea. Green tea.

Angela (*To offstage persona, caring*): The lady wants green tea. Can we accommodate her?

(*Lights cross-fade to two spotlights in which Evelyn and Hiro stand, talking on imaginary phones, in mid-conversation. Hiro waits for her to speak as Shizuko embraces him from behind. She struggles with tears.*)

Hiro: How did you get this number?

Evelyn: T-t-they tried to call you.

Hiro (*Impatient*): Are you all right?

Evelyn: They couldn't find you. She had them call me.

Hiro: Yasako? What's happened? Where are they?

Evelyn (*Fresh tears*): O-oyako shinju.

Hiro: . . . they're dead? They're both dead?

Evelyn: K-Kuniko. She . . . drowned . . .

(*Shikuzo studies his distraught state with concern. She pulls away.*)

Hiro: Kuniko is drowned? My daughter is drowned?

(*Shizuko gasps and turns away.*)

Evelyn: They saved Yasako.

Hiro: What hospital is she in?

Evelyn (*Pressing him*): She came to me, Mr. Yamashita, very upset. She said she had to go back to Japan.

Hiro: What hospital is she in?

Evelyn: She's not in a hospital. She's in jail.

Hiro: Jail? Why jail? What did she do wrong?

Evelyn: This is America, Mr. Yamashita. They call it murder.

Hiro: No! I must go to her. I must see her.

Evelyn: Mr. Yamashita, what made her think there was no other choice? (*Then*) Why was she so distraught? Was something happening between the two of you?

Hiro: That is none of your business.

Evelyn: You're wrong, Mr. Yamashita. And, after today, it's going to be everybody's business.

(*Lights cross-fade to a prison. Yasako sits. Evelyn arrives with a small box. Yasako is so ashamed that she will not raise her head. She stares down at her hands.*)

Evelyn: When I read the article in the paper and all the horrible things they said about you, I said to myself, "That doesn't sound like my neighbor." So I came to bring you this. (*Hands Yasako the box*) They're torn because they had to inspect them.

Yasako: Thank you. Sorry for the trouble. (*Bows*)

Evelyn: You sound just like my mother. (*Beat*) I made them myself.

Yasako: You made this o-manju? I have never known Americans to even eat these.

Evelyn: My father was American, but my mother was from Japan.

Yasako: You never told me.

Evelyn: I never told you she was Japanese because, well, it seemed unnecessary to point it out. Unless you had asked.

(*Yasako leans forward, as does Evelyn in response.*)

Yasako: Do you think what I did was wrong?

Evelyn (*Troubled*): My mother probably wouldn't have thought so.

Yasako: But what about you?

Evelyn: I don't know. I understand, but then I don't understand. Because I'm not in your situation. Also, I don't look Japanese, so it's easier for me. Sometimes.

Yasako: Miss Lauderdale, I want you to bring me some . . . special tea. (*Looks over her shoulder*) The kind that will allow me to . . . travel.

Evelyn: Mrs. Yamashita, I can't do that.

Yasako: In the cabinet to the left of the stove, there is a teacup painted gold and rust. In that teacup, I wish to drink my tea.

Evelyn (*Overlapping, evading*): I brought you a book. Here. You can rest and read. (*Shaken, a pause*) I-it's too late, Mrs. Yamashita.

Yasako: My family travels the universe now. Before you said you would do anything to help me. Please.

Evelyn: Last year, my mother died. I don't want you to die, too. You're meant to live.

Yasako: But how? How am I supposed to do that?

Evelyn: Let me help you. Let me be your friend.

Yasako: You should go now.

Evelyn: I'm sorry.

Yasako: Just go. Please do not come again.

(*Evelyn fades into the darkness upstage. As lights cross-fade, a sound bite cuts in.*)

Sound Bite: Mrs. Rossetti? We understand that you're a mother. How can you begin to justify your client's actions? How can you even stand to represent the case of an alleged child murderer?

(*Lights cross-fade downstage as Angela and Yasako enter the cell. Yasako manipulates a black tea bag in her hands.*)

Yasako: Those white guards out there. They called me "baby killer."

Angela (*Beat*): Fuck 'em.

(*This responses brings a faint smile to Yasako's lips.*)

Angela: Okay, Mrs. Yamashita. I'm a white woman on the jury from, say, Topeka, Kansas. I'm Catholic with balls of iron and I've got one very precious child. Convince me that what happened was not, according to your system of beliefs, something bad. What'd you call it again?

Yasako: Oyako-shinju.

Angela: Parent-child suicide, right?

Yasako: Until a certain age, the child is inseparable from the mother. The egg and what it has created are one. If I had taken my life and left my child behind to be raised by substitute mothers, I would have dishonored my family.

Angela: I don't buy that. Not in any culture. Let me tell you, Mrs. Yamashita, if anybody tried to harm my child, I'd kill them without a second thought. And probably with my bare hands.

Yasako: So would I. That is why I took her with me. Bun-shin. "Bun" means divide and "shin" means part of the body. I consider my child bun-shin; my body divides to create the child and we are one. Here you believe that the child is an individual, separate from you.

Angela: And Kuniko Yamashita was not an individual in your eyes?

Yasako: Bun-shin is like a tree. The child is the branch that needs to stay connected to grow. So, if you—the tree—dies, the branch dies.

Angela: But if just the branch dies, can't the tree continue to live, grow new branches and leaves?

Yasako (*Without self-pity*): Who cares about the tree? No one needs the tree.

Angela: There was a woman in Kansas City, white; she killed her son and was about to join him when her husband caught her. She went to jail for life. And the American public wouldn't've even flinched if she'd been burned at the stake.

Yasako: An American woman? You would have killed her for . . . for doing this?

Angela: I wouldn't do it. But the People might.

Yasako: What people?

Angela: The People of the United States.

Yasako: You mean a whole gang? A whole gang of Americans?

Angela: It's a phrase, Yasako. The People, capital "P." The government. The good of our society. (*Beat*) I found three cases of Japanese women who ended up with lesser charges of manslaughter. So in arguing for a reduced sentence, I'll use cultural defense to make our case.

Yasako: Cultural defense?

Angela: Laotian man beats up his wife and, when he gets arrested, he looks at the police in surprise—maybe even shock—and says, "What do you mean I'm in trouble because I beat up my wife? I own her. I can do whatever I want with her." To him, see, the wife is as good as a dog. But this is America. He goes to jail and she gets a divorce.

Yasako: American men do not beat up their wives?

Angela (*Looks at her as if to say touché and sighs*): The Laotian man has an easier time of it in the courts because, in Laos, his behavior is within the law. The courts ask him to realize that he must adapt to the American way, but they give him a break.

Yasako: But then he is no longer Laotian if he exchanges his culture for yours.

Angela: . . . I'm still Italian.

Yasako: . . . and I am still the tree.

(*The women stare at each other over a confounding impasse.*)

Yasako: What is your daughter's name?

Angela: . . . Samantha.

Yasako: That is a nice name.

Angela: Thank you. (*Beat*) I'll bring you some good tea next time.

Yasako (*Hands her the tea bag with an apologetic bow*): Sorry. I do not like American black tea. It is so bitter. Like everything else here, you have to sweeten it or it is impossible to swallow.

Angela: So sweeten it. Is that so difficult?

Yasako (*Nods*): Kuniko means child of the country. I named her that because I wanted her to feel like a child of Japan even though she had to grow up here. (*Begins to cry*)

Angela (*With sadness*): She didn't grow up, Mrs. Yamashita. She didn't grow up.

(*Yasako's tears grow fervent. Angela's impulse is to comfort her, but she cannot bring herself to do so. Exit Angela. Lights cross-fade downstage. Hiro stands to give a speech. Evelyn sits nearby holding a clipboard full of petitions.*)

Hiro: Thank you all for coming to this important community meeting this evening.

(*Shizuko appears in an upstage spotlight. She looks exhausted. Her clothes look slept-in. Hiro and Evelyn continue to function, unaware of Shizuko's presence. She also is unaware of theirs.*)

Hiro: There are many reasons why we are gathered here tonight.

Shizuko: The room is cold. He's still here, but not really. Not now.

Hiro: I-I wasn't the best husband or father that my family deserved.

Shizuko: . . . Hiro collapses to his knees screaming, "KUNIKO, KUNIKO," and tells me that he killed his child. . . .

Hiro: Japanese culture is different from American culture. But what I want to make clear is that my wife, Yasako Yamashita, is not a murderer.

Shizuko: Winter in his eyes.

Hiro: Especially considering the incredible bond my wife had with our daughter, Kuniko.

Shizuko: Winter . . .

Hiro: All of your ancestors originally came from other lands and, as they struggled to carve a place for themselves in America, they, too, had trouble coming to terms with new cultural views of right and wrong. In this way, we are all the same.

Shizuko: I gather all my things and leave without a note.

Hiro: This has been a terrible accident. I hope you will forgive us.

Shizuko: I cannot compete with ghosts. (*Looks out toward the audience*)

Hiro: Please sign this petition asking for leniency for Yasako. Please, for the sake of my child.

Shizuko: Yasako?

Hiro: This is our neighbor, Miss Lauderdale. She is Japanese and American. She can understand both sides of this. I ask your help, because the media, the public is against us. Ask your friends to sign them as well.

Shizuko: Yasako-san? I leave all my secrets to you. Keep them for me, okay? Keep them. (*Bows all the way to floor*)

Hiro: Thank you.

(*Evelyn mimics handing out petitions as she exits. Lights fade and Shizuko rises. For a brief moment, her eyes and Hiro's meet. Lights cross-fade to the prison, where Angela and Yasako sit on a cot.*)

Angela: She said she was Godzilla? Miss Mizoguchi's quite a piece of work. One doesn't often hear of such aggressiveness in Japanese women.

Yasako: Let me guess. You merely saw *Shogun* on American TV and now you are expert, ne? I saw *Shogun*. It was like *Gone with the Wind*, but Japanese style. Are you Scarlett O'Hara?

Angela: I'm sorry. Please, Yasako. I'm here to help you.

Yasako: Do you believe you possess a soul?

Angela: What? Well, yes, I think so.

Yasako: Then you believe you have lived before and will live again.

Angela: I'm not so sure. I'm a recovering Catholic, reinventing my faith. But I know I have a soul.

Yasako: Where have you lived before?

Angela: Cincinnati.

Yasako (*Disappointed in her*): I see.

Angela: Before that, I lived in Des Moines.

Yasako: Well, I lived in ninth-century Kyoto.

Angela: I see.

Yasako: Do you?

Angela: Yes. I understand. Traveling . . . in a vessel. Is that a Japanese belief?

Yasako: I don't know. It is my belief.

Angela: I guess there are many metaphysical possibilities.

Yasako: Now I want to . . . live somewhere else.

Angela: A life is a precious thing, Yasako. Your life was precious even to a stranger. I want to believe that if this had happened in Japan, a Japanese also would have dragged you from the sea.

Yasako: I failed as a wife. And now I have failed as a mother, too. (*Beat*) And all you know of life is that yesterday you lived in Cincinnati and today you live in San Diego.

Angela: Yasako, you have to stop wanting to die and start wanting to live.

Yasako: . . . what happens in San Diego when you are convicted of murder? Is it absolutely certain I would be put to death?

Angela: You think it's that easy to get yourself killed? Listen to me very carefully: it means you're admitting guilt. That's like getting up in front of all your Japanese relatives and saying, "I murdered Kuniko."

Yasako: No! I did not and I will not say that. But I want the death sentence. It's the only way I can catch up with Kuniko.

Angela: A guilty sentence doesn't mean you waltz to the gas chamber and join your daughter. It means you might get to go. But it also means that, in the eyes of the world—including a lot of Japanese—you are disgraced, you are the cold-blooded killer of the child you brought into this world.

Yasako (*Momentarily stunned, then draws into herself, stony*): . . . someone once told me that, in America, only soldiers and superheroes get to die with honor.

(*Yasako and Angela stare at one another as lights cross-fade to another spotlight. Evelyn sits. Angela and she are in mid-interview.*)

Evelyn: A few days later, he finally broke down and told me that he'd been having an affair with a Miss Mizoguchi. He said he loved her, but he also loved his wife.

Angela: How special.

Evelyn: The woman left abruptly. He hasn't seen her. He wants to see Yasako. Has she changed her mind?

(*Angela shakes her head.*)

Evelyn: Does she know about his efforts to help her?

Angela: She doesn't want to be helped, saved or pitied. She just wants to die.

(*With a touch of guilt, Evelyn looks away.*)

Angela: Tell me, Ms. Lauderdale. Mr. Yamashita's Japanese; he's adapted. Why can't Yasako?

Evelyn: She was raised by a woman who grew up before the war. That means old customs, old-fashioned ways.

Angela: But I don't get it. Does that mean a lot of Japanese resort to suicide when something goes wrong?

Evelyn: It may surprise you to know that Americans have a higher suicide rate than Japanese, especially American young people.

Angela: Okay. Fine. Good point.

Evelyn: So what are you going to do?

Angela: The cultural defense isn't enough. To get the jury to be lenient, I have to plead temporary insanity, Ms. Lauderdale.

Evelyn: Insanity? Why?

Angela: To save my client.

Evelyn: But she's not insane. Why can't we plead not guilty?

Angela: Plead that and the jury will grind their heels in her face. In the eyes of that jury, she's psychologically disturbed. They can buy that, maybe even feel sorry for her. I want you to convince her that the insanity plea's the best way to go. I brought it up with her and she asked me to leave.

Evelyn: Is that how it's going to be? If you can't be like everybody else, then let's call you mentally deviant and shove you out of the way? Are you her friend or enemy, Mrs. Rossetti?

Angela: Neither. I'm her attorney. Look, if it makes you feel any better, I don't think she was thinking about murdering her child when she walked into the ocean. God help me, I think she was thinking about saving her child.

Evelyn: You mean you really believe she was innocent?

Angela: She's not innocent. But she's not guilty either. Here's a riddle for you: is it more crazy for people to expect everyone to behave just like them or for someone like Yasako to expect to behave in another way, but still live among the people? (*Beat*) What am I saving Yasako for? A lifetime of insomnia as she curses herself for not getting it right? Now that's insane. Good day, Ms. Lauderdale. I think I'll go take my daughter out for a root beer float.

Evelyn (*As Angela crosses*): I've done some research . . . It's not right for Yasako to be labeled as insane or in any way be painted as a cold-blooded baby-killer. (*Beat*) So I think we should let the judge decide and plead no contest.

Angela: You think I haven't thought of that? Don't you know it's the same thing as a guilty plea to the prosecution?

Evelyn: But it's not the same thing to Yasako. And that's what matters, isn't it?

Angela: Thanks for the advice, counselor.

(*Angela exits and then Evelyn exits. A sound bite of court hallway noises and busy reporters cuts in.*)

Sound Bite: Mrs. Rossetti! Mrs. Rossetti! We understand that the defendant has lived in this country for six years. Isn't it true that if we let every new immigrant keep their customs and not assimilate that we're asking for trouble for the future of this country?

(*Angela enters the cell where Yasako sits as lights cross-fade.*)

Yasako: Thank you for green tea.

Angela: You're welcome. So you wanted to see me. What's up?

Yasako: I have come up with my own plan, Mrs. Rossetti.

Angela: All right. Let's hear it.

Yasako: . . . I will pretend hysteria. You will say I need special tests. Then they will let me leave to go to a hospital. And you can take me back to the ocean.

(*Yasako bows to the floor. Angela gently pulls her up. Overwhelmed, Angela removes several newspaper articles from a packet and shows them to Yasako.*)

Angela: I think you should see these news stories. You've become a celebrity. Some Americans feel sympathy for you.

Yasako (*Visibly shaken*): But "Medea"? Why do they call me this "Medea"?

Angela: Do you know Medea? Like you, she was a foreigner. Popular myth says Jason brought her back from the East and she helped him obtain a treasure, the Golden Fleece. When Jason deserted her, she killed their children and fed them to him. There're many different versions of the myth. In another case similar to yours, the attorney argued a Medea-like compulsion exists among Japanese women to react to infidelity by killing their children.

Yasako: Now we are cannibals, too?

Angela: No. Although Medea is despised in the West, I believe she killed because she knew Jason's new wife would enslave her children.

Yasako: The point is to go together. Mrs. Rossetti, please. Help me with this plan.

Angela: What about returning to Japan after this, Yasako? Your family would understand.

Yasako: Maybe, but they will not necessarily forgive. Many may despise me, gossip about me over milk-tea or soda pop. Because children are sacred and I have abandoned mine to the afterlife without a mother. You have to understand, Mrs. Rossetti. In Japan, we have no crib death because we sleep with our children from the day they are born. We honor, no, we worship our children. In America, you have Mother's Day, Father's Day. We have Children's Day.

Angela: Yasako, you say the universe is out of balance because your daughter's spirit is fragmented without you. I say this is the only universe we've got. (*Quick beat*) I can't take you to the beach, Yasako. I believe too much in freedom. I believe that people have to live and let live, especially in America. I believe you didn't understand the ramifications of what you were doing, at least not in this cultural context. So don't let me do all this hard work for nothing, Yasako. You said the point is to go together. Well, she's already gone, so you can't have that. Let's concentrate on what you can have. (*Angela gathers the articles and returns them to the packet. Yasako espies one that has a photograph of her and Kuniko, a reprint of a family snapshot. She grabs it, stares at the photo.*) It's a good picture of you and your daughter.

Yasako: Yes. It is.

(*Yasako hands back the photo. Angela looks at it, gives it back to her as a gift. Yasako bows deeply in appreciation and looks up at Angela, who hesitates and then decides to bow. Angela exits, acknowledging Hiro as she passes him in the hall. Hiro enters the cell.*)

Yasako: Get out.

Hiro: I know you don't want to see me, but—

Yasako: Get out or I'll scream.

Hiro: Stop it. Remember. I'm the only one who knows you really aren't crazy.

Yasako (*This remark has an impact on her. Her anger subsides momentarily.*): Of course. After all, you celebrate what I am.

(*Hiro doesn't understand what she means.*)

Yasako: You celebrate your perfect Japanese wife. You got what you wanted, right? Fine brain, small heart, good sex, clean floors . . . and so traditional that your "perfect" wife is all you have left. (*Beat*) Go. Just go.

Hiro: It's very quiet at home, Yasako. (*No response*) I can't go into the restaurant. Everyday someone asks, "How are you doing? Are you okay?" I can't smile anymore and say I'm fine. Because it's a lie and there have been too many lies already. So I stay home and clean Kuniko's room. I read her books and take a nap in her bed.

Yasako (*Quietly*): You must fix it if you sleep in it.

Hiro (*Nods*): I wish . . . I wish none of this would have happened. I'm sorry that I failed you and Kuniko. I should be in jail now, not you.

Yasako: You should not sleep in her bed.

Hiro: I understand, Yasako. You tried. (*Beat*) You had responsibility for three lives. Now you only have two.

Yasako: One. And you have to let me go.

Hiro: You look tired, Yasako. But so beautiful. You must sleep and dream again.

Yasako: Dream of what? What do you want from me? To make you another baby and fix our miserable lives? Forget it. If I could rip my womb out with my bare hands, I would.

Hiro: I just want you. I . . . (*Beat*) I need you.

Yasako: What for? What could you possibly want me for but to be what I've always been? I'm not willing to live that way again.

Hiro: It's just about you, Yasako. To think I almost lost you.

Yasako: You did lose me, Hiro. I disappeared that day at the beach and I'm not coming back. . . . you're looking at a ghost.

Hiro: Yasako, listen. We can go back to Japan and—

Yasako: I don't want to go back to Japan. Not like this.

Hiro: Okay. Then we can stay. We can stay right here and learn to live a new way.

Yasako: How strange that you are now the dreamer and all I can see are the necessary order of things.

Hiro: Yasako, listen. You can help me at the restaurant. We can be together all the time. And we can talk like we used to when we first met. Who we were is what's dead. Not us. We must go on, learn and repair. (*Beat*) Have I ever needed you before?

Yasako (*Looks at him for a beat and then slowly shakes her head*): Make certain when you fix the bed that you get the blankets in the right order. She likes the pink-flowered futon on top and the mint one underneath. Make sure you get it right.

Hiro (*Beat*): Okay.

(*Spotlight out and then downstage center, into which Yasako enters and stares at the audience as faint ocean sounds are heard.*)

Yasako (*Recites*):
　　She swims so long at sea,
　　so strong in the current
　　looking for me.

　　But the web of the net
　　detains me as worlds overlap
　　and I consider the trap.
　　Whether to die to live
　　or live in death,
　　a mother in exile,
　　a daughter's last breath.

The sea is she
and if I do not go,
then who am I,
what do I know.

(*Ocean sounds and lights out. A gavel thuds exaggeratedly in the darkness. A judicial voice reverberates from the darkness.*)

Judicial Voice: You have been arraigned in this court on the charges as specified. (*Beat*) Is the defendant ready to enter a plea?

(*Yasako and Angela stand in separate spotlights looking at each other from across the stage.*)

Angela:	Yasako:
She is, Your Honor.	I am, Your Honor.

Judicial Voice: And how do you plead?

Angela: The defendant pleads no contest.

Yasako (*Haltingly*): . . . no . . . contest.

(*Lights fade out. Angela and Yasako exit. There is a hubbub of voices, cameras clicking, and footsteps criss-crossing. They crescendo and then blend with the ocean sounds that overwhelm them. Lights fade up on the cell. Yasako crosses to the light and sits. A nervous Evelyn enters. Yasako is not happy to see her visitor.*)

Evelyn: Hello.

Yasako: Why do you keep coming to the courtroom every day? I asked you to leave me alone.

Evelyn: You've been handling yourself so well, Yasako. You're going to get through this.

Yasako: Am I? (*Beat*) When I was returning from the courthouse, an American yelled "murderer" and threw a tomato at me. I didn't wipe it off. She was Japanese American.

Evelyn: Well, their mothers aren't from Japan. They don't look at things the Japanese way. They don't even use chopsticks.

Yasako: Shame, ne. Even in Japan, children do not want to use chopsticks anymore. I hope you use them.

Evelyn: Before I used a fork.

Yasako: Your mother was smart to teach you the old ways.

Evelyn: When I have children, I'll teach them, too. (*Beat*) Oh. I'm sorry.

Yasako: About what?

Evelyn: I shouldn't talk about. . .

Yasako: Children? Oh, no, it's all right.

Evelyn: We have over five thousand names on the petitions. Mr. Yamashita is very excited about it.

Yasako: Hiro?

Evelyn: He didn't tell you? He's been the driving force to get signatures on petitions that he's giving to the media and to the court to show that Americans understand your dilemma.

Yasako: Hiro did that?

Evelyn: It was his idea. The papers have picked up the story, so even the media seems to be more sympathetic toward your case.

Yasako: But I do not want sympathy.

Evelyn: Yasako . . . what honor is there in dying by someone else subjecting you to gas or the chair?

Yasako: Please get out. You dishonor me with your persistence. You are so American sometimes.

Evelyn: And sometimes too Japanese for my own good.

(*This remark sparks interest, curiosity in Yasako. Evelyn takes from her clothing a small container.*)

Evelyn: . . . I brought you tea. Special tea. (*Evelyn passes the tea to Yasako and Yasako stares at the can.*)

Yasako: A-a-are you sure you want to do this?

Evelyn: No.

Yasako: You could get in trouble.

Evelyn: I've thought about that.

Yasako: Thank you.

Evelyn: Yasako-san, is suicide so honorable—when it really isn't about shame, but about running away from facing life . . . without Kuniko?

Yasako: I'm running to her. I think.

Evelyn: Are you sure? Are you certain you're not running away?

(*Quick beat*) She's gone, but we have to go on living . . . somehow. Don't you think that's what Kuniko would want?

Yasako: Kuniko . . .

Evelyn: She would say, "Mommy, don't hurt yourself. Papa needs you." And then she'd sing.

Yasako: Yes. She would . . .

Evelyn: You know, I think Kuniko came to my yard and took my cat away just so she could be the hero and rescue her. I think that's what she did.

Yasako: . . . how does one go on living after this?

Evelyn: I don't know, but can't we answer that question together?

(*Evelyn and Yasako stare at each other with clarity and affection. Evelyn exits. Lights close to a tight spotlight. Yasako enters the light, kneels, and studies the teacup as Fuyo enters and urges her to drink.*)

Yasako: Who cares about the tree when the branch is gone?

Angela's Voice (*Offstage*): It must be you who cares. You must start to love yourself, be yourself apart from husband and child . . .

Evelyn's Voice (*Offstage*): We just do it. We just get up in the morning and start walking into the wind.

Hiro's Voice (*Offstage*): I can't remember which blanket goes on top of Kuniko's bed. Is it the green one or the flowered one? Help me.

Kuniko's Voice: Mommy?

Yasako: Kuniko?

Kuniko's Voice: Where's Papa? Make him walk on the beach with you, Mommy. Make him sing like this (*Sings*): "Down the river oh down the river oh down the river we go-o-o!" (*Ends singing and giggling*) Come on, Mommy, you can do it. Bye, Mommy!

(*Yasako stares outward, toward the audience, as she struggles with a decision. The wishes of Kuniko's spirit cause her to contemplate life over death.*)

Yasako:
> Bare of branches, the tree in winter forever.
> But alive, as she would want me to be,
> breathing her dreams through me.

Who cares about the tree when the branch dies?
The women say it is I who must rise above
this misery that I have wrought,
I who must face the future
no matter what I've been taught.

And so I go, but it will always be cold.
And ever with me travels her precious soul.

(*Yasako picks up the cup, stares at it, turning it around, and then slowly places it on the ground. The placement is not easy, as if a force pushes it upward, too. She bows to her mother.*)

Yasako: Mother, do not linger here. Go. Please. Your fate is blessed; mine is cursed. Kuniko needs you.

(*With disappointment, Fuyo caresses Yasako's face, her hand coming close but never touching, her face full of longing. Fuyo exits in defeat as Kuniko's voice sings a bit of "Down the River": "The river is up and the channel is deep, the wind is steady and strong . . . ," and then fades out as Fuyo disappears and Yasako turns toward Kuniko's fading voice.*)

Yasako (*Slow cadence*): "The river is up and the channel is deep, the wind is steady and strong. Oh won't we have a jolly good time as we go sailing along. Down the river, oh down the river, oh down the river we go-o-o, Down the river, oh down the river, oh down the Ohio."

(*The exaggeratedly loud slamming of a gavel startles Yasako as a judicial voice reverberates from the darkness. Lights begin a slow tightening, ending up as a small spotlight on Yasako's face.*)

Judicial Voice (*Voiceover*): Yasako Yamashita. The Superior Court of the County of San Diego, State of California, has found you guilty of one count of voluntary manslaughter. (*Beat*) You will be sentenced to five years' probation with psychiatric treatment and a year in County Jail. (*Beat*) Do you understand the gravity of what has happened to you and, indeed to us all, Mrs. Yamashita?

(*She does. Her eyes reveal that she does. Extremely slow fade on Yasako's resolute face.*)

END OF PLAY

In the

Heart of

America

NAOMI WALLACE

And I await those who return,
who come knowing my times of death.
I love you when I love you not.
The walls of Babylon are close
in the daylight, and your eyes
are big, and your face looms
large in the light.

It is as if you have not been born yet,
we have not separated, and you
have not felled me, as if above
the storm tops every speech is
beautiful, every reunion,
a farewell.

—Mahmoud Darwish

In the Heart of America had its first
performance on August 3, 1994, at the
Bush Theatre in London. Creative
contributors were Richard Dormer, Robert
Glenister, Sasha Hails, Toshie Ogura, and
Zubin Varla. It was directed by Dominic
Dromgoole, set design by Angela Davis,
lighting direction by Paul Russell.

Cast of Characters

Craver Perry

Fairouz Saboura

Lue Ming

Remzi Saboura

Boxler

Setting

*The present and the past. A motel
room, a military camp in Saudi
Arabia, another room, the Iraqi
desert.*

Production Notes

Minimal and not "realistic" set.

ACT 1

SCENE 1

(*Lights up on Craver doing a headstand. Fairouz is standing in the shadows, watching.*)

Fairouz: He sent me a horn in a box. It was a ram's horn.

Craver: He is a funny guy.

Fairouz: Do you laugh at him?

Craver (*Gets to his feet*): What did you say your name was?

Fairouz: I don't laugh at him.

Craver: What's your background? He's never clear where he's from.

Fairouz: Can you tell me how he's doing?

Craver: I told you over the phone I haven't heard from him in months.

Fairouz: You are his best friend.

Craver: I'm sorry to hear that.

Fairouz: Where is he? (*Beat*) Mr. Craver.

Craver: Perry. Mr. Perry. Craver's my first name. C-R-A-V-E-R. How did you get my address?

Fairouz: Remzi wrote in a letter . . .

Craver: I hardly know him.

Fairouz: He wrote: "Craver and I are never separate."

Craver: People get lost. Call the Army.

Fairouz: I did.

Craver (*Does another headstand*): This kid over in Saudi taught me how to do this. It's not keeping your legs in the air; it's how you breathe. See? You got to push the air up through your lungs and into your feet. Then your feet will stay up, float like balloons.

Fairouz: Can Remzi do that? Stand on his head like you?

Craver (*Stands*): Remzi has no balance.

Fairouz: He wrote me that he loved you.

Craver: And who do you love?

Fairouz: I threw it out. The ram's horn.

Craver: We must have bought a dozen horns while we were over there, but not one of them was good enough to send her. He wrote her name on the inside of it. F-A-I-R-O-U-Z. Fairouz. That was the name he wrote.

Fairouz: It had a bad smell.

Craver: Fairouz isn't anything like you.

Fairouz: Horns make noise.

Craver: He said she was like a flower.

Fairouz: I don't like noise. Remzi knows that.

Craver: No, he said she was like milk, sweet, fresh milk.

Fairouz: He likes to race. Did he race with you? He's not fast but he won't believe it.

Craver: Fairouz would have appreciated his gift.

Fairouz: Do you expect me to beg you?

Craver: Know what we call Arabs over there?

Fairouz: I'm not afraid of you, Mr. Perry. When I find out, I'll be back.

(*She exits.*)

Craver (*Calls after her*): Fairouz! (*Beat*) He was my friend.

SCENE 2

(*Craver asleep, worn out. A figure of a woman—an apparition or perhaps something more real—enters. Craver wakes.*)

Craver: Are you looking for him too?

Lue Ming: I might be. Who?

Craver: Remzi. Remzi Saboura.

Lue Ming: Are you Mr. Calley?

Craver: No. I'm not.

Lue Ming: Oh my. I'm in the wrong house.

Craver: How did you get in?

Lue Ming: I was homing in on a small jewelry store in Columbus, Georgia. Is this Georgia?

Craver: Kentucky. Motel 6.

Lue Ming: And you're not Calley?

Craver: Are you Chinese?

Lue Ming: Oh no. I was born in Hanoi.

Craver: What are you doing here?

Lue Ming: I've never left my country. I'm a real homebody.

Craver: You speak good English.

Lue Ming: Haven't tried it before, but it's going nicely, isn't it?

Craver: What do you want?

Lue Ming: He's about five foot ten, red in the face, and likes colorful fish. He should be in his fifties by now.

Craver: I'm not Calley. I can't help you.

Lue Ming (*Sniffs*): A trace. Yes. You smell of him. He's your buddy. Who are you?

Craver: Craver Perry.

Lue Ming: What do you do?

Craver: Not much right now. I'm . . . on leave.

Lue Ming: Ah. An Army fellow. Where were you stationed in Vietnam?

Craver: Vietnam? I wasn't in Vietnam. I was in the Gulf. In Saudi. In Iraq?

Lue Ming: How can they fight in Vietnam and the Gulf at the same time?

Craver: We're not fighting in Vietnam.

Lue Ming: Of course you are. Why, just yesterday my grandfather was out in the fields trying to pull a calf out of the mud. The rains. So much rain. You flew over with your plane and bang, bang, bang, one dead cow and one dead grandfather.

Craver: I've never even been to Vietnam.

Lue Ming: Of course you have.

Craver: The Vietnam war ended over fifteen years ago, lady.

Lue Ming: Are you sure?

Craver: Positive.

Lue Ming: Who won? My God, who won?

Craver: You did.

Lue Ming: Oh I wish I could have told Grandpa that this morning. (*Beat*) So I missed the house and the year. But not the profession. How many gooks have you killed?

Craver: I don't kill gooks; I kill Arabs.

Lue Ming: Really? Arabs?

Craver: Not just any Arabs, Iraqi Arabs. Saddam Arabs. But that war is over now too.

Lue Ming: Who won?

Craver: We had a kill ratio of a thousand to one.

Lue Ming: Oh my! (*Beat*) What's it like to kill a woman?

Craver: I never killed anyone.

Lue Ming: Such modesty! In my village alone you killed sixteen people, seven pigs, three cows, and a chicken.

Craver: I never killed anyone in my life. I never got that close.

Lue Ming: Does it feel the same to shoot a cow in the back as it does to shoot a man in the back?

Craver: Get the fuck out of my room.

Lue Ming: Lue Ming. (*Caresses his face*) I can't leave now! I think we're falling in love.

SCENE 3

(A year earlier in the Saudi desert. Craver and Remzi in position to sprint.)

Remzi: I get more traction running on this sand.

Craver: Get on your mark.

Remzi: Like a streak of light I'll pass you by, Craver. Just watch.

Craver: Get set!

Remzi: You just watch me.

Craver: Go!

Remzi: Wait! Wait! Cramp. Shit.

Craver: Bad luck to get beat before we start.

Remzi: I'm going to visit the village where my parents were born. When I get my first leave. Want to come with me?

Craver: Nope.

Remzi: Don't like to be seen with Arabs. Look. I've got more money than you. You're broke and I'm Arab. That about evens it out, doesn't it?

Craver: The CBU-75 carries eighteen hundred bomblets, called Sad Eyes. Sad Eyes.

Remzi: What do you think it's like . . .

Craver: One type of Sad Eyes can explode before hitting the ground.

Remzi: . . . to kill someone?

Craver: Each bomblet contains six hundred razor-sharp steel fragments.

Remzi: I wonder what I'll feel like after I do it?

Craver: It's nothing personal. We're not just here to get them out of Kuwait, but to protect a way of life.

Remzi and **Craver:** Flawed it may be, but damn well worth protecting!

Craver: Those poor bastards are so brainwashed by Saddam, they need to kill like we need oxygen.

Remzi: When I went in for the interview, the recruiter asked me was I against taking another person's life.

Craver: If you are, you could fuck up an entire war.

Remzi: I just went in for the interview to piss my mother and sister off. The recruiter said: "What you need, son, is all right here." He looked at me, and I looked back. Then he said something that changed my life: "The Army will give you a quiet sense of pride."

Craver: "A quiet sense of pride." (*Beat*) I'm not going to die.

Remzi: I am.

Craver: It's hot here. Why does it have to be so hot here? Can't we just turn the sun up a few degrees and roast those motherfuckers! All these weeks with our ass frying in the sun, crawling through the sand like mutts, and the drills, drills, drills. Tomorrow might be the real thing. (*Beat*) We've got eight types of guided bombs.

Remzi: I wonder if you'll see it.

Craver: There's the GM-130, an electro-optically or infrared two-thousand-pound powered bomb. See what?

Remzi: How I die.

Craver: Then there's the GBU-10 Paveway II, a two-thousand-pound laser-guided bomb based on an MK-84.

Remzi: Let's say I'm lying over there, dead as can be, and then you see it's me, from a distance. But you still have to walk over to my body to check it out. So, how would you walk?

Craver: We've got Harm missiles, Walleyes, Clusters, and guided anti-tanks.

Remzi: Craver. This is something important I'm talking about. Let's say I'm you and I see me lying up ahead, dead. I stop in my tracks. I'm upset. We were friends, and I've got to cross the thirty or so feet between us. (*Does a "walk" over to the imaginary dead body*) No. That feels too confident.

Craver: And you wouldn't feel confident because . . .

Remzi: Because I'd be thinking: That could just as easily be me lying there as him.

Craver: Right. So maybe you'd do it like this. Kind of . . . (*Does his "walk" up to the imaginary body*)

Remzi: That's too careful.

Craver: Yeah. And too scared. I mean, I might be feeling in a pretty nice way, thinking about being alive and not quite as dead as you.

Remzi: You've got a point there. You might be feeling pretty Okay.

Craver: And fucking lucky too, 'cause the blood's still rolling through my veins.

Remzi: Something like this maybe. (*Does another "walk," a sort of combination of his others*)

Craver: Yes! That's it! That's it! Let me try. Okay. I see you up ahead of me, twenty feet, maybe thirty, and I want to get closer to you . . . Why do I want to get closer if you're dead and I know it's you? I mean, there's nothing else to figure out then, is there?

Remzi: Because . . . I'm your friend, and you'd rather be the one to report my death than some jerk who doesn't know I exist.

Craver: Right. So here I go.

Remzi: Get on your mark.

Craver: Get set.

Remzi: Go!

Craver (*Copies Remzi's walk, but not quite as well*): That didn't feel right.

Remzi: Your shoulders are too tight. Loosen up. See it before you, my body up ahead.

Craver: How did you die?

Remzi: This Iraqi we shot dead isn't dead. He's almost dead, but he's got just enough strength to fire one more time. When I turn my back— bang!—he shoots me.

Craver: Where?

Remzi: In the neck.

Craver: Got it.

Remzi: So there I am in the sand, a bullet in my neck.

Craver: And it's hot. A fucking hot day, and the sun is pissing a hole through my fucking hot head.

Remzi: Exactly, and I'm dead.

Craver: But I'm alive.

Remzi: And glad to be that way.

Craver: But you were my buddy. We were friends . . . just friends or good friends?

Remzi: Pretty good friends.

Craver: Pretty good friends.

Remzi: Right. And now you have to cross the distance between us.

Craver: About thirty-five feet.

Remzi: And then you do it. The walk. The shortest and most important walk of your life. And you have to believe you can do it, with dignity in your stride, power, and above all, a quiet sense of pride.

Craver: I'm ready.

Remzi: So am I.

(*They link arms and walk in unison.*)

SCENE 4

(*Fairouz is also practicing a walk.*)

Fairouz: Keep your chin in the air at all times. As though your chin has a string attached to it that is pulling it up.

(*Lue Ming appears and walks in unison behind her. Fairouz doesn't yet notice her.*)

Fairouz: No, a hook is better, a hook in your chin like a fish. Beauty lesson number seven: walking with grace.

Lue Ming: It's all a matter of balance.

Fairouz: Not you again. I told you I don't know Calley.

Lue Ming: Your friend Craver said you might know.

Fairouz: He's not my friend.

Lue Ming: Are we still in Kentucky?

Fairouz: Yes.

Lue Ming: American boys are so interesting! Full of secrets. All roads lead through him. My road. Your road. Dominoes in the dark.

Fairouz: Have you tried the other motel, across the street?

Lue Ming: Calley's a soldier. A lieutenant. Of Charlie Company. A unit of the American Division's 11th Light Infantry Brigade. Very light. So light some thought he was an angel when he came home.

Fairouz: How do the women walk in your country?

Lue Ming: Not as upright as we'd like. Hunched over a bit most of the time.

Fairouz: Show me.

Lue Ming (*Shows her*): The lower a body is to the ground, the less of a target.

Fairouz: I can't move without making noise. Clump, clump, clump. My mother always wanted me to walk with what she calls "presence." When I was in the fourth grade I had to walk home from school.

Lue Ming: Show me. How you walked home from school.

Fairouz: It was only three blocks. (*Walks again*)

Lue Ming: Yes. I think I remember it now.

(*Now they are both practicing their walks.*)

Fairouz: There were some older children in the seventh grade. Two boys and a girl. They stopped me on the sidewalk. They wanted me to take off my shoes.

Lue Ming: You should meet my mother; she has one foot.

Fairouz: To see the toes.

Lue Ming: She stepped on a mine on her way for a piss.

Fairouz: Not the toes, but the hooves. They said I had hooves for toes. Devil's feet.

Lue Ming: It was March 16, 1968.

Fairouz: Devil's feet.

Lue Ming: Why, you weren't even born then, were you?

Fairouz (*Chants*): Devil's feet. Devil's feet.

Lue Ming: Devil's feet?

Fairouz: Yes. (*Chants*): Fairouz has devil's feet.

Lue Ming (*Chants*): Dirty Arab devil, you go home.

Fairouz (*Chants*): Dirty Arab devil, you go home!

Lue Ming: Get her shoe. Pull off her shoe.

Fairouz: Hold her down and pull off her shoe!

Fairouz and **Lue Ming** (*Chant*): Dirty Arab, dirty Arab, you go home!

Fairouz: Remzi! (*Beat*) Remzi.

Lue Ming: Arab! Slope! Dink!

Fairouz: No. They didn't call me that: slope.

Lue Ming: Thought I'd throw it in. Slope. Dink. Gook.

Fairouz: "Gook" I've heard of.

Lue Ming: The Philippines war. It was used again for Korea, and then recycled for Vietnam. How did they get your shoe off?

Fairouz: I can't remember. I can figure the distance from right here, where we're standing, to the center of the earth, but I can't remember just how the shoe came off.

Lue Ming: But it did come off? And when they saw you didn't have devil's feet did they let you be their friend?

Fairouz: A happy ending? It was for them. I think they were scared of me. Afterward, they weren't.

Lue Ming: And now you have a devil's foot?

Fairouz: It does look a bit like a hoof now. The bones curved wrong. Do you know what's happened to my brother?

Lue Ming: I think we met each other once, but we were headed in different directions.

Fairouz: My God, where? Where did you see him?

Lue Ming: I don't know anymore. We passed each other in a rather bad storm, and he reached out and touched my sleeve. Then he was gone.

Fairouz: Thank God. He's alive.

Lue Ming: I didn't say that, my dear.

Fairouz (*Not listening*): He's alive!

SCENE 5

(A year earlier. Remzi and Fairouz are talking. Fairouz is polishing Remzi's combat boots.)

Fairouz: You're becoming a stranger.

Remzi: Look. I'm sorry about the occupation and that you don't feel you have a homeland, but I do. And it's here. Not over there in some never-never land.

Fairouz: I hardly recognize you.

Remzi: Iraq invaded a sovereign country. That's against international law.

Fairouz: International law? Ha! Your own land is overrun, occupied, slowly eaten up . . .

Remzi *(Mocks)*: Village by village, orchard by orchard. Decades and decades of UN resolutions . . .

Fairouz: And no one's ever smacked a Desert Shield on those bastards!

Remzi: There's just no parallel.

Fairouz: There's always a parallel. Did mother ever tell you how she broke her hip before she came to America?

Remzi: She fell down when she was running away from the soldiers . . .

Fairouz: No. She was running toward the soldiers.

Remzi: I've heard this so many times it's a sweet little lullaby that could rock me to sleep. So mother saved father and they broke her hip with a rifle butt. Crack, crack. Bone broke. Hobble, hobble for the rest of her life. What do you expect me to do, hobble around for the rest of my life? You're so serious. Open your mouth and laugh for a change. You used to do that, remember? Get out of the house. Throw a party. Go to the Burger King on the corner and order some fries. *(Beat)* You're an American girl. Enjoy it.

Fairouz: I'm an Arab woman.

Remzi: You've never even been there.

Fairouz: Neither have you!

Remzi: If you walked into our village today, they'd tar and feather you.

Fairouz: Fuck you. I'd put on a veil.

Remzi: The veil's not the problem. You haven't been a virgin since you were thirteen.

Fairouz: How dare you!

Remzi: I'm sorry.

Fairouz: I was at least fourteen! (*They laugh.*) Mother still says to me, "The honor of a girl is like a piece of glass. If it's broken, you can never glue it together again."

Remzi: Why don't you tell her the truth?

Fairouz: It's my truth. Not hers. You hardly know her, and she lives five minutes away!

Remzi: I can't talk to her.

Fairouz: Learn Arabic.

Remzi: No. She should learn English. She's been here over twenty years.

Fairouz: She speaks English. She just won't.

Remzi: You're still doing the shopping for her, aren't you?

(*Fairouz doesn't answer.*)

Remzi: You should move out.

Fairouz: In the stores, for years, she'd lift me in her arms, and whisper in my ear "chubbes."

Remzi: "Chubbes."

Fairouz: And I would say "bread." "Habib," and I would say "milk."

Remzi: "Habib."

Fairouz: She's our mother.

Remzi: You were going to be a nurse, a doctor, or something. Get your degree. Get a job. I want a quiet life. As an American citizen. That's good enough for me. Beats living in the past.

Fairouz: An American citizen. What is that? This government pays for the guns that force us off our land.

Remzi (*Interrupts*): Allah, spare me! Jesus Christ! It's not my land. I'm not into redrawing maps or being trapped in the minds of crusty grandparents.

Fairouz: We're your family.

Remzi: Some family. More like a selection of Mesopotamian ruins.

Fairouz: Why don't you learn a little something about—

Remzi: About ruins?

Fairouz: The Intifada?

Remzi: What? They're finally letting the women out of their houses to throw stones?

Fairouz: We throw stones. We run unions. We go to prison. We get shot.

Remzi: Oh, martyrdom! Why don't you get out of the house and throw a few stones around here! You've got a big mouth, Fairouz, but your world is this small. I'm sick of being a hyphen: the Palestinian, the gap between Arab-American. There's room for me here. Where I have my friends.

Fairouz: Ah, yes. Your friends. You tell your friends I was born that way.

Remzi: You're going to blame me that no one wants to marry a girl with a gimpy foot.

Fairouz: My foot is deformed, but my cunt works just fine!

Remzi: You have a mouth full of dirt, sister. What is it you want from me?

Fairouz: What I want? (*Speaks some angry lines to him in Arabic*)

Remzi: Gibberish, Fairouz. Save it for the relatives.

(*Fairouz speaks another line of Arabic to him.*)

Remzi: I'm not a refugee. It's always somewhere else with you, always once removed. I am not scattered.

Fairouz: If I could go to war with you, I'd shoot my enemies first, then I'd shoot the ones who made them my enemies.

Remzi: Enemies. Always the enemies.

Fairouz: There are three kinds of people. Those who kill. Those who die. And those who watch. Which one are you, Remzi? Which one are you? I know. I know which one you are, don't I?

Remzi: Go to hell. I was a kid. A child. You'll never let it go, will you?

Fairouz: I just don't want you to join up without knowing that sometimes I still hate you.

SCENE 6

(*A year earlier in the Saudi desert. Remzi and Craver are doing jumping jacks. Boxler enters.*)

Boxler: That's enough. Take a rest.

Remzi and **Craver:** Yes, Lieutenant.

Boxler: At ease.

Craver: Thank you, sir.

Boxler: No sirs and thank-yous. We're equal when I say at ease. Where are you girls from? Haven't seen you around.

Craver: Echo Company A, 2, 3, sir.

Remzi: Those fatigues you have on. I don't think I've seen those kind before.

Boxler: Special Forces.

Craver: I can smell the mothballs.

Boxler: I like a sense of humor. (*To Remzi*) Where are you from, babe?

Remzi: The States.

Boxler: I mean, where are your parents from?

Remzi: My father died when I was just a kid. My mother never told me where she was from.

Boxler: Now that's not nice . . . Parents owe the knowledge of their roots to their sons. A root must know its origins. You, my son, are a root living in the dark without a compass, and you have no idea what kind of tree is going to sprout forth from your skull. I'd say, American Indian, maybe. No. Could be your mommy is from Pakistan. Then again, could be South of the Border. It's hard to tell these days.

Remzi: Yes. It is.

Boxler: But never mind. We're all family here, aren't we?

Craver: Do you know about the Sad Eyes, sir?

Boxler: Boxler's my name. And of course I know about the Sad Eyes. I've seen them on the faces of many a soldier who comes back without his buddy at his side.

Craver: The weapon. Sad Eyes is a weapon.

Boxler: That's what I love about war. The creativity of it. (*Beat*) Shall we?

Craver and **Remzi:** Ready, sir.

Boxler (*As he speaks he takes out a blindfold and puts it on. He gets to his knees.*): Now, let's say you have a situation. A delicate situation. You've taken an Iraqi prisoner. He has a secret, and you need to get this secret without breaking international law, the Geneva Constrictions, etc. Prisoners must be treated humanely. Please tie my hands behind my back. (*No response*) Do as I tell you. Use your handkerchief. (*Remzi does so.*) All right. Interrogate me. (*Neither Craver nor Remzi responds.*) Bang, crash! Rat-tat-tat-tat! Howl! There are bullets flying all around you. This camel jockey knows where the reserve forces are located, and if they aren't destroyed, you and your buddies are minced meat. (*Beat*) Interrogate me!

Remzi: What's your name? I said: What's your name? He won't talk, Craver. What do we do?

Boxler: Be firm.

Craver: Tell us your name, shitbag, and we'll go easy on you. (*No response from Boxler*) Give him a push.

Boxler: That's an idea. Go on. (*Remzi pushes him, but not hard.*) That's a start. (*Craver does so, but harder.*) You two Barbies, you think just because you push me around a little I'm going to spill my guts? You're nothing but pissants with one hand tied behind your back. (*Craver shoves him, and he falls over.*)

Remzi: One hand tied behind our backs? (*Strikes Boxler. Craver strikes him too.*)

Boxler: You two dandelions aren't getting anywhere. Hey, baby doll, yeah you, the one with the dark skin, are you a half-breed?

Remzi: No. But you are. (*Kicks Boxler in the stomach.*) You fucking sandnigger.

Boxler: From what I can see of your face, you're a sandnigger yourself. (*Remzi kicks Boxler again.*) What a farce: a sandnigger killing sandniggers. (*Remzi keeps kicking until Boxler lies still.*)

(*Some moments of silence*)

Remzi: Sir? Did I hurt you, sir?

(*Boxler doesn't move.*)

Craver: Oh shit.

(*Remzi and Craver free Boxler's wrists and eyes. Boxler springs to his feet, unharmed.*)

Boxler (*To Remzi*): That was good. For a first time. (*Suddenly he punches Remzi in the stomach.*) Pity is what you leave behind you, son, back home, tucked under your pillow with your teddy bear and girly magazine. Now get to your feet, you stinking Arab. (*Remzi starts to get up, but Boxler pushes him over with his foot. Remzi attacks Boxler, but Boxler restrains him.*) That's it. That's it. Now hold on to it! Hold on to that anger. Stoke it. Cuddle it, and when the right moment comes, take aim and let it fly. A soldier without anger is a dead soldier.

Craver: What about me, sir?

Boxler: What about you?

Craver: How do I get that anger when I need it?

Boxler: Where are you from?

Craver: Town of Hazard. Kentucky. Sir.

Boxler: Let me see your teeth? Hmmm. Trash, are you?

Craver: Yes, sir.

Boxler: Joined up because you couldn't get a job.

Craver: Yes, sir.

Boxler: Father dead?

Craver: Yes, sir. The mines, sir.

Boxler: Burned to a crisp in an explosion?

Craver: Suffocated. His lungs, sir.

Boxler: A pity you weren't with him when he died.

Craver: It was like something sawing through wood. His breathing, sir. I couldn't stand to hear it. But the Company wouldn't let him retire. He kept working. For the money, sir. We had to tie him into his chair to keep him at home.

Boxler: Shat right there in his chair, did he? And you let your mother clean up his mess. Never offered her a hand. Tsk, tsk. Went out with your friends and got drunk on Pabst Blue Ribbon. But one night you came home early, and he was still sitting there, tied to his chair. Your mother was passed out on the couch.

Remzi: Sir, this is ridicu—

Boxler (*Interrupts*): Yes, it is, isn't it? Because Craver then leaned over and said into his father's ear: "I'm sorry, Dad. I am so sorry." And do you know, Remzi, just what his father did to show his acceptance and respect for his prodigal son? He pissed. Right then and there. Pissed where he sat, and Craver didn't even know it until he looked down and saw he was standing in it. The piss soaked through his shoes, right into his socks.

Craver: When he went into the mines he was my father. When he came back out, he was something else. I couldn't love something else.

Boxler: And you were out fucking some pretty little box in the back of his Ford pickup truck the night he drew his last painful breath. You shot your cum the moment his heart stopped.

Remzi (*To Craver*): Don't listen to him, Craver.

Craver: That's where you're wrong. I didn't come. I never came.

Boxler: And why not? (*Beat*) What was the problem? Are you a funny little boy, one of those ha-ha little boys?

Craver: What are you going to do about it? Report me? I'll break your fucking neck.

Remzi: Let's get out of here, Crave.

(*Craver shoves Remzi away.*)

Boxler (*To Craver*): My, my. I can call your father a broken-down, coal-shitting, piss-poor excuse for the American dream and you don't bat an eye, but when I detect that you're a bit on the queer side . . .

Remzi: Craver?

(*Craver suddenly turns on Remzi. They push each other. Craver knocks Remzi down and begins to choke him.*)

Remzi: Craver! Fuck! Craver!

Boxler (*Whispers*): Faggot. Shit-fucker.

Remzi: Stop it! Get off of me.

Boxler: Sodomite. Fairy. (*Beat*) Feel it? Feel it inside you, Mr. Perry? Now grab hold of it. (*Pulls Craver off Remzi.*) Catch it. Hold it like a bullet between your teeth. And when the right moment comes, when you've spotted your enemy, let it rip, my son. Let it rip. But remember, aim is everything and unbridled anger is of no use to you, it's like crude oil: worthless without refinement. But you've got to know where to direct it. Out there, my friend. Out there, in Indian territory, beyond the sand dunes where the camels lie in wait. Think of them as culprits in the death of your father. If the ragheads hadn't shot our buffalo, we could have swapped them for their camels, and then we wouldn't have needed the coal mines to begin with, and your father would have worked in an auto factory, and he'd still be alive today.

Craver: That's not how it happened. (*Beat*) Sir.

Boxler: You can give his death any reason you want. Facts are not infallible. They are there to be interpreted in a way that's useful to you. Why, your President does it, and he is no smarter than you. President Johnson says—

Remzi: President Bush.

Boxler: Whatever the hell his name is, he said: "Our troops . . . will not be asked to fight with one hand tied behind their back." As you did in Vietnam. (*Begins to laugh*) Do you know how many tons of bombs were dropping on Vietnam? Four million six hundred thousand. It's awesome, isn't it?

Remzi: This is a different war, sir.

Boxler: The tonnage dropped by the Allies in World War II was only three million. Now, my hands won't be tied behind my back when we go into Panama City. Operation Just Because, it will be called.

Craver: It was called Operation Just Cause. Just Cause.

Remzi: That was in '89. In December.

Boxler: I'll be driving a tank there. They promised me I could drive a tank this time. The only nuisance is that crunching sound under my treads. A crunching sound, like this. (*Makes the sound*) Civilians have so little consideration.

Craver: You were never in Panama, sir.

Remzi: There were no civilian deaths to speak of.

Boxler: But not to speak of, I'd say about three thousand. Now, when we went into the barrios of Grenada . . .

Remzi: Just where haven't you been, sir?

Craver: To hell. He hasn't been to hell, but he's on his way there.

Boxler: Oh, there you're wrong. I stood outside the gates for a very long time. In rain and snow, fire and brimstone, but they wouldn't let me in. I don't know why they won't let me in.

(*We hear Lue Ming's voice offstage calling.*)

Lue Ming: Fairouz! Fairouz!

Boxler: Now we're ready for lesson two. How to handle women in combat.

(*Lue Ming calls "Where are you?" in Vietnamese.*)

Boxler: Hear it? (*Remzi and Craver do not hear it. Boxler begins to slink away.*) Can't you hear it? Poor hound. She's still after me. Still sniffing at my tracks.

Fairouz (*Offstage*): Remzi! Remzi!

SCENE 7

(*Fairouz is blindfolded. She moves about the dark stage carrying small paper lanterns. Throughout the scene Lue Ming moves about the stage, taking up different positions in relation to Fairouz—here, now there—sometimes surprising Fairouz with her voice. Just prior to Fairouz speaking, Lue Ming begins to sing a Vietnamese lullaby.*)

Fairouz: I can see through it anyway.

Lue Ming: This is how we must operate: able to pinpoint the enemy even though we are almost blind. Night vision. Strategy where there should be none.

Fairouz: Like a bat?

Lue Ming: If you like. Now. Think past the obstacles, that which hides your objective. Map out the lay of the land as you remember it and have never seen it.

Fairouz: And forget the motel carpet?

Lue Ming: Hands up! Don't you know there's a war on? Keep your head. Look for what is not there.

Fairouz: Imagine the land I can't see.

Lue Ming: Once, an American soldier called himself my brother.

Fairouz: Sounds like a friendly war.

Lue Ming: In the first years the soldiers gave us toffee and boiled sweets.

Fairouz: By the rice paddies? In Saigon?

Lue Ming: Tu Cung, actually. By the coast. (*Beat*) Rush always gave me gum, Juicy Fruit gum. He called me his little sis. Once he gave me a ribbon to put in my hair. I had very long hair, beautiful, thick hair that I wore in a braid down my back. (*Beat*) But one day Rush didn't bring any gum and he took out his knife and cut off my braid.

Fairouz: Was it a slow knife? Serrated are slow.

Lue Ming: Oh no, it was a quick knife, a Rush knife, and he strapped my hair to the back of his helmet. His friends laughed and laughed. Rush looked so very silly with his camouflage helmet on and this long, black braid hanging down his back.

Fairouz: It was only hair.

Lue Ming: I'd be careful if I were blindfolded.

Fairouz: I like it. I could go anywhere in the world right now, and to do it I wouldn't have to lift a finger.

(*From the shadows, we hear the sound of Remzi's footsteps.*)

Lue Ming: Or a foot.

Fairouz: I'm four hundred and thirty miles from home. This is the first time I've been outside of Atlanta. The first time I've flown in a plane.

Lue Ming: I despise flying. It puts my hair in a tangle.

Fairouz: Could you get a message to Remzi?

Lue Ming: Your brother's not accepting messages these days.

Fairouz: I'm sorry, but I don't have time for your lost braid. What's done is done. My brother is alive, and we must think about the living and wait for my brother to send word. (*Beat*) I'm sick of waiting. And I can't stop waiting.

Lue Ming: Those who wait, burn.

SCENE 8

(*Fairouz and Remzi, a year earlier*)

Fairouz: Did you get the vaccines you needed?

Remzi: Yesterday.

Fairouz: Then everything's in order?

Remzi: All set to leave. The big adventure awaits me. Little brother goes to war.

Fairouz: When we were small, the children from our school would come to our house to have a look at my funny foot. You made them pay a dime each time they had a look.

Remzi: I split the profit with you, fifty-fifty.

Fairouz: It was my foot.

Remzi: It was my idea.

Fairouz: I used to lie awake at night, for years, dreaming of ways to kill you. I thought: If I kill him, there will be no one to hate. I was investing my hatred in you. It was a long-term investment. Really, I think you owe me some thanks.

Remzi: For hating me?

Fairouz: Yes. Then you wouldn't be surprised by the hate of the world.

Craver (*Offstage*): Remzi! Remzi!

(*Craver, offstage and "somewhere else," calls Remzi's name, and Remzi exits. Lue Ming enters.*)

Fairouz: Listen to me. You don't have the right balance. I do. You see, I love you, but I hate you too. I have to. Tightly, tightly. As though at any moment either of us could slip off this earth. Are you listening to me?

Lue Ming (*Answering as Remzi*): Yes, I am, Fairouz. I'm listening.

Fairouz: Go say good-bye to Mother. She's in her room, and she won't come out. She says they'll kill you. Just like they killed Father.

Lue Ming: That was an accident, and you know it. He fell onto the lily pads and into the pond and drowned.

Fairouz: His face was messed up. As though he'd been hit many times.

Lue Ming: Water can do that to a face.

Fairouz: I've told Mother that, Remzi. Over and over I've told her that it's the Iraqis you're going off to fight, but she keeps saying (*Speaks in Arabic and then translates*), "They'll kill him. The Yankees will kill him." Silly old woman. She's all mixed up.

SCENE 9

(*A military camp in Saudi Arabia. Remzi is sitting alone and reciting.*)

Remzi: Tabun. Mawid. Zbib, trab ahmar, dibs.

(*Craver enters. He listens to Remzi for a while.*)

Remzi: Maya, zir, foron.

Craver: Sounds like you had a good leave.

Remzi: Zbib, trab ahmar, dibs. Raisins. Red soil. Molasses.

Craver: Really? How amazing . . .

Remzi: I went to visit my father's village. On the western side of the Hebron Mountains. Al-Dawayima. According to my mother, there were five hundred and fifty-nine houses there.

Craver: I didn't know you were back.

Remzi: Tall grasses, wildflowers, scrubs. That's all that's there now. Dozers have flattened the houses.

Craver: When did you get back?

Remzi: I went to the refugee camp nearby, but I couldn't speak the language. I could point, though.

Craver: We went on alert a couple of times. Lucky we didn't start without you.

Remzi: A Palestinian farmer explained to me that there are three varieties of fig suitable for preserving—asmar, ashqar, abiyad. The black fig, the blonde, and the white. Craver, I was a tourist there. An outsider.

Craver: You're a Palestinian.

Remzi: One old woman took me in for coffee, because I didn't know anyone and had nowhere to go. She called me "Yankee Palestina." These people lose their homes. They live in poverty, and they're the enemies of the world. (*Throws Craver a bag of figs*) I brought that for you.

Craver: Nice you remembered I existed. I think of the three, I'm the white fig variety. How do you say it?

Remzi: Abiyad.

Craver: Yeah. Abiyad. (*Tastes a fig*) These are nasty.

Remzi: You're not eating them right. You don't just plug them in your mouth like a wad of chewing tobacco. You've got to eat them with a sense of purpose. (*Eats one*) With a sense of grace.

Craver (*Picks out another fig*): With a quiet sense of pride?

Remzi: Exactly.

Craver (*Eats the fig*): Nastier than the first one.

Remzi: No. Look. You're gobbling.

Craver: Why didn't you buy me a souvenir, like a nice little prayer rug?

Remzi: Eating is like walking. My sister taught me that. There's a balance involved. You have to eat the fig gently. As though it were made of the finest paper. (*Puts a fig in his own hand*) Look. I'll put the fig in my hand, and without touching my hand, you pick it up. Gently.

(*Craver starts to use his fingers, but Remzi stops his hand.*)

Remzi: With your mouth. (*Beat*) Go on. See if you can do it.

(*Craver leans down and very carefully and very slowly lifts the fig from Remzi's open hand. Craver holds the fig between his lips.*)

Remzi: Now take it into your mouth. Slowly. (*Helps the fig inside Craver's mouth*) Slowly. There . . . Well. How does it taste now?

Craver (*After some moments of silence*): Did you take a lot of pictures?

Remzi: On the streets of Atlanta I've been called every name you can think of: pimp, terrorist, half-nigger, mongrel, spic, wop, even Jew-bastard. And to these people in this camp it didn't matter a damn that I was some kind of a mix. Some kind of a something else, born someplace in a somewhere else than my face said. Or something like that. Do you know what I mean?

Craver: Haven't any idea.

Remzi: So. What's on for tomorrow?

Craver: Drills. Red Alert. Stop. Go. Stop. Go.

Remzi: Every day it's any day now.

Craver: I just want it to start.

SCENE 10

(*Lue Ming and Fairouz are rehearsing for Fairouz's travels. Lue Ming is wearing Remzi's boots.*)

Lue Ming: Your shoulders are too tight. That's what they look for. Tight shoulders, pinched faces.

Fairouz: My face isn't pinched.

Lue Ming: If you're going to find your brother, you have to cross borders. But not with sweat on your upper lip. Try it again. Not a care in the world. Right at home. (*Assumes the posture of an immigration officer*) Passport? Hmmm. North American?

Fairouz: Yes, sir.

Lue Ming: Tourist?

Fairouz: Yes.

Lue Ming: How long? How long have you been a tourist?

Fairouz: Most of my life, sir.

Lue Ming (*Speaks as herself*): Don't be perverse. (*Speaks as officer*) First time out of the United States?

Fairouz: Yes.

Lue Ming: Relatives here?

Fairouz: Yes. I mean, no. I mean I do, but they—

Lue Ming (*Interrupts*): Just what do you mean, Miss . . . Saboura?

Fairouz: My parents were born here.

Lue Ming: Here? Born here?

Fairouz: Yes.

Lue Ming: You mean right where I'm standing? (*Lifts her feet and looks under them*)

Fairouz (*Looks at Lue Ming's boots*): Yes. (*Beat*) Where did you get these?

Lue Ming: Do you think they're stuck to my shoes?

Fairouz: I know these boots. What?

Lue Ming: Your parents. Do you think they're stuck to my shoes?

Fairouz: I don't understand.

Lue Ming: I assure you it was an accident. One minute they're alive, and, well, the next minute they're under my shoes.

Fairouz: My brother is lost.

Lue Ming: Lucky man.

Fairouz: I'm Palestin—

Lue Ming: Don't say it! Don't say it! It's like a bee that flies into my ear and fornicates there.

Fairouz: Don't you think you're overdoing it?

Lue Ming: You must be prepared for them to throw anything at you. (*Beat*) Purpose of your visit?

Fairouz: Your ruins.

Lue Ming: Yes. Lots of ruins. I like ruins. Your voice reminds me of one. Are you sad? Are you missing someone close to your heart? Pull up your shirt. I don't have all day.

(*Fairouz raises her shirt.*)

Lue Ming: Education?

Fairouz: Doctor. I haven't finished the degree.

Lue Ming: Ah, a person who quits?

Fairouz: I plan to go back.

Lue Ming: You can't go back to Al-Dawayima. There's no place to go back to. (*Beat*) So you're Arab?

Fairouz: American.

Lue Ming: American?

Fairouz: Arab.

Lue Ming: Make up your mind!

Fairouz: I'm a Palestinian-Arab-American. From Atlanta. Sir.

SCENE 11

(*Fairouz enters Craver's motel room.*)

Fairouz: Did he talk to you about his visit to the Territories?

Craver: Not a word.

Fairouz: He never likes to learn anything new.

Craver: Ever heard of the Beehive? It's the ultimate concept in improved fragmentation. It spins at high velocity, spitting out eighty-eight hundred fléchettes.

Fairouz: Fléchettes?

Craver: Tiny darts with razor-sharp edges capable of causing deep wounds.

Fairouz: What is a deep wound? How deep exactly?

Craver: To the bone. You should leave now.

Fairouz: I got a letter from the army.

Craver: Know the DU penetrator? Cigar-shaped, armor-piercing bullets. The core of the bullet is made from radioactive nuclear waste.

Fairouz: They say he's missing.

Craver: When fired, the DU's uranium core bursts into flame. Ever had forty tons of depleted uranium dumped in your backyard?

Fairouz: Not in action, just missing.

Craver: Things get lost. People—

Fairouz: Get lost. But why not you? Why didn't you get lost?

Craver: Because I fell in love. In our bunkers at night, Remzi used to read the names out loud to us, and it calmed us down. He must have read that weapons manual a hundred times. All those ways to kill the human body. Lullabies. It was like . . . they were always the same and always there, and when we said them to ourselves there was nothing else like it: Fishbeds, Floggers and Fulcrums. Stingers, Frogs, Silkworms, Vulcans, Beehives, and Bouncing Bettys.

Fairouz: Did you love my brother?

Craver: I can't remember.

Fairouz: But you can. You will. Remember!

Craver: I remember . . . what my first . . . favorite was: the B-52, the Buff. B-U-F-F. The Big Ugly Fat Fellow, it can carry up to sixty thousand pounds of bombs and cruise missiles.

Fairouz: All right. Let's try something more simple.

Craver: It has survived in front-line service for three generations.

Fairouz: Not about numbers, but about flesh.

Craver: It has an engine thrust of thirteen thousand seven hundred and fifty pounds and a maximum speed of five hundred and ninety-five miles per hour. It's slow but it's bad.

Fairouz: If you could give his flesh a velocity?

Craver: The Buffs, the B-52s, won the Gulf War. Not the smarts. Not the smarts.

Fairouz: Or a number, what would it be?

Craver: Ninety-three percent of the bombs dropped were free-falls from the bellies of Fat Fellows.

Fairouz: If you could give his flesh a number?

Craver: Only seven percent were guided, and of these half-wits, forty percent missed their targets.

Fairouz: A number that's short of infinity? Was that your desire for him?

Craver: Forty . . . forty-five percent of the smarts . . . they missed . . .

Fairouz: Something short of infinity?

Craver: They missed their targets.

Fairouz: Did you or did you not fuck him?

Craver: That (*Beat*) is a lot of missed targets.

Fairouz: Okay. Mr. White Trash likes Arab ass, yes? Is it good? Is it sweet like white ass? Do you find it exotic?

Craver: I'm not that kind of a soldier.

Fairouz: He could be a bastard, my brother. But if you fucked him and then hurt him in any way, I'll tear your heart out.

Craver: Remzi never said he had a sister with a limp. His sister, he said, she walked like a princess.

Fairouz: Was he gentle with you? Sometimes when we were children he would soak my foot in a bowl of warm water, with lemon and orange rinds. He would blow on my toes to dry them. He thought if he cared for my foot, day by day, and loved it, that somehow it would get better. (*Beat*) What was it like to kiss him?

Craver: After the Buffs it was the GR. MK-1 Jaguar with two Rolls Royce Adour MK-102 turbofans. A fuselage pylon and four wing pylons can carry up to ten thousand pounds of armaments . . .

(*Remzi now "appears." Fairouz moves away and watches, as though watching Craver's memory.*)

Craver: The Jag can carry a mix of cannons, smarts, and gravity bombs. And get this: maximum speed, Mach 1.1. Then there's the brain of the electronic warfare central nervous system: the E-3 Sentry, Boeing.

Remzi: If there ever was an indispensable weapon, it is the E-3 AWACS, capable of directing UN forces with tremendous accuracy. Improvements include—

Craver: A better Have Quick radar jamming system and an upgraded JTIDS. Able to manage hundreds of warplanes airborne at any given moment.

Remzi: At any given moment?

Craver: Any given moment.

Remzi: How about now?

Craver: We could go to jail. It's illegal in the Army.

Remzi: So are white phosphorous howitzer shells. So are fuel-air explosives.

Craver: We don't decide what gets dropped.

Remzi: Would you kiss me if I were dead?

Craver: Why would I kiss you if you were dead?

Remzi: Would you kiss me if I were alive?

Craver: I had a thing for the Sentry jet, but how long can love last, after the first kiss, after the second, still around after the third? I dumped the Sentry jet and went on to the Wild Weasel, F-4G. Like a loyal old firehorse, the Weasel was back in action.

Remzi: Have you ever touched the underbelly of a recon plane? Two General Electric J79-15 turbojets.

Craver: If you run your hand along its flank, just over the hip, to the rear end, it will go wet. Not damp, but I mean wet.

Remzi: Have you ever run your face over the wing of an A-6 Intruder, or opened your mouth onto the tail of a AV-8B Harrier II? It's not steel you taste. It's not metal.

Craver: Ever had a Phoenix missile at the tip of your tongue? Nine hundred and eighty-five pounds of power, at launch. (*Moves to kiss Remzi, but Remzi moves away*)

Fairouz: Is that how you kissed him?

Craver: I kissed a girl for the first time when I was twelve. She had a mouth full of peanut butter and jelly and that's what I got. Have you ever seen an airplane take off vertically? That's what I was when I kissed Remzi, like the AV-8B Harrier II, straight up into the air, no runway, no horizontal run, but VTO, vertical takeoff.

Fairouz: Why don't you say it?

Craver: One Rolls Royce turbojet going up, engine thrust twenty-one thousand five hundred pounds maximum speed.

Fairouz: Please. Just say it.

Craver: Forever. Remzi said to me the first time he kissed me: "What are you now, Craver Perry? A White Trash, River Boy, who kisses Arabs and likes it?" I said, "I'm a White Trash, River Boy, Arab-kissing Faggot." And the rest, as they say, is history. (*Beat*) Remzi was, as they say, history too.

Fairouz: Remzi is dead, isn't he?

Craver: I said he was history. That's something else.

Fairouz: How can this be funny to you?

Craver: If you saw your brother lying dead in the sand, just what would you say to him? Imagine it. There he is. Dead on the sand. A bullet in his neck.

Fairouz: Bled to death?

Craver: Maybe. What would you do? (*Fairouz touches his face.*) Like that? Would you touch Remzi like that? What if he didn't have a face? What if his face were gone too? (*She kisses him on the cheek.*) That would take a lot of guts if he didn't have a face.

Fairouz: What was it for? You're of no use to me. Just a dead brother now. Zero. No more Remzi to hate. No more Remzi . . .

Craver: . . . to love. That's right. Do you think we're doing it too, falling in love?

Fairouz (*Moves away from Craver*): Would Remzi like that? (*Beat*) Do you like to watch or do you like to kill? You haven't tried dying yet, have you? Perhaps you should.

Craver: There's nothing wrong with your foot.

Fairouz: You're kind. I see why Remzi was so attached to you.

(*Remzi enters, unobserved by either of them.*)

Fairouz: My brother was the kind that watched. Is he the other kind now, Mr. Perry? (*Beat*) I think I'm going to scream.

(*Craver backs away, watching the two of them, as though he is seeing them both in the past. Remzi holds her foot.*)

Remzi (*Talking to her gently*): Just once more.

Fairouz: I can't. I can't

Remzi: You've got to do it or you'll never walk right. Just once more.

Fairouz: Just once more. Only once more. Will it be better then?

Remzi: Soon. It will be better soon.

(*Remzi twists her foot, and she lets out a sound of pain that is part scream and part the low, deep sound of a horn.*)

ACT 2

SCENE 1

(*Lue Ming appears. She summons up the Gulf War: the sounds of jets, bombs, guns. The war sounds continue through the following invocation.*)

Lue Ming: My sweet. My love. Come out from your hiding. Oh, my little angel, my tropical fish. Swim to me through the corridors of air. I am waiting for you. Come home. Come home.

(*The war sounds stop.*)

Lue Ming: Yes. Yes. It's you.

(*Boxler appears.*)

Lue Ming: It is always, only you, could ever be you.

Boxler: Boxler.

Lue Ming: Is that it now, "Boxler"?

Boxler: I have nothing to say to you.

Lue Ming: You're looking so well. So robust. So alive. And happy?

Boxler: When I'm training my girls.

Lue Ming: And what do you teach them?

Boxler: Are you enjoying your visit?

Lue Ming: Some of your cities make me feel right at home. Burned out, bodies in the street, the troops restoring order. They're so much like Vietnam.

Boxler: You're Vietcong, aren't you?

Lue Ming: I hear your record sold over two hundred thousand copies. You're a pop star.

Boxler: That was thirty . . . twenty-five . . .

Lue Ming: Twenty-one years ago. Just how much time did you get?

Boxler: I got labor for life, but three days later I was out of the stockade, courtesy of President Nick. Then I got thirty-five months in my bachelor pad at Fort Benning with my dog, my myna bird, and my tank full of tropical fish.

Lue Ming: Could you sing it for me? That song?

(*Sings the following to the tune of "The Battle Hymn of the Republic":*)

My name is Rusty Calley
I'm a soldier of this land!

Boxler: I'm a hero, you know. I'm a hero, and you're a dead gook.

Lue Ming: Don't try to sweet-talk me. It won't work.

Boxler: They took care of me. Friends in high places. I have a jewelry store and a Mercedes. I have a lot to be grateful for.

Lue Ming: Have you missed me terribly?

Boxler: I'm sorry, but I can't place you.

Lue Ming: Take a look at my face, closely.

Boxler: Nope.

Lue Ming: You'll remember the walk. There is no one in the world who walks like Lue Ming. (*Walks*)

Boxler: Sorry.

Lue Ming: How is it I can remember you and you can't remember me?

Boxler: What's done is done.

Lue Ming: And what's done is often done again and done again.

SCENE 2

(*Remzi and Craver are watching the bombs dropping over Baghdad from a long distance. We hear the muffled thuds of the bombs and see beautiful flashes of light far off.*)

Remzi: One, two. And there. Three. Look at it. Cotton candy. Carnival. Dancing. Craver. You're missing it. That one! (*Beat*) "And all the king's horses and all the king's men . . ."

Craver: "Couldn't put Humpty together again."

(*An even bigger flash of lights. Craver joins him. They both watch.*)

Remzi: Do you think he really wanted to be whole again?

Craver: Who?

Remzi: The egg.

Craver: What?

Remzi: Do you think he wanted to be put back together?

Craver: How the hell should I know what an egg wants?

Remzi: I should be dead but I'm not.

(*They see an awe-inspiring explosion.*)

Craver (*Sings*): Happy birthday, Baghdad.

Remzi: I think he was tired of being a good egg.

Craver: Make a wish.

Remzi: Yeah. A birthday.

Craver: If you sit out in the dark, they light up all around you. Like that. Back in Hazard. Just like that. All over the sky. Fireflies. There—

Remzi: That first time.

Craver: And then gone. There—

Remzi: Like. It was like—

Craver: And then gone.

Remzi: I was a window, and you put your hand through me.

SCENE 3

(*Boxler and Lue Ming*)

Boxler: You're not bad-looking.

Lue Ming: I know.

Boxler: But I could never touch you. I mean really touch you. I mean I know you are human, but, well . . . (*Beat*) I was a child once. Hard to believe, isn't it? I had blocks and crayons, and when it snowed I'd open my mouth to catch the flakes on my tongue. I had a favorite blanket. I liked most to roll the corner of it into a little point and stick it in my ear. Then I'd fall asleep. All the sounds around me were muffled and soft.

Lue Ming: My three-year-old daughter had a blanket, made from two scarves my mother sewed together.

Boxler: I had a father I loved and a mother I loved, and then I went to school.

Lue Ming: Show me what you teach the boys. Show me.

Boxler: My teacher made us sit in a formation, with the whitest faces up front in the first row, then the second and third rows for the olive skins and half-breeds, and the fourth and fifth rows for the dark ones.

Lue Ming: Remember: You have a situation. (*She puts on a blindfold.*) You've captured a Vietcong, and you need to know the whereabouts of the others. Now be polite. You're an American soldier, and that means something.

Boxler: Did you know they made bumper stickers with my name on it?

Lue Ming: You know who I am.

Boxler: Shut your squawking, bitch. (*Calls*) Hey, you two troopers. Over here on the double.

(*Remzi and Craver enter.*)

Boxler: Remzi, what's the best way to make a woman talk?

Craver: The dozers are clearing the area, sir.

Boxler: Get on with it. What dozers?

Remzi: We're mopping up.

Boxler: I said make her talk!

Craver: Can you tell us where Saddam's minefields are?

Boxler: This is Vietnam, son.

Remzi: We're in Iraq, sir.

Boxler: This is Panama City!

Craver: We have the Dragon M-47 assault missile, sir. Couldn't we use that instead?

Boxler: Duty is face-to-face confession, son. Between two people. You and this prisoner. Well, go on. Take down your pants.

Craver: Sir?

Boxler: Take down your pants. (*To Lue Ming*) Suck him.

Lue Ming (*To Craver*): Haven't we met before?

Boxler: Suck him, or I'll cut your head off.

(*Craver unzips his pants. Lue Ming begins to sing a Vietnamese lullaby.*)

Boxler: Jesus. Can't you even give her something to suck?

Craver: It's the singing, sir.

Boxler: Remzi. Go get her kid. It's in the hut.

Remzi: What hut, sir? We're in the middle of a desert.

Boxler: Get her fucking kid and bring it here, or I'll cut his dick off.

Remzi: What kid, sir?

Boxler: What kid? There's always a kid.

Lue Ming: The child is right here. In my arms.

(*They all look at Lue Ming.*)

Remzi: We're moving out. Now, sir.

Craver: Remzi.

Remzi: Let's go.

(*They exit. Silence.*)

Lue Ming: I so much prefer it like this. The two of us. Alone.

Scene 4

(*A U.S. military camp somewhere in the Iraqi desert. Remzi and Craver are stunned and worn out.*)

Remzi: Ancient Mesopotamia.

(*Craver begins to whistle to the tune of "Armour Hot Dogs." Then Remzi joins him.*)

Craver (*Sings*): Hot dogs. Armour hot dogs. What kind of kids eat Armor hot dogs?

Remzi (*Sings*): Fat kids, skinny kids, kids that climb on rocks.

Craver (*Sings*): Tough kids, sissy kids, even kids with—

Remzi and **Craver** (*Sing*): —chicken pox! Love hot dogs. Armour hot dogs. The dogs kids love to bite.

Craver: I always loved that song when I was a kid.

Remzi: It made me feel included.

Craver: Yeah.

Remzi: Which kid were you, the fat kid?

Craver: The tough kid.

Remzi: Of course.

Craver: Some of those fuckers were still moving.

Remzi: Right here, where we're sitting, long ago they gave us the zero and the wheel.

Craver: Civilians.

Remzi: Irrigation and organized religion and large-scale trade.

Craver: But there are no civilians in Iraq.

Remzi: Laws and cities and schools. (*Beat*) That was in 2000 B.C.

Craver: Bad fucking luck.

Remzi: The first poet known in history.

Craver: Those pilots took whatever bombs they could get their hands on, even the clusters and five-hundred-pounders.

Remzi: A woman called Enheduanna.

Craver: Imagine dropping a five-hundred-pound bomb on a Volkswagen! Every moving thing. Terminated. Thirty fucking miles of scrap metal, scrap meat. All scrapped. (*Lets out a howl that is half celebration and half terror*) And I've never seen guys dig that fast. Forty-nine holes.

Remzi: They were going home. We shot them in the back. There are laws regarding warfare.

Craver: You're going to get out of the truck this time.

Remzi: I can't.

Craver: Yes you can, and I'll make you.

Remzi: Don't ask me to do it, Craver. I'm warning you.

Craver: But I have to. Get out of the truck this time and walk along the road with me. Get out of the truck this time and help me. Help me.

Remzi: No.

Craver: Someone has to do it.

Remzi: But not you!

Craver: Fuck off.

Remzi: What was it like, you son of a bitch? To carry a man's leg?

Craver: We were ordered to pick up—

Remzi (*Interrupts*): To carry a man's leg when the man is no longer attached?

Craver: To pick up the pieces and put them in the holes. The dozers covered the pieces we found with sand.

Remzi: Is that what you think we're doing, burying them?

Craver: We buried them.

Remzi: We're covering them up. So no one will ever know. I saw you, Craver. I saw you.

Craver: It was like a limb of a tree. No. It was like the branch of a tree. That's how heavy it was. I said to myself: Craver, you're not carrying what you think you're carrying. It's just a piece of tree. For the fire. And you're out in your backyard in Hazard, Kentucky, and he's still alive, my father, and my mother still laughs, and we're having a barbecue. And I can smell the coals.

Remzi: One of the bodies I saw . . . it was very . . . burned. In one of the vans. For a minute I thought, well, he looked like . . . Maybe it was the sun on my head. I don't know. I put my finger inside his mouth. I wanted to touch him someplace where he wasn't (*Beat*) burned.

Craver: Touch me.

Remzi: Every fucking time it tastes different with you. No.

Craver: You didn't try and stop it, did you? (*Shouts*) Did you?

(*Some moments of silence*)

Remzi: Why are we here (*Beat*) killing Arabs?

Craver: For love? Say it's for love. Don't say for oil. Don't say for freedom. Don't say for world power. I'm sick of that. I'm so fucking sick of that. It's true, isn't it? We're here for love. Say it just once. For me.

Remzi: We're here for love.

(*They kiss.*)

SCENE 5

(*Boxler appears with a black box. Lue Ming stands in the shadows watching him. Boxler speaks to the audience.*)

Boxler: Trust me. I'm the man with the box. The Amnesty Box. And this time I'm in . . . Iraq. Is that right? (*Beat*) This box you see before you is a very special box. It's a common device we use here within the military, a receptacle in which soldiers can relieve themselves of contraband, no questions asked. Would you like to drop something in it? You can't take those bits and pieces home with you. No, no, no. I've already made the rounds with the other troops. You're not alone. (*Lifts the lid just a bit but then slams it shut*) What distinguishes this particular box is its stench. Now some soldiers are more attached to their souvenirs than others; in one instance, a severed arm was discovered on a military flight leaving the base for Chicago. One might assume that someone somewhere would be disciplined for anatomical trophy-hunting, but no, not this time. Lucky, lucky. Are you listening? I'm ready for hell, but they won't have me and that's where they're wrong. (*Beat*) All that nasty shit, it took place all the time, before I even killed my first one. But they weren't interested then. And then when they were, bingo, there I was. (*Beat*) Yes, I did it. I never denied it.

(*Lue Ming steps forward.*)

Lue Ming: March 16, 1968. Charlie Company . . .

Boxler: A unit of the America Division's 11th Light Infantry Brigade entered—

Lue Ming: Attacked.

Boxler: Attacked an undefended village on the coast of Central Vietnam and took the lives—

Lue Ming: Murdered.

Boxler: And murdered approximately five hundred old men, women, and children. The killing took place over four hours. Sexual violations . . .

Lue Ming: Rape, sodomy.

Boxler: Anatomical infractions.

Lue Ming: Unimaginable mutilations.

Boxler: Unimaginable. Yes. By the time I went to trial, public opinion was in my favor. T-shirts, buttons, mugs. One company wanted to put my face on a new cereal.

Lue Ming: And my daughter?

Boxler: It's over now. They say it's over.

Lue Ming: The past is never over.

Boxler: The war is over.

Lue Ming: Which one?

Boxler: Do you have anything you want to put in the box?

Lue Ming: Can I take something out?

Boxler: It's supposed to be a one-way thing.

Lue Ming: Give the box to me. Give the box—

Boxler (*Interrupts*): I can't do that.

Lue Ming: Give the box to me, or I'll hunt you across this desecrated world forever. (*Beat*) You owe me a favor.

(*He hands it over to her. She opens the lid and feels about inside. She pulls out her braid.*)

Lue Ming: It's my braid. My braid!

Boxler: Can we call it quits?

(*Lue Ming looks at him but doesn't respond.*)

SCENE 6

(*Remzi and Fairouz are together the night before he leaves for the Mideast. Fairouz is tickling him.*)

Fairouz: I'm going to tickle you until you pee in your pants.

Remzi: Stop it. Get off of me! Stop it!

Fairouz: What will the other soldiers say?

Remzi (*Wrestles her off and now tickles her*): You're so jealous. You can't stand me leaving.

Fairouz: Let's meet up in the Territories.

Remzi: You'll have to come out of the house!

Fairouz: We could look for the village where we might have been born. We could go exploring, find relatives, take photos and—

Remzi (*Interrupts*): If I get a leave, I'm going to go somewhere . . . fun. With my buddies. (*Beat*) Hey. But I'll tell you what. I am going to send you back something very special.

Fairouz: Send something for Mother, too.

Remzi: Maybe I'll even fall in love over there and bring somebody home with me. They do that in wars. Come back with lovers and wives.

Fairouz: If you fall in love, will you let me meet him?

(*Some moments of silence*)

Remzi: Now you're going to be punished for your foul and lecherous tongue! (*Grabs her foot and begins to tickle it*)

Fairouz: Not that one, you fool! I can't feel it.

Remzi (*Playfully*): Oops. Sorry! (*Grabs her other foot and tickles it*)

Fairouz: Stop it. Stop it! Now go on or you'll miss your bus. (*Kisses him on the cheek to shut him up*) Nothing more. Just go. Go on.

(*He exits.*)

Fairouz: Get out of here!

(*Lue Ming appears. Fairouz talks to her as though she were Remzi.*)

Fairouz: No. Wait a minute . . . It doesn't matter now . . . We were children then. Are you listening to me? I'm thinking of leaving too, you know. Perhaps I'll make a trip, all on my own. Yes. I might even start a clinic out there, at the edge of the world. You don't believe me? Well, you just wait. When I—

Lue Ming (*Interrupts*): Fairouz. I get leave in a few months. Don't do anything rash. Just wait 'til I get back.

Fairouz: Those who wait, burn. (*Knowing now that it is Lue Ming*) They won't send home the body.

SCENE 7

(*Fairouz and Craver are in his motel room.*)

Fairouz: The Army won't send home the body.

Craver: What's it matter? It's just a body. It's not him.

(*Split scene: Remzi and Boxler elsewhere on stage. Boxler ties Remzi's hands and blindfolds him. Lue Ming stands watching.*)

Fairouz: I want to see his body. It belongs to us.

Craver: It. It. Just what the fuck are you talking about? He's gone. I don't want anything to do with the it.

(*Fairouz's foot hurts her.*)

Fairouz: I think I twisted it again.

Craver: You should see a doctor. (*Beat*) Let me see.

Fairouz: I don't usually show men my foot unless I take my pants off first. (*Craver takes a look at her foot.*) It doesn't smell very good, does it? Remzi used to crush grass and dandelions, sweet clover, sometimes even the wings of insects, all together in a bowl. He was quite a medic.

Lue Ming (*To Remzi*): Devil's feet, devil's feet, devil's feet.

Craver: May I?

Fairouz: You want to kiss my foot?

Craver: Yes.

Remzi (*Chants with a deadpan voice*): Fairouz Saboura has devil's feet.

Fairouz: Because you want to make it better?

Lue Ming (*Chants*): Dirty Arab devil, you go home!

Fairouz: Or because I told you he used to do that?

Remzi (*Chants*): Dirty Arab devil, you go home!

Lue Ming (*Chants*): Get her shoe. Pull off her shoe.

Craver: Both.

Remzi (*Chants*): Hold her down and pull off her shoe.

Craver: For both reasons.

Fairouz: All right.

(*Craver leans to kiss her foot.*)

Remzi: No!

Fairouz (*Pulls her foot away from Craver*): Don't.

Remzi (*Remzi cannot get loose. He is again "seeing" his sister being beaten.*): Get the fuck off her, you motherfuckers!

Fairouz: Remzi!

Boxler (*To Remzi*): We had an Iraqi prisoner. I stuck the knife in, just below the sternum.

Craver: I won't hurt you.

Boxler: And I slit him all the way down.

Remzi: All of you! Back off!

Boxler: I pulled his rib cage wide open . . .

Remzi: Leave her alone!

Boxler: . . . and stood inside his body. I said—

Remzi: Fairouz!

Boxler: Hey, boys, now I'm really standing in Iraq.

Craver: I promise you, I won't hurt you. (*Fairouz lets him kiss her foot, then she kicks him.*) Bitch.

Remzi: Get away from her!

Craver: Fucking . . . Arab whore.

Remzi: Get away from her. I'm warning you!

Fairouz: Take a look, Craver. This isn't a B-52. This isn't a Buff. This is a hammer. I could do to your face what they did to my foot.

Craver: Go on then. You fucking gimp. Go on. Do it! Hit me! Hit me, you fucking cunt! Please. (*Drops to his knees*) Please. Hit me.

Fairouz (*Raises the hammer as if to strike him but instead runs the hammer over his cheeks*): How do you remember him now? (*Presses the face of the hammer to his mouth and moves it sexually*) Like this?

Remzi: No!

Craver (*Pushes the hammer away*): No.

(*Remzi goes "unconscious." Fairouz and Craver are alone.*)

Craver: A plague. A flood. An ice age. That's what I expected when it was over and I got back here. An earthquake. Something that would rip this country wide open. Eighty-eight thousand tons of explosives dropped. That country is like a body with every bone inside it broken.

Fairouz: How did he die?

Craver: Every single bone. We tried. Day after day, but there were too many pieces. We couldn't get them all. Do you know how many pieces make up the human body? Two, three hundred thousand. (*Beat*) Dead. Maybe half of them civilians. We bombed the sewers, the electricity, the water. They'll die in the thousands because of bad water. Just bad water.

Fairouz: Give me an answer.

Craver: They came for us. Both of us.

Fairouz: But you're still alive.

Craver: The question here isn't how many feet were between Remzi and I. It could have been thirty feet. Or twenty-five. I think it was more like twenty.

Fairouz: Tell me.

Craver: I had practiced it with him. I got it down just right. Do you want to see how I walked? (*Does his "walk" for her as she watches him*) Are you watching me? (*Continues his "walk"*)

SCENE 8

(*Boxler and Lue Ming are alone.*)

Boxler: I remember you. I think I do. Is that what you want? An apology? Why didn't you just say so? Hey. Really. I'm sincerely sorry. I've always been sorry. Besides, I wasn't completely heartless. You didn't know I shot your kid, because I shot you first.

Lue Ming: You said you'd let her live if I did what you wanted. You couldn't get it up. That's why you killed us both.

Boxler: I had a war on my mind.

Lue Ming: What is it like to kill a child?

Boxler: You're sick.

Lue Ming: I have to know.

Boxler: It's simple: A bit of . . . a clump of . . . a piece of . . . (*Beat*) a piece of the future is alive, and then it isn't.

Lue Ming: Were you ever in love?

Boxler: Oh, yes. Long ago. I was born a human being, you know. But one can't stay that way forever. One has to mature. (*Beat*) Maybe it was you I fell in love with. I mean, it could have happened, couldn't it? (*Kisses her. She does not respond.*)

Lue Ming: Why wasn't one time enough?

Boxler: Because I wanted to kiss you again. Naturally.

Lue Ming: Why did you have to shoot her twice? Three times? Just to make sure?

Boxler: Just to make sure, I did it four times. And shooting a child, if you must know, is rather exceptional. It's like shooting an angel. There's something religious about it.

Lue Ming: I woke up after you and your troops were gone. I woke up with my child in my arms. A dead child weighs so much more than a live one. I carried her back to the village. When I was well again, I continued my work with the Vietcong. I was one of their top commanders. I searched for you everywhere. Everywhere. With more passion than one would a lost lover. But I never found you.

Boxler: Just how did you die?

Lue Ming: I can't remember. How long have you been dead?

Boxler: Calley is still alive and well in Georgia, only I've run out on him. I'm his soul. Calley's dead soul.

Lue Ming: His soul?

Boxler: Yes, his soul, and I'm homeless.

Lue Ming: I don't believe in souls.

Boxler: Neither do I, but here I am. I go from war to war. It's the only place that feels like home. I didn't kill your daughter. Calley did. I was inside him, looking out, but I didn't do it. I didn't pull the trigger.

Lue Ming: You watched.

Boxler: What else can a soul do but watch? We're not magicians.

Lue Ming: Are you suffering?

Boxler: I can't suffer. I can't, and it hurts me.

Lue Ming: Is it terrible?

Boxler: It tears me apart.

Lue Ming: How long will this go on?

Boxler: World without end.

Lue Ming: Delightful. More than I'd hoped. (*Beat*) But I want you to make a sound for me.

(*Split scene: Fairouz is watching Remzi and Craver, who do not "see" her watching them.*)

Boxler: No.

Lue Ming: You owe it to me.

Fairouz (*Calls*): Remzi.

Boxler: I don't know what you're talking about.

Fairouz and **Lue Ming:** The sound—

Fairouz: . . . you made inside you. Not the second time.

Lue Ming: Not the third or fourth. But the first time you died.

Boxler: The first time I died.

Lue Ming: Yes.

Boxler: That would be sometime in November 1967. There was an old man. He was wounded. He wouldn't have made it anyway. I threw him down a well.

Remzi (*To Craver*): I couldn't say it any louder. I whispered her name. (*Whispers*) Fairouz.

Craver (*Whispers*): Fairouz.

Remzi: There were five of them.

Fairouz: Go on.

Boxler: I threw him down a well. An old man. I heard his head go crack against the stone wall and then splash.

Remzi: One of the boys had just come out of woodshop. He'd been making an end table for his mother for Christmas. He had a hammer.

Craver: You were a kid, Remzi.

Boxler: I was a child once. Did you know that? I liked to run naked and jump up and down on the bed. I had a bath toy. A blue bath toy. I can't remember what it was.

Remzi: They got one of her shoes off. Then the sock. I stood behind the bushes and watched.

Craver: You looked out for yourself. That was right.

Remzi: I was afraid that if I tried to stop them they'd do the same to me.

Craver: Shhhhhhhhh.

Boxler: I threw him down the well. I heard a crack. I heard a splash. I heard a crack and a splash, and I died.

Craver: You were just a kid.

(*Craver and Remzi kiss, and Craver removes Remzi's shirt.*)

Fairouz: You were just a child.

Boxler: When I killed him, I died, though I didn't make a sound when I died. My body just turned and walked back into the village to finish the rest of the job.

Lue Ming: But I heard it. I heard the splash. And I heard you die.

Fairouz: Do you want to know what it sounds like?

Lue Ming: What it sounds like to go on living and the child in your arms is so heavy and she is dead and you are dead and I am dead but—

Fairouz: We just keep living.

Boxler: Forever and ever.

Lue Ming: It sounded like this—

(*Lue Ming, Fairouz, and Boxler all scream "no." Their screams are deafening and mixed with the sound of thundering jets. Remzi and Craver look up at the jets above them, which are awe-inspiring.*)

SCENE 9

(*Craver and Fairouz are in his motel room. Craver is still holding Remzi's shirt.*)

Craver: That's beautiful. Sad Eyes. The CBUs were prohibited weapons, like the napalm, cluster, and fragmentation. But Sad Eyes. Who would have had the heart to try and stop a weapon named Sad Eyes? Eyes like his. Not sad, really. But confused. Or furious. Or scared. (*Remzi appears as a vision. Craver speaks to him.*) The first time we made love, we were so scared and I started to cry. It was a first time for both of us, and it hurt. You leaned over me and kissed the back of my neck and you said over and over . . .

Remzi: You are my white trash, and I love you.

(*Craver mouths the words along with Remzi.*)

Craver and **Remzi:** You are my white trash, and I love you.

Craver: They caught us together, out behind the barracks. They were lower ranks. Just kids. Like me. Kids who grew up with garbage in their backyards. Kids who never got the summer jobs, who didn't own CD players. They knocked us around. After a while, they took us to a room. Handed us over to an upper rank. There was a British officer and an Iraqi prisoner in there too, and they were laughing and saying sandnigger. Indian. Gook. (*Beat*) Remzi. Well. He went wild. He jumped one of those officers. I was standing there. I couldn't move. I couldn't . . . Then somebody hit me over the head, and I went out. (*Beat*) The first time I came to, the prisoner was down and he kept waving his arms like he was swimming, doing the backstroke, and Remzi was there and I could hear his voice, but it was like trying to see through a sheet of ice. (*Beat*) My head was spinning, and it was snowing stars. In that room. In the middle of the biggest bunch of hottest nowhere in the world and it was snowing stars and Remzi in the center of it and this one officer or maybe it was two and there was a knife and the Iraqi had stopped moving—I think he was dead—and they were all over him and having a good time at it. Like kids in the snow. (*Beat*) Do you want to know how you died, Remzi?

Remzi: Friendly fire.

Craver: One of them had his arm around my neck, choking me, while another one held you down. I shouted for you to stay down but you wouldn't stay down. Each time he knocked you down you stood up. He hit you in the mouth so many times I couldn't tell anymore what was your nose and what was your mouth. (*Beat*) What did you call the other soldiers when you first joined up?

Remzi: Family.

Craver: When I woke up, I took him in my arms. The blood had stopped coming out. (*Beat*) Five foot . . . eleven inches. That's how tall you were. I used to run my hand up and down your body like I was reading the bones.

Remzi: I wanted to travel everyplace on your body. Even the places you'd never been. Love can make you feel so changed you think the world is changed. Up 'til then, we'd survived the war.

Remzi (*To Craver*): What are you?

Fairouz (*To Craver*): What are you?

Remzi (*Louder*): What are you, Craver?

Craver (*Whispers*): What are you? What are you? (*Shouts*) What are you, Craver?

(*Remzi says the following words with Craver, beginning with "Indian." Remzi's words are spoken just a fraction sooner than Craver's.*)

Craver: I am a White Trash,

Craver and **Remzi:** Indian, Sandnigger, Brown Trash, Arab, Gook Boy, Faggot—

Remzi (*To Fairouz*): From the banks of the Kentucky river.

SCENE 10

(*Remzi as a vision, as a child, making a "mix" for Fairouz's foot. Fairouz watches him, as though from a long distance. Craver listens from the shadows.*)

Fairouz: He and I. We were never children. We were pieces of children. After that. But what is a piece of a child?

Remzi: Grass. Black pepper. Gold. From a gold crayon.

Fairouz: Sweetness doesn't last. Bitter lasts. Bile lasts. I am looking. Yes. I am looking for him.

Remzi: Pancake syrup. Lots of that.

Fairouz: And I don't want to find him. Not now. Not tomorrow. But I'm looking.

(*Craver exits.*)

Fairouz: I don't want him to come back to me as him, but as a boy wearing my face. *(Beat)* Where you ended, I began.

Remzi: Ready, Fairouz? *(Calls)* Are you ready? *(To himself)* This one's just right. Won't sting.

Fairouz: And the sand. I can't sleep because of it. Everywhere. Inside my pillow. Inside my sleep. I'm walking. Walking and calling for you. But the sand slides below my feet, stopping me, keeping me in place. And the wind throwing handfuls. But then in the distance. I see. Something. Dark. Moving. Moving toward me.

Remzi: Eggshells. Mint.

Fairouz: And it seems hours, years, until I can see. What. Yes. That it's a child. Five or six. A boy. The wind has torn small pieces from your body. With each step you take toward me you are less whole. When we reach each other, you are almost transparent.

Remzi: It's too dry. *(Calls)* Bring me some water.

Fairouz: Almost nothing left. I know I must say your name. Now. But I can't. There's no sand in my mouth. No wind. But I can't say it.

Remzi *(Calls)*: Are you coming?

Fairouz: I can't. Say it. And then you're moving away from me, moving back. I open my mouth. To say it. I say: Fairouz.

Remzi *(Calls)*: Fairouz.

Fairouz: My own name. Not yours. And in that moment, the sun drills brilliant through your chest. And then you are. Gone.

SCENE 11

(Craver and Fairouz are in his motel room.)

Fairouz: The ram's horn. Why did he send me the ram's horn?

Craver: He carved your name on the inside. It took him three hours to do it. His sister would have appreciated it. You should have given it to her.

Fairouz: I am his sister.

Craver: Yes. You are. *(Does a headstand)*

Fairouz: Why do you do that?

Craver: I'm training my balance.

Fairouz: Remzi had no balance.

Craver (*Comes out of the headstand*): No?

Fairouz: He said balance could be a bad thing, a trick to keep you in the middle, where things add up, where you can do no harm.

Craver: Remzi said that?

Fairouz: No. But he might have. (*Beat*) I'll go wherever I need to go. I won't leave them in peace.

Craver: Remzi said you were the best sister any brother—

Fairouz (*Interrupts*): Don't. Please. (*Beat*) It's terrible, isn't it? To be freed like this. Are you going to talk?

Craver: I'm going to try.

Fairouz: But what is it for?

Craver: It might keep me alive. Talking about it might keep me alive.

Fairouz: I mean the ram's horn. What is it for?

Craver: He said.

(*Remzi appears and gets in position to race.*)

Remzi: I want to race.

Craver: He said if you blow on it, it will make a noise.

Remzi: I haven't had a good race in almost . . .

Craver: You're on! (*Joins Remzi. Gets down in a starting position to run with him.*) Motherfucker. Ready?

(*Craver is in two realities now and speaks to both Remzi and Fairouz with ease.*)

Fairouz: A noise.

Remzi: I'm going to beat you this time!

Fairouz: All right.

Craver: On your mark.

Fairouz: Will it be loud?

Remzi: I'm going to pass you by so fast, I'm going to, bang, disappear right in front of you!

Craver (*To Fairouz*): Fucking loud. (*To Remzi*) Get set?

Remzi: You just watch me.

Fairouz: Fucking loud. I like that.

Remzi: Just watch me!

Fairouz: Goddamn, fucking loud!

Craver and **Remzi:** Go!

(*As the two men move to run, the lights go black.*)

END OF PLAY

Marisol

JOSÉ RIVERA

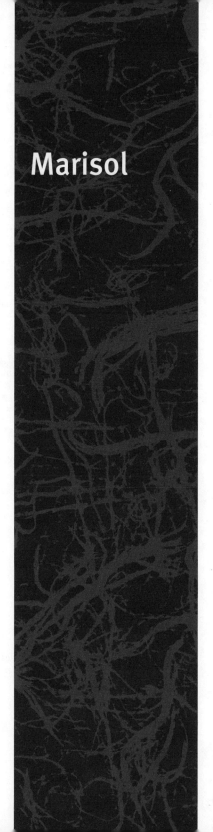

Marisol received its world premiere at the Humana Festival of New American Plays at the Actors Theatre of Louisville, in Louisville, Kentucky, on March 13, 1992. The producing director was Jon Jory; director, Marcus Stern; set designer, Paul Owen; costume designer, Laura A. Patterson; lighting designer, Mary Louise Geiger; sound designer, Darron West; state manager, James Mountcastle. The cast included Karina Arroyave as Marisol; V. Craig Heidenreich as Man with Golf Club, Man with Ice Cream, Lenny, Man with Scar Tissue; Esther Scott as Angel; Susan Knight as June; and Carlos Ramos as Homeless Person.

Marisol was subsequently produced by the New York Shakespeare Festival (George C. Wolfe, producer), in association with the Hartford Stage Company (Mark Lamos, artistic director), in New York City, May 1993. It was directed by Michael Greif.

Marisol was originally commissioned and developed by INTAR Hispanic American Arts Center (Max Ferra, artistic director) through a grant from the Rockefeller Foundation.

Cast of Characters

Marisol, a Puerto Rican woman, 26

Angel, Marisol's guardian angel, a young black woman

Subway Announcer

Man with Golf Club

First Voice

Second Voice

Third Voice

June, Marisol's friend, Irish-American, 36

Radio Voice

Man with Ice Cream

Lenny, June's brother, 34

Woman with Furs

Man with Scar Tissue

Homeless People

Setting

New York City. The present. Winter.

ACT 1

SCENE 1

(*New York City. The present.*

Lights up on an upstage brick wall running the width of the stage and going as high as the theater will allow. The windows in the wall are shielded by iron security gates. The highest windows are boarded up.

Spray-painted on the wall is this graffiti-poem:

> "The moon carries the souls of dead people to heaven.
> The new moon is dark and empty.
> It fills up every month with new glowing souls
> then it carries its silent burden to God. WAKE UP."

The "WAKE UP" looks like it was added to the poem by someone else.

Downstage of the wall is a tall ladder coming down at an angle. Sitting on the ladder is Marisol's Guardian Angel.

The Angel is a young black woman in ripped jeans, sneakers, and black T-shirt. Crude silver wings hang limply from the back of the Angel's diamond-studded black leather jacket. Though she radiates tremendous heat and light, there's something tired and lonely about the Angel: she looks like an urban warrior, a suffering burnt-out soldier of some lost cause. She watches the scene below with intense concern.

Floating in the sky is a small gold crown inside a clear glass box.

Lights up on the subway car: a filth-covered bench.

It's late night. Late winter.

Marisol Perez, an attractive Puerto Rican woman of twenty-six, sits in the subway car. Marisol has dark hair and deep, smart, dark eyes. She is a young urban professional: smartly dressed, reading the New York

Times, *returning to her Bronx apartment after a long day at her Manhattan job. She wears heavy winter clothing. She has no idea she's being watched by an angel.*)

Subway Announcer: . . . and a pleasant evening to all the ladies. 180th Street will be the next and last stop. Step lively, guard your valuables, trust no one.

(*The Man with Golf Club enters the subway car. He's a young white man, twenties, in a filthy black T-shirt and ripped jeans; his long matted hair hangs over blazing eyes. His shoes are rags and his mind is shot.*

The Man with Golf Club looks at Marisol and "shoots" the club like an Uzi. Marisol has taught herself not to show fear or curiosity on the subway. She digs deeper into her paper. The Man talks to Marisol.)

Man with Golf Club: It was the shock that got me. I was so shocked all I could see was pain all around me: little spinning starlights of pain 'cause of the shocking thing the angel just told me. (*He waits for a reaction. Marisol refuses to look at him.*) You see, she was always *there* for me. I could *count* on her. She was my very own God-blessed little angel! My own gift from God! (*No response. He makes a move toward Marisol. She looks at him, quickly sizing him up . . .*)

Marisol: God help you, you get in my face.

Man with Golf Club: But last night she crawled into the box I occupy on 180th Street in the Bronx. I was sleeping: nothing special walking through my thoughts 'cept the usual panic over my empty stomach, and the windchill factor, and how, oh *how*, was I *ever* gonna replace my lost Citibank MasterCard?

Marisol: I have no money. (*Marisol tries to slide away from The Man with Golf Club, trying to show no fear. He follows.*)

Man with Golf Club: She folded her hot silver angel wings under her leather jacket and creeped into my box last night, reordering the air, waking me up with the shock, the bad news that she was gonna *leave me forever . . .*

Marisol (*Getting freaked*): Man, why don't you just get a job?!

Man with Golf Club: *Don't you see?* She once stopped Nazi skinheads from setting me on fire in Van Cortlandt Park! Do you get it now, lady?! I live on the street! I am dead meat without my guardian angel! I'm gonna be *food* . . . a fucking *appetizer* for all the Hitler youth and their cans of *gasoline* . . . (*He lunges at Marisol and rips the newspaper from her. She's on her feet, ready for a fight.*)

Marisol (*To God*): Okay, God! Kill him now! Take him out!

Man with Golf Club (*Truly worried*): That means you don't have any protection either. Your guardian angel is gonna leave you too. That means, in the next *four or five seconds*, I could change the entire course of your life . . .

Marisol (*To God*): Blast him into little bits! Turn him into salt!

Man with Golf Club (*Calm, almost pitying*): I could turn you into one of me. I could fix it so every time you look in the mirror . . . every time you dream . . . or close your eyes in some hopeless logic that closed eyes are a shield against nightmares . . . *you're gonna think you turned into me* . . .

(*The Man with Golf Club makes a move toward Marisol. The Angel reacts.*

There's an earsplitting scream as the subway stops. Marisol and the Man are thrown violently across the subway car. The Man falls.

Marisol seizes her chance, pushes the disoriented Man away, and runs out of the subway car into the street.

Lights to black on the subway. The Man exits in the dark.)

SCENE 2

(*Lights up on the street: a small empty space with a battered city trash can. It's snowing lightly. The shivering Marisol stops to look up at the sky. She crosses herself.*)

Marisol: Thank you.

(*No response from the Angel. It stops snowing as Marisol leaves the street and enters her apartment.*)

SCENE 3

(*Lights up on Marisol's apartment: bed, table, lamp, clock, offstage bathroom, and large romanticized picture of a traditional Catholic guardian angel on the wall.*

Marisol quickly runs in, slamming and locking the door behind her. She runs to the window to make sure the security gates are locked.

She tries to catch her breath. She takes off her coat. She notices an army of cockroaches on the floor. She stomps them angrily until every last one is dead. This seems to make her feel a little better.

She collapses on the bed. She pounds her pillow angrily. Exhausted, she checks a knife she keeps under her pillow. She puts it back and lies on her bed, trying to calm herself and just breathe.

As she changes her clothes she fixes herself a drink and downs it. She checks the crucifix, horseshoe, rabbit's foot, prayer cards, milagros, medicine bundles, statuettes of Buddha, and other good luck charms kept under the bed. She crosses herself and closes her eyes.]

Marisol:
Matthew, Mark, Luke and John.
Bless the bed that I lie on.
Four corners to my bed.
Four angels 'round my head.
One to watch and one to pray.
And two to bear my soul away.

(Marisol crosses herself, opens her eyes, and lies down.

Then the noises begin. They come at Marisol from apartments all around her. Doors are slammed, bottles smashed, radiator pipes pounded, stereos played loud. Then the Voices join in.)

First Voice *(Female)*: *Ave Maria purisima, donde esta el* heat?

(Marisol sits up. She can't believe this bullshit is starting again . . .)

Second Voice *(Female, a high-decibel shriek)*: Matthew? It's Sandy! I KNOW YOU'RE IN THERE. STOP HIDING FROM ME, YOU MALIGNANT FUCK!

(Marisol starts rubbing her pounding head.)

Third Voice *(Male)*: Ah yeah yeah man you gotta help me man they broke my fuckin' *head* open . . .

Marisol *(Runs to her window, shakes the iron gates)*: *Mira,* people are trying to sleep!

Second Voice: YOU'RE PISSING ME OFF, MATTHEW, OPEN THE DOOR!

First Voice: *Donde esta el* heat?? *NO TENGO* HEAT, *CONO!*

Second Voice: MATTHEEEEEEEEEEEEEEEEEW!

(*Marisol dives back into bed, covering her head, trying not to hear. The noises increase and the Voices come faster, louder, overlapping . . .*)

Third Voice: . . . I was jus' tryin' to sell 'em some dope man . . .

Second Voice: MATTHEW, GODDAMMIT, IT'S SANDY! SANDY! YOUR GIRLFRIEND, YOU WITLESS *COCK*!

First Voice: *Me vas a matar* without *el* fucking heat!!

Second Voice: MATTHEEEEEEEEEEWWWWWWW! OPEN THIS DOOOOOOOOOOOOR!

Third Voice: . . . so they hadda go bust my fuckin' head open oh look haha there go my busted brains floppin' 'round the floor I'm gonna step right on 'em I'm not careful man I shouldda got their fuckin' *badge* numbers . . .

Marisol (*Bangs on the floor with a shoe*): Some people work in the morning!!

Third Voice: . . . think I'll pick up my brains right now man get a shovel 'n' scoop up my soakin' brainbag off this messy linoleum floor man sponge up my absentee motherfuckin' *mind* . . .

Second Voice: THAT'S IT, MATTHEW! YOU'RE DEAD. I'M COMING BACK WITH A GUN AND I'M GONNA KILL YOU AND THEN I'M GONNA KILL EVERYONE IN THIS APARTMENT BUILDING INCLUDING THE CHILDREN!

(*The Voices stop. Marisol waits. Thinking it's over, Marisol gets into bed and tries to sleep. Beat. Marisol starts to nod off. There's suddenly furious knocking at Marisol's door.*)

Second Voice: MATTHEW! I'M BACK! I'VE GOT MY DADDY'S GUN! AND YOU'RE GONNA DIE RIGHT NOW!

Marisol (*Runs to the door*): Matthew doesn't live here! You have the wrong apartment!

Second Voice: Matthew, *who's that*???

Marisol: Matthew lives next door!!

Second Voice: IS THAT YOUR NEW GIRLFRIEND, MATTHEW???! OH YOU'RE DEAD. YOU'RE REALLY DEAD NOW!!

(*A gun is cocked. Marisol dives for cover. The Angel reacts. Suddenly, the stage is blasted with white light.*

There's complete silence: the rattling, banging, screaming all stop. We hear crickets.

Marisol, amazed by the instant calm, goes to the door, looks through the peephole. She cautiously opens the door.

There's a small pile of salt on the floor. At first, Marisol just looks at it, too amazed to move. Then she bends down to touch the salt, letting it run through her fingers.)

Marisol: Salt?

(Frightened, not sure she knows what this means, Marisol quickly closes and locks the door. She gets into bed and turns out the light.

Lights down everywhere except on the Angel.)

SCENE 4

(Lights shift in Marisol's apartment as the Angel climbs down the ladder to Marisol's bed.

Marisol feels the tremendous heat given off by the Angel. The Angel backs away from Marisol so as not to burn her. The Angel goes to the window and looks out. Her voice is slightly amplified. She speaks directly to Marisol, who sleeps.

Throughout the scene, the light coming in through Marisol's window goes up slowly, until, by the end, it's the next morning.)

Angel: A man is worshiping a fire hydrant on Taylor Avenue, Marisol. He's draping rosaries on it, genuflecting hard. An old woman's selling charmed chicken blood in see-through Ziplock bags for a buck. They're setting another homeless man on fire in Van Cortlandt Park. *(The Angel rattles the metal gate.)* Cut that shit out you fucking Nazis! *(The Angel goes to Marisol's door and checks the lock. She stomps cockroaches. She straightens up a little.)* I swear, best thing that could happen to this city is immediate evacuation followed by fire on a massive scale. Melt it all down. Consume the ruins. Then put the ashes of those evaporated dreams into a big urn and sit the urn on the desks of a few thousand oily politicians. Let them smell the disaster like we do. *(The Angel goes to Marisol's bed and looks at her. Marisol's heart beats faster and she starts to hyperventilate.)* So what do you believe in, Marisol? You believe in me? Or do you believe your senses? If so, what's that taste in your mouth? *(The Angel clicks her fingers.)*

Marisol (*In her sleep, tasting*): Oh my God, *arroz con gandules*! Yum!

Angel: What's your favorite smell, Marisol? (*Click!*)

Marisol (*In her sleep, sniffing*): The ocean! I smell the ocean!

Angel: Do you like sex, Marisol?

(*Click! Marisol is seized by powerful sexual spasms that wrack her body and nearly throw her off the bed. When they end, Marisol stretches out luxuriously: exhausted but happy.*)

Marisol (*Laughing*): I've got this wild energy running through my body!

Angel (*Gets closer to Marisol*): Here's your big chance, baby. What would you like to ask the Angel of the Lord?

Marisol (*In her sleep, energized*): Are you real? Are you true? Are you gonna make the Bronx safe for me? Are you gonna make miracles and reduce my rent? Is it true angels' favorite food is Thousand Island dressing? Is it true your shit smells like mangos and when you're drunk you speak Portuguese?!

Angel: Honey, last time I was drunk . . .

Marisol (*Gets a sudden, horrifying realization*): *Wait a minute—am I dead?* Did I die tonight? How did I miss that? Was it the man with the golf club? Did he beat me to death? Oh my God. I've been dead all night. And when I look around I see that Death is my ugly apartment in the Bronx. No this can't be Death! Death can't have this kind of furniture!

Angel: God, you're so cute, I could eat you up. No. You're still alive.

(*Marisol is momentarily relieved—then she suddenly starts touching her stomach as she gets a wild, exhilarating idea.*)

Marisol (*In her sleep*): *Am I pregnant with the Lord's baby?!* Is the new Messiah swimming in my electrified womb? Is the supersperm of God growing a mythic flower deep in the secret greenhouse inside me? Will my morning sickness taste like communion wine? This is amazing— *billions* of women on earth, and I get knocked up by God!

Angel: No baby, no baby, no baby, no baby—No. Baby.

(*Beat. Marisol is a little disappointed.*)

Marisol (*In her sleep*): No? Then what is it? Are you real or not? 'Cause if you're real and God is real and the Gospels are real, this would be the perfect time to tell me. 'Cause I once looked for angels, I did, in every shadow of my childhood—but I never found any. I thought I'd find you hiding inside the notes I sang to myself as a kid. The songs that put me to sleep and kept me from killing myself with fear. But I didn't see you then. (*The Angel doesn't answer. Her silence—her very presence—starts to unhinge Marisol.*) C'mon! Somebody up there has to tell me why I live the way I do! What's going on here, anyway? Why is there a war on children in this city? Why are apples extinct? Why are they planning to drop human insecticide on overpopulated areas of the Bronx? Why has the color blue disappeared from the sky? Why does common rainwater turn your skin bright red? Why do cows give salty milk? Why did the Plague kill half my friends? AND WHAT HAPPENED TO THE MOON? Where did the moon go? How come nobody's seen it in nearly *nine months* . . . ? (*Marisol is trying desperately to keep from crying. The Angel gets into bed with Marisol. Contact with the Angel makes Marisol gasp. She opens her mouth to scream, but nothing comes out. Marisol collapses—her whole body goes limp. Marisol rests her head on the Angel's lap. Electricity surges gently through Marisol's body. She is feeling no pain, fear, or loneliness. The Angel strokes her hair.*)

Angel: I kick-started your heart, Marisol. I wired your nervous system. I pushed your fetal blood in the right direction and turned the foam in your infant lungs to oxygen. When you were six and your parents were fighting, I helped you pretend you were underwater: that you were a cold-blooded fish, in the bottom of the black ocean, far away and safe. When racists ran you out of school at ten, screaming . . .

Marisol (*In her sleep*): . . . "kill the spik" . . .

Angel: . . . I turned the monsters into little columns of salt! At last count, one plane crash, one collapsed elevator, one massacre at the hands of a right-wing fanatic with an Uzi, and sixty-six thousand six hundred and three separate sexual assaults never happened because of me.

Marisol (*In her sleep*): Wow. Now I don't have to be so paranoid . . . ?

(*The Angel suddenly gets out of bed. Marisol curls up in a fetal position. The Angel is nervous now, full of hostile energy, anxious.*)

Angel: Now the bad news. (*The Angel goes to the window. She's silent a moment as she contemplates the devastated Bronx landscape.*)

Marisol (*In her sleep, worried*): What?

Angel (*Finds it very hard to tell Marisol what's on her mind*): I can't expect you to understand the political ins and outs of what's going on.

But you have eyes. You asked me questions about children and water and war and the moon: the same questions I've been asking myself for a thousand years.

(*We hear distant explosions. Marisol's body responds with a jolt.*)

Marisol (*In her sleep, quiet*): What's that noise?

Angel: The universal body is sick, Marisol. Constellations are wasting away, the nauseous stars are full of blisters and sores, the infected earth is running a temperature, and everywhere the universal mind is wracked with amnesia, boredom, and neurotic obsessions.

Marisol (*In her sleep, frightened*): Why?

Angel: Because God is old and dying and taking the rest of us with Him. And for too long, much too long, I've been looking the other way. Trying to stop the massive hemorrhage with my little hands. With my prayers. But it didn't work and I knew if I didn't do something soon, it would be too late.

Marisol (*In her sleep, frightened*): What did you do?

Angel: I called a meeting. And I urged the Heavenly Hierarchies—the Seraphim, Cherubim, Thrones, Dominions, Principalities, Powers, Virtues, Archangels, and Angels—to vote to stop the universal ruin . . . by slaughtering our senile God. And they did. Listen well, Marisol: angels are going to kill the King of Heaven and restore the vitality of the universe with His blood. And I'm going to lead them.

(*Marisol takes this in silently—then suddenly erupts, her body shaking with fear and energy.*)

Marisol (*In her sleep*): Okay, I wanna wake up now!

Angel: There's going to be war. A revolution of angels.

Marisol (*In her sleep*): GOD IS GREAT! GOD IS GOOD! THANK YOU FOR OUR NEIGHBORHOOD!

Angel: Soon we're going to send out spies, draft able-bodied celestial beings, raise taxes . . .

Marisol (*In her sleep*): THANK YOU FOR THE BIRDS THAT SING! THANK YOU GOD FOR EVERYTHING!

Angel: Soon we're going to take off our wings of peace, Marisol, and put on our wings of war. Then we're going to spread blood and vigor across the sky and reawaken the dwindling stars!

Marisol (*In her sleep, reciting fast*): "And there was war in Heaven; Michael and his angels fought against the dragon; and the dragon fought—"

Angel: It could be suicide. A massacre. He's better armed. Better organized. And, well, a little omniscient. But we have to win. (*Beat*) And when we do win . . . when we crown the new God, and begin the new millennium . . . the earth will be restored. The moon will return. The degradation of the animal kingdom will end. Men and women will be elevated to a higher order. All children will speak Latin. And Creation will finally be perfect. (*Distant thunder and lightning. The Angel quickly goes to the window to read the message in the lightning. She turns to Marisol, who is struggling to wake up.*) It also means I have to leave you. I can't stay. I can't protect you anymore.

(*Beat*)

Marisol (*In her sleep*): What? You're *leaving* me?

Angel: I don't want to. I love you. I thought you had to know. But now I have to go and fight—

Marisol (*In her sleep*): I'm going to be alone?

Angel: And that's what you have to do, Marisol. You have to fight. You can't *endure* anymore. You can't trust luck or prayer or mercy or other people. When I drop my wings, all hell's going to break loose and soon you're not going to recognize the world—so get yourself some *power*, Marisol, whatever you do.

Marisol (*In her sleep*): What's going to happen to me without you . . . ?

Angel (*Goes to Marisol and tries to kiss her*): I don't know.

(*Marisol lashes out, trying to hit the Angel. Marisol spits at the Angel. The Angel grabs Marisol's hands.*)

Marisol: *I'm gonna be meat!* I'M GONNA BE FOOD!! (*By now the lights are nearly up full: it's the next morning. The Angel holds the struggling Marisol.*)

Angel: Unless you want to join us—

Marisol: NOOOOO!!

(*Marisol fights. Her alarm clock goes off.*

The Angel lets Marisol go and climbs up the ladder and disappears.

Marisol wakes up violently—she looks around in a panic—instantly goes for the knife under her pillow.

It takes her a few moments to realize she's home in her bed.

She puts the knife away. Turns off the alarm clock. She thinks: I must have been dreaming. She shakes her head, catches her breath, and tries to calm down. She wipes the sweat from her face.

Marisol gets out of bed. She goes to the window and looks down at the street—her eyes filled with new terror. She runs to her offstage bathroom.)

SCENE 5

(Lights up on Marisol's office in Manhattan: two metal desks facing each other covered in books and papers. One desk has a small radio.

June enters the office. She's an Irish American, thirty-six, bright, edgy, hyper, dressed in cool East Village clothes. Her wild red hair and all-American freckles provide a vivid contrast to Marisol's Latin darkness. June tries to read the New York Post *but she can't concentrate. She keeps waiting for Marisol to appear. June turns on the radio.)*

Radio Voice: . . . sources indicate the President's psychics believe they know where the moon has gone to. They claim to see the moon hovering over the orbit of Saturn, looking lost. Pentagon officials are considering plans to spend billions on a space tug to haul the moon back to earth. The tug would attach a long chain to the moon so it never strays from its beloved earth again. One insider has been quoted as saying the White House hopes to raise revenues for Operation Moon Rescue by taxing lunatics. Responding to allegations that cows are giving salty milk because grass is contaminated, government scientists are drafting plans to develop a new strain of cow that lives by eating Astroturf.

(June turns off the radio. Marisol enters the office in a change of clothes. June sees her and lets out a yell of joy. She goes to Marisol and embraces her.)

June: Marisol! Thank God! I couldn't sleep all night because of you!

(Marisol, still shaken by the night's strange visions, is dazed, unhappy. She pulls away from June.)

Marisol (*Wary*): What's the matter?

June (*Grabbing her*): You died! You died! It was all over the networks last night! You're on the front page of the *Post*! (*June shows Marisol the paper. On the cover is a closeup of a young woman's battered corpse. June reads:*) "Twenty-six-year-old Marisol Perez of 180th Street in the Bronx was bludgeoned to death on the IRT Number Two last night. The attack occurred at 11:00 P.M." (*Marisol tries to remain calm as she looks at the hideous picture.*) I thought it was you. And I tried to call you last night but do you have any idea how many Marisol Perezes there are in the Bronx phone book? Only seven pages. I couldn't sleep.

Marisol (*Barely calm*): How did he kill her?

June: Fucking barbarian beat her with a *golf club*, can you believe that? Like a caveman kills its *dinner*, fucking freak. I'm still upset.

Marisol (*Numb, she gives the paper back to June.*): It wasn't me, June.

June: It could have been you, living alone in that marginal neighborhood, all the chances you take. Like doesn't this scare you? Isn't it past time to leave the Bronx behind?

Marisol (*Marisol looks at June fully for the first time, trying to focus her thoughts.*): But it wasn't me. I didn't die last night.

(*Marisol sits at her desk. June looks at the paper.*)

June (*Not listening*): Goddamn vultures are having a field day with this, vast closeups of Marisol Perez's pummeled face on TV, I mean what's the *point*? There's a prevailing sickness out there, I'm telling you, the Dark Ages are here, Visigoths are climbing the city walls, and I've never felt more like raw food in my life. Am I upsetting you with this?

Marisol (*Rubs her throbbing head*): Yeah.

June: Good. Put the fear of God in you. Don't let them catch you not ready, okay? You gotta be prepared to really *fight* now!

Marisol (*Looks at her, surprised*): Why do you say that? Did somebody tell you to say that?

June (*Gives Marisol a long look*): Something wrong with you today? You look like shit. You, Miss Puerto Rican Yuppy Princess of the Universe, you never look like shit.

Marisol (*Tries to smile, to shake off her fear*): It's nothing. Let's get to work. If I don't get this manuscript off my desk . . . (*Marisol opens up a manuscript and tries to read it. June closes the manuscript.*)

June: Something happen to you last night?

Marisol: No—it's—nothing—it's—*my body*—it feels like . . . like it fits into my clothes all wrong today. Every person on the subway this morning gave me the shivers. They all looked so hungry. I keep hearing children crying. I keep smelling burnt flesh. And now there's a woman with my exact name killed on my exact street last night. (*Beat*) And I had this dream. A winged woman. A black angel with beautiful wings. She came to my bed and said she loved me.

June (*Very interested*): Oh?

Marisol: She seemed so real. So absolute. Virtuous and powerful, incapable of lying, exalted, sublime, radiant, pure, perfect, fulgent.

June: Fulgent? (*June takes Marisol by the shoulders and looks in her eyes.*) Whoa! Marisol! Yo! That didn't happen. You dreamed it. It's Roman Catholic bullshit.

Marisol: . . . now I feel sorry. I just feel so sorry for everything . . . (*Marisol goes downstage and looks up at the sky, expecting to see something but not knowing what. She's fighting tears. June looks at her: Marisol's definitely not herself today. June goes to her, embraces her. Marisol holds June for dear life. June tries to cheer Marisol up.*)

June: Lookit, I think your dream is like the moon's disappearance. It's all a lot of premillennium jitters. I've never seen so much nervousness. It's still up there but paranoia has clouded our view. That shit can happen you know.

Marisol (*Pulls away from June*): I don't think the moon's disappearance is psychological. It's like the universe is senile, June. Like we're at the part of history where everything breaks down. Do you smell smoke?

June (*The lights begin to subtly go down. June notices the darkness right away. She looks at her watch.*): Wait! It's nine-thirty! They're expecting the smoke from that massive fire in Ohio to reach New York by nine-thirty. (*June and Marisol look out the window. The lights go darker and darker.*) Jesus! Those are a million trees burning! (*June and Marisol calmly watch the spectacle.*) Christ, you can smell the polyester . . . the burnt malls . . . the defaulted loans . . . the unemployment . . . the flat vowels . . . (*Lights begin to go up. Marisol and June* *stand at the window and watch the black smoke begin to drift toward Europe. Silence. They look at each other. The whole thing suddenly strikes them as absurd—they laugh.*) Fuck it, I'm going on break. You want something from downstairs? Coffee? I'm going for coffee.

Marisol: Coffee's extinct, June.

June (*She hates tea.*): *Tea*—I meant *tea.* I'll get us both a cup of tea, try to carry on like normal. I swear, one more natural cataclysm like that and I'm going home. Are you okay?

(*Marisol nods yes. June leaves the office. Marisol quickly starts reading from her manuscript.*)

Marisol (*With growing surprise*): ". . . Salt is in the food and mythology of cultures old and new. Ancient writers believed that angels in heaven turned into salt when they died. Popular mythology holds that during the Fall of Satan, angels who were killed in battle fell into the primordial ocean, which was then fresh water. Today, the oceans are salted by the decomposed bodies of fallen angels . . ."

(*The Man with Ice Cream enters the office. He wears a business suit and licks an ice cream cone. He smiles at Marisol, who looks at him, instantly sensing trouble.*)

Man with Ice Cream: I was in the movie *Taxi Driver* with Robert De Niro and the son-of-a-gun never paid me.

Marisol: Uhm. Are you looking for someone?

Man with Ice Cream: The Second A.D. said this is where I go to collect my pay for my work in *Taxi Driver.*

Marisol: This isn't a film company, sir. We publish science books. I think there's a film company on the tenth floor.

Man with Ice Cream: No, this is the place. I'm sure this is the place.

Marisol: Well . . . you know, sir . . . maybe if I called security for you . . .

Man with Ice Cream: I worked real hard on that picture. It was my big break. And of course, working with a genius like De Niro is like Actor Heaven, but, c'mon, I still need the money!

Marisol: I'm a busy woman, sir, I have a department to run—

Man with Ice Cream: I mean, I don't want to get temperamental, but *Taxi Driver* came out a long time ago and I still haven't been paid!

Marisol: Yeah, I'll call security for you—

Man with Ice Cream (*In despair*): Christ, I have bills! I have rent! I have a toddler in a Catholic preschool! I have an agent screaming for his ten percent! *And how the fuck am I supposed to pay for this ice cream cone? Do you think ice cream is free? Do you think Carvel gives this shit out for nothing?*

Marisol (*Calling out*): June?! Is somebody on this floor?!

Man with Ice Cream: Don't fuck with me, lady. I once played a Nazi skinhead in a TV movie-of-the-week. I once set a man on fire in Van Cortlandt Park for CBS! *And I really liked that role!* (*The Man throws the ice cream into Marisol's face. June runs in.*)

June: LEAVE HER ALONE YOU SCUMBAG! (*June hits the Man with Ice Cream as hard as she can. She pummels him. He howls like a dog and runs out of the office. June runs after him.*)

(*Offstage*) SOMEBODY HELP ME GET HIM

(*As Marisol wipes the ice cream from her face, we hear footsteps going into the distance. Then footsteps returning. June runs back in, panting.*)

He's gone. (*June picks up the phone.*) Security? YOU FUCKING BOZOS! WHY DON'T YOU DO YOUR JOB AND STOP LETTING MANIACS INTO THE BUILDING?! (*June slams down the phone. She goes to Marisol, who is still wiping ice cream from her clothes. She's trembling.*)

Marisol: Vanilla almond. I'll never be able to eat vanilla almond again.

June: Okay, that's IT, you and I are taking the rest of the day off, going to my house where it's safe, fuck everybody, I've had it with this deathtrap . . .

(*June starts to hustle Marisol out of the office.*

Marisol looks up—she's frozen by a vision.

Lights up, far above Marisol. The Angel is there, cleaning an Uzi, humming quietly. Marisol isn't sure she's really seeing what she's seeing.

June looks up, sees nothing, and pulls Marisol offstage. Lights down on the Angel, who disappears in the dark.)

SCENE 6

(*Lights up on June's apartment: a marbleized formica table and matching red chairs.*

It's later that day. June and Marisol enter. June automatically stomps cockroaches as she enters.)

June: . . . so we agitated for them to install metal detectors in all the buildings on this block. That'll definitely cut down on the random homicides.

Marisol: That's civilized.

June (*Brightly*): That's Brooklyn.

Marisol: What's that huge, ugly, windowless building with the smokestacks and armed guards across the street?

June: Me? I think it's where they bring overthrown brutal right-wing dictators from Latin America to live, 'cause a friend's a friend, right?

Marisol: I really appreciate this, June.

June: Good, 'cause now I have to issue you a warning about my fucked-up brother who lives with me.

Marisol: You do?

June: Uhm. Lenny's a little weird about women. His imagination? It takes off on him on the slightest provocation and, uh, he doesn't know, you know, a reasonable way to channel his turbulent sexual death fantasies . . .

Marisol: This is a long warning, June.

June: He knows about you. Shit, I've told him for two years. And so he's developed this *thing* for you, like he draws *pictures* of you, in crayon, covering every inch of his bedroom. He's thirty-four, you know, but he has the mental capacity of a child.

(*Lenny enters. Lenny has uncontrollable hair that makes him look a little crazy. He can stand very, very still for a very long time. He goes immediately to the window without looking at June or Marisol.*)

Lenny (*Indicating window*): Wrong. It's a federally funded torture center where they violate people who have gone over their credit card limit.

June (*Wary*): Marisol, this is Lenny, the heat-seeking device. Lenny, this is Marisol Perez, and you're *wrong*.

Lenny (*At window*): I've seen them bring the vans, June, so shut up. People tied up. Guards with truncheons. Big fat New York City police with dogs. It happens late at night. But you can hear the screams. They cremate the bodies. That's why Brooklyn smells so funny.

Marisol (*Nervous*): I owe a lot of money to the MasterCard people.

(*Lenny suddenly turns to Marisol. He is utterly focused on her.*)

June (*To Marisol*): What he says is not proven.

Lenny: *Everybody* knows, June. It's a political *issue*. If you weren't so right-wing—

June: I am not right-wing, you punk, don't EVER call me that! I happen to be the last true practicing communist in New York!

Lenny (*Keeps staring at Marisol*): You were on the news. You died on the news. But that was a different one.

Marisol: She and I have the same name. Had.

Lenny (*Approaching Marisol*): I'm so glad you didn't die before I got a chance to meet you. (*Lenny suddenly takes Marisol's hand and kisses it. June tries to step in between them.*)

June: That's enough, Lenny—I didn't bring her here to feed on . . .

Lenny (*Holding Marisol's hand*): I went to your neighborhood this morning. To see the kind of street that would kill a Marisol Perez. I walked through Van Cortlandt Park. I played in the winter sunlight, watched perverts fondling snowmen, and at high noon, the dizziest time of the day, I saw a poor homeless guy being set on fire by Nazi skinheads—

June: That's *it*, Lenny. (*June pulls Lenny aside. He knows he's in for a lecture.*)

Lenny: What?

June: We had a hard day. We came here to relax. So take a deep breath—

Lenny: She talked to me first—

June: Listen to me before you say anything more. Are you listening—?

Lenny: *Yes. Okay.*

June: Let's cool our hormones, okay? Before the psychodrama starts in earnest—?

Lenny: Yes. All right.

June: Are we really—?

Lenny (*Pulls away from June. Talks to Marisol.*): Hey, honey, you wanna see my sculpture?

(*Lenny runs to his offstage bedroom before Marisol can reply. June grabs her coat angrily.*)

June: You wanna get outta here? He's raving.

Lenny (*Offstage*): I'm an accomplished sculptor, Marisol. Before that I was a Life and Growth Empowerment Practitioner. Before that I worked for the Brooklyn Spiritual Emergence Network.

(*Lenny quickly reenters with his sculpture, a ball of nails welded together in a formless shape. It's an ugly little work of art and everyone knows it.*)

This one's called "Marisol Perez." The nails symbolize all the things I know about you. Spaces between the nails are all the things I don't know about you. As you see, you're a great mystery . . . (*Marisol looks at the sculpture, trying hard to see some beauty in it.*) No one else is working like this. It's totally new. But it's only a small step in my career. I'm going to need a lot more *money* if I'm going to evolve past this point. (*Lenny looks hard at June. June buttons up her coat, hoping to avoid a confrontation.*)

June (*Tight*): I don't think Marisol wants to hear us talk about money.

Lenny: Well, I'm not gonna get a job, June, so you can fuck that noise.

June (*To Marisol*): Who said "job"? When did I say "job"?

Lenny (*To Marisol*): I promised myself to never work for anyone again. She heard me say that—

June: Gee, Lenny, fuck you, we're going—

(*June starts to go. Lenny blocks her path to the door.*)

Lenny (*To June*): Why do you hate my sculpture? Why do you hate everything I do?!

June (*Trying to control herself*): Man, man . . . Lenny . . . you don't want to learn *anything* from me, do you? You want to be a pathetic invertebrate your whole life long. Fine. Just don't waste my precious time!

Lenny: Who gives a fuck about your time. I HAVE PROJECTS!

June: Yeah? What ever happened to the CIA, Lenny? Didn't they want you for something *really special* in Nicaragua? What about the electric guitars you were gonna design for the Stones? What about *Smegma: The Literary Magazine of Brooklyn*? Huh?

(*Lenny runs back into his offstage room.*)

I swear, the cadavers of your dead projects are all over this goddamn apartment like Greenwood Cemetery. I can't eat a bowl of cereal in the morning without the ghosts of your old ideas begging me for a glass of milk!

(*Lenny reenters with stacks of homemade magazines and several unusual homemade guitars. He throws this trash at June's feet.*)

Lenny: *You wish Mom had drowned me!* I know that's what you wish! Well, you don't have to feel sorry for me anymore!

June: Sure I do. You're pathetic. The only thing separating you from a concrete bed on Avenue D is *me*.

Lenny (*To Marisol*): She thinks I'm a loser, Marisol! Can you believe that? Sometimes I want to kill her!

June: Oh get out of my face, Lenny. You're never gonna kill me. You're never gonna get it together to kill *anybody*—

(*Lenny exits into his offstage room again. June turns to Marisol angrily.*)

Can I list for you just a few of the things I don't have because I have him? Lasting friendships. A retirement account. A house. A career. A night life. Winter clothing. Interest on checking. Regular real sex.

(*Lenny returns with a long kitchen knife and tries to cut June's throat. June and Marisol scream.*)

Lenny: *I was supposed to be somebody!* That's what I learned right after I died!

June: YOU NEVER DIED—!

(*June scrambles from Lenny and goes for the door. There's chaos as Marisol starts throwing things at Lenny and Lenny continues to chase June. Lenny pulls June from the door and throws her back into the room.*)

Lenny: The doctors all said I died! There's medical evidence! It's on the charts! My heart stopped for seven minutes and my soul was outta Lenox Hill at the speed of light! (*Lenny is almost out of control as he stalks June, slashing the air.*)

June: Your whole *life*, everything I do is to *bolster* you, build you up—

Lenny: After my death . . . my soul was cruising up and up . . . and it was intercepted by angels and sucked back into my body, *and I lived*!

Marisol: Give me that knife!

Lenny: . . . I was resurrected, I returned to the living to warn the world that big changes are coming . . . and we have to be ready . . . (*Fighting tears*) . . . I've been warning people for years, but no one listens to me . . . (*Lenny starts to cry. Marisol and June jump him, grabbing the knife away. Lenny throws himself on the ground like a toddler in a rage and cries. June and Marisol look at him.*)

June (*Takes a moment to catch her breath and gather her thoughts*): I can't do this shit no more. I can't mother you. Carry you around protected in my Epic Uterus anymore. This is final. Biology says you're a grown man. I don't love the law of the jungle, Lenny, but you're adult, you're leaving the nest and living in the real world from now on, eat or be eaten, I'm sorry, that's the way my emotions are built right now 'cause you *architectured* it that way! (*Beat*) I'm calling our mother, tell her not to take you in either. This is not a transition, Leonard. This is a break. A severing. So get up. Collect your mutant trash. Give me your fucking keys. Leave right now. And don't look back at me or I'll turn you to salt right where you stand with my eyes, so help me God.

(*Lenny stands, gathers his trash, and exits to his room. Marisol goes to comfort June but she's interrupted by Lenny, who has reentered wearing a coat and carrying a bag of golf clubs. June gives Lenny all the money she has on her. Marisol is unable to look at Lenny. He turns angrily to June.*)

Lenny: I almost had Marisol married to me, June. We practically had babies! Now I'm alone. Whatever happens to me out there, it's totally specifically on you.

(*Lenny leaves the apartment. June sits at the table. Marisol looks at June.*)

Marisol: So where do you want to have dinner? (*No answer. Marisol sits with June, takes her hand. Tears on June's face.*)

June: You think I'm a shit for throwing him out?

Marisol: Maybe people will throw him some change. Maybe this will force him to get a job.

June: Is he gonna dissolve in the fucking street air? (*June runs to the door. She calls out.*) Lenny! I'm SORRY! Come back, I'm sorry!! (*No answer. June sits.*) Shit. (*June looks at Marisol, wiping her tears, getting an idea.*) You wanna live with me? 'Cause if you wanna live with me, in Lenny's empty bedroom, I'll rent it to you, it's available right away.

Marisol (*Smiles, surprised*): Wait—where did that come from?

June: Hey, c'mon girlfriend, they're killing Marisol Perezes left and right today, we gotta stick together!

Marisol (*Wanting to*): Wow. I don't know what to say . . .

June: You think the Bronx needs you? It doesn't. It needs blood. It needs to feed. You *wanna* be the blood supply for its filthy habits?

Marisol: But the Bronx is where I'm from.

June: So friggin' what? Come here. We'll survive the millennium as a team. I'll shop. You can clean the chemicals off the food. I know where to buy gas masks. You know the vocabulary on the street. We'll walk each other through land mines and sharpen each other's wits.

Marisol (*Smiles and looks at June*): You're not saying that just because you're scared to be alone, right? You really want me here, right?

June: Of course I do, hey.

Marisol: Then let's do it, girlfriend.

June (*Delighted, June embraces Marisol.*): Oh great!

(*June and Marisol hold each other. June is about ready to cry. Marisol gently rocks her a little bit, then looks at June.*)

Marisol: I'm gonna go home and pack right now. We have to be fast. This town knows when you're alone. That's when it sends out the ghouls and the death squads.

June (*Nods understandingly, kisses Marisol, and gives her Lenny's keys*): What a day I'm having, huh?

(*Marisol takes the keys, leaves, goes back to her own apartment and immediately starts packing.*)

SCENE 7

(*Later that night. Marisol is in the Bronx packing. Her singing is heard underneath the others' dialogue.*)

Marisol (*Softly*):
Madre que linda noche
cuantas estrellas
abreme la ventana
que quiero verlas . . .

(*June sits at the table in her apartment, facing downstage. She talks to herself.*)

June: Maybe someone'll throw Lenny some change, right?

(*Lenny appears upstage, on the street, warming his hands at a burning trash can. His clothes are filthy and his eyes are glazed. The golf club is at his side. He looks at Marisol.*)

Lenny: I've been on the street, Marisol. I know what it's like.

June: Yeah, maybe people will throw him some change.

Marisol (*Smiling, remembering*): "The flat vowels . . ."

Lenny: It's incredible there. Logic was executed by firing squad. People tell passionate horror stories and other people stuff their faces and go on. The street breeds new species. And new silence. No spoken language works there. There are no verbs to describe the cold air as it sucks on your hands. And if there were words to describe it, Marisol, you wouldn't believe it anyway because, in fact, it's literally unbelievable, it's another reality, and it's actually happening *right now*. And *that* fact—the fact that it's happening right *now*—compounds the unbelievable nature of the street, Marisol, adds to its lunacy, its permanent deniability. (*Beat*) But I know it's real. I've been bitten by it. I have its rabies.

June: I know someone will throw him some change.

(*Lenny raises the golf club over June's head. June is frozen. Blackout everywhere but Marisol's apartment. June and Lenny exit in the dark.*)

SCENE 8

(There's loud knocking at Marisol's door. Marisol stops packing and looks at the door. The knocking continues—loud, violent, louder.)

Marisol: Who is it?

(Before Marisol can move, her door is kicked open. Lenny comes in wielding a bloody golf club and holding an armful of exotic wildflowers.)

Lenny: So how can you live in this neighborhood? Huh? You got a death wish, you stupid woman?

Marisol: What are you doing here? *(Marisol goes to her bed and scrambles for the knife underneath her pillow.)*

Lenny: Don't you love yourself? Is that why you stay in this ghetto? Jesus, I almost got killed getting here!

Marisol *(Points the knife at Lenny)*: Get out or I'll rip out both your fucking eyes, Lenny!

Lenny: God, I missed you. *(Lenny closes the door and locks all the locks.)*

Marisol: This is not going to happen to me in my own house! I still have God's protection!

Lenny *(Holds out the flowers)*: Here. I hadda break into the Bronx Botanical Garden for them, but they match your eyes . . . *(Lenny hands Marisol the flowers.)*

Marisol: Okay—thank you—okay—why don't we—turn around—and go—down to Brooklyn—okay?—let's go talk to June—

Lenny: We can't. Impossible. June *isn't*. Is *not*. I don't know who she is anymore! She's out walking the streets of Brooklyn! Babbling like an idiot! Looking for her lost mind!

Marisol: What do you mean? Where is she?

Lenny: She had an accident. Her head had an accident. With the golf club. It was weird.

Marisol *(Looking at the bloody club)*: What did you do to her?

Lenny: She disappeared! I don't know!

Marisol *(Panicking)*: Please tell me June's okay, Lenny. Tell me she's not in some bodybag somewhere—

Lenny: Oh man, you saw what it's like! June *controlled* me. She had me *neutered*. I squatted and stooped and served like a goddamn house eunuch!

Marisol: Did you hurt her?

Lenny (*Starts to cry. He sobs like a baby, his body wracked with grief and self-pity.*): There are whole histories of me you can't guess. Did you know I was a medical experiment? To fix my asthma when I was five, my mother volunteered me for a free experimental drug on an army base in Nevada. *I was a shrieking experiment in army medicine for six years!* Isn't that funny? (*He laughs, trying to fight his tears.*) And that drug's made me so friggin' loopy, I can't hold down a job, make friends, get a degree, *nothing*. And June? June's had *everything*. She loved you. That's why she never brought you home to meet me *even after I begged her for two years.* (*Marisol is silent—and that silence nearly makes him explode.*) DON'T BE THIS WAY! We don't have to be enemies. We can talk to each other the right way—

Marisol: We have no right way, Lenny.

Lenny (*Jumps up and down, very happy*): We do! We do! 'Cause we have *God*, Marisol. We have God in common. Maybe it's God's will I'm with you now. On this frontier. Out in this lawless city, I'm what he designed for you.

Marisol: I don't know what you're talking about . . .

Lenny: It's why God brought me here tonight—to offer you a way to survive. I know you don't love me. But you can't turn your back on God's gift.

Marisol (*Exhausted*): Jesus Christ, just tell me what you want . . .

Lenny (*Moves closer*): I want to offer you a deal. (*Beat*) You controlled your life until now. But your life's in shambles! Ruins! So I'm gonna let you give me control over your life. That means I'll do everything for you. I'll take responsibility. I'll get a job and make money. I'll name our children. Okay? And what you get in return is my protection. (*Beat. Lenny gives Marisol the golf club.*) I can protect you like June did. I can keep out the criminals and carry the knife for you. I can be your guardian angel, Marisol.

Marisol: You're asking—

Lenny: A small price. Your faith. Your pretty Puerto Rican smile. No. I don't even want to sleep with you anymore. I don't want your affection. Or your *considerable* sexual mystery. I just want you to look up to me. Make me big. Make me central. Praise me, feed me, and believe everything I tell you. (*Lenny steps closer to Marisol.*) You once tried to give these things to June. And June would have said yes because she loved you. Well, I'm June. June and I are here, together, under this hungry skin. You can love us both, Marisol.

(*Marisol looks at Lenny a long moment, studying him, thinking of a way out. She makes a decision. She tosses her knife on the bed and drops the golf club. She takes a step toward Lenny. They stare at each other. Marisol lets herself be embraced. Lenny, amazed, revels in the feel of her body against his.*)

Marisol: Okay. I'll believe what you say. I'll live inside you.

(*Lenny is oblivious to everything but Marisol's warm hands. She kisses him. It's the most electrifying feeling Lenny's ever known. He closes his eyes.*)

But . . . before we set up house, live happily ever after, we're going to go outside, you and me, and we're going to find out what happened to your sister . . .

Lenny (*Oblivious*): She's lost. She can't be found.

Marisol (*Kissing him*): . . . that's my condition . . .

(*Lenny starts to push Marisol to the bed. She starts to resist.*)

Lenny: It's too dangerous for a girl out there.

Marisol: . . . but if you don't help me find her, Lenny, . . . there's no deal . . .

(*He pushes her. She resists. Lenny looks at her, hurt, a little confused.*)

Lenny: But I don't want to share you.

(*Beat*)

Marisol: Too bad. That's the deal.

(*Beat*)

Lenny (*Hurt, realizing*): You don't love me. You're just fucking with me. That's not okay! WELL, I'M GLAD I HIT HER! (*Lenny grabs Marisol. Marisol tries to escape. They struggle. He holds her tightly, trying to kiss her. He throws her to the floor. He rips at her clothes, trying to tear them off. Marisol struggles with all her strength—until she finally* *pulls free and goes for the golf club. He tries to grab it from her and she swings at him.*) You're lying to me! Why are you always lying to me?!

Marisol: Because you're the enemy, Lenny. I will always be your enemy, because you will always find a way to be out there, hiding in stairwells, behind doors, under the blankets in my bed, in the cracks of every bad dream I've had since I've known there were savage differences between girls and boys! And I know you'll always be hunting for me. And I'll never be able to relax, or stop to look at the sky, or smile at something beautiful on the street—

Lenny: But I'm just a guy trying to be happy too—

Marisol: I want you to tell me, RIGHT NOW, where June is—*right now!* (*Marisol swings at Lenny. He panics and falls to his knees in front of her. Marisol pounds the floor with the golf club.*)

Lenny: She's on the street.

Marisol: Where?

Lenny: Brooklyn.

Marisol: Where?

Lenny: I don't know!

Marisol: What happened?

Lenny: I hit her on the head. She doesn't know who she is. She went out there to look for you. (*Marisol stands over him, poised to strike him. He's shaking with fear.*) Look at me. I'm a mess on the floor. Just asking you to look at me. To give me compassion and let me live like a human being for once. Marisol, we could have a baby . . . and love it so much . . .

(*Marisol only shakes her head in disgust and turns to the door. Lenny springs to his feet and lunges at her. She turns and swings the club and hits Lenny.*

He falls to the ground.

Marisol looks at Lenny's fallen body. Has she killed him? She panics and runs out of the apartment with the golf club.

Blackout everywhere except on the street area.)

SCENE 9

(*Marisol runs to the street area.*

It starts to snow. There's blood on Marisol's clothes. She's extremely cold. She shivers. She kneels on the ground, alone, not knowing what to do or where to go.

Lights up over Marisol's head, against the brick wall. The Angel appears. The Angel wears regulation military fatigues, complete with face camouflage and medals. She looks like a soldier about to go into battle. The Uzi is strapped to her back.

Marisol sees her and gasps.

There's blood coming down the Angel's back: the Angel has taken off her silver wings—her wings of peace. She holds the bloody wings out to the audience, like an offering. Then she drops the wings. They float down to the street.

Marisol picks them up.)

Marisol: War?

(*The wings dissolve in Marisol's hands. Blackout everywhere.*)

ACT 2

(*Darkness. All the interiors are gone. The entire set now consists of the brick wall and a huge surreal street that covers the entire stage.*

The Angel is gone. The gold is crown still there.

Street lighting comes up, but there's something very different about this light. On this street, reality has been altered—and this new reality is reflected in the lighting.

We see a metal trash bin, overflowing with trash and a fire hydrant covered in rosaries. There are several large mounds of rags onstage; underneath each mound is a sleeping Homeless Person.

Marisol is onstage exactly where she was at the end of act 1. She's holding out her hands as if holding the Angel's wings. But they're gone now; she holds air.

She looks around and notices that the street she's now on is nothing like the street she remembers. She registers this weird difference and picks up the golf club, ready to defend herself.

She looks up to see the Angel, but she's gone.

She thinks she hears a sound behind her and swings the club. There's nothing there. She tries to orient herself, but she can't tell north from south.

And even though it's the dead of winter, it's also much warmer than it was before. Startled, Marisol fans herself.

Bright sparkling lights streak across the sky like tracers or comets. The lights are followed by distant rumblings. Is that a thunderclap? Or an explosion? Marisol hits the ground. Then the lights stop. Silence.

The Woman with Furs enters. The Woman is prosperous—long fur coat and high heels—but there are subtle bruises and cuts on her face, and it looks like there's dried blood on her coat. She stands to the side, very, very still. She holds an open newspaper, but she stares past it, no emotion on her shell-shocked face.

Marisol looks at the Woman, hesitates, and then goes to her.)

Marisol: Excuse me. Miss? *(No answer from the Woman with Furs, who doesn't look at her.) Where the hell are we? (The Woman ignores her. Marisol gets closer.)* I'm . . . supposed to be on 180th Street. In the Bronx. There's supposed to be a bodega right *here.* A public school *there.* They sold crack on that corner. It was cold this morning!

Woman with Furs *(Speaks out to the air, as if in a trance)*: God help you, you get in my face.

Marisol *(Begins to examine the altered space with growing fear)*: No buildings. No streets. No cars. No noise. No cops. There are no subway tokens in my pocket!

Woman with Furs: I have no money.

Marisol *(Realizing)*: It's what she said would happen, isn't it? She said she'd drop her wings of peace . . . and I wouldn't recognize the world . . .

Woman with Furs: Don't you know where you are either?

Marisol *(Trying to think it through)*: I have to . . . I have to . . . reclaim what I know. I need June. Where's June? Brooklyn. South. I gotta go south, find my friend, and restore her broken mind.

(*Marisol tries to run away, hoping to find the subway to Brooklyn, but it's impossible to find anything familiar in this radically altered landscape.*)

Woman with Furs: I had tickets to *Les Misérables*. But I took a wrong turn. Followed bad advice. Ended up on this weird street.

(*Marisol sees something in the distance that makes her freeze in her tracks.*)

Marisol (*To herself*): The Empire State Building? *What's it doing over there?* It's supposed to be south. But that's ... north ... I'm sure it is ... isn't it? (*In her panic, Marisol runs to the Woman with Furs and tries to grab her arm.*) You have to help me!

(*The Woman with Furs instantly recoils from Marisol's touch. She starts to wander away.*)

Woman with Furs: I have to go. But I can't find a cab. I can't seem to find any transportation.

Marisol: You're not listening! There's no transportation; forget that, the city's *gone.* You have to help me. We have to go south together and protect each other.

(*Marisol roughly grabs the arm of the Woman with Furs, trying to pull her offstage. The Woman seems to snap out of her trance and pull back. The Woman is suddenly shaking, tearful, like a caged animal.*)

Woman with Furs: Oh God, I thought you were a nice person—!

Marisol (*Grabbing the Woman with Furs*): I am a nice person, but I've had some bad luck—

Woman with Furs (*Struggling*): Oh God, you're hurting me—

Marisol (*Letting go*): No, no, no, I'm okay. I don't belong out here. I have a job in publishing. I'm middle-class—

Woman with Furs (*Freaking out, pointing at the golf club*): Oh please don't kill me like that barbarian killed Marisol Perez!

(*Marisol lets the Woman with Furs go. The Woman is almost crying.*)

Marisol: I'm not what you think.

Woman with Furs: ... Oh God, why did I have to buy that fucking hat?! God ... God ... why?

Marisol: Please. June's not used to the street, she's an indoor animal, like a cat ...

Woman with Furs: I bought a fucking hat on credit and everything disintegrated!

Marisol: South. Protection.

Woman with Furs (*Takes off her fur coat. Underneath, she wears ripped pajamas. We can clearly see the bruises and cuts on her arms.*): There is no protection. I just got out of hell. Last month, I was two hundred dollars over my credit card limit because I bought a hat on sale. And you know they're cracking down on that kind of thing. I used to do it all the time. It didn't matter. But now it matters. Midnight. The police came. Grabbed me out of bed, waving my credit statement in my face, my children screaming. They punched my husband in the stomach. I told them I was a lawyer! With a house in Cos Cob! And personal references a mile long! But they hauled me to this . . . huge, window-less brick building in Brooklyn . . . where they tortured me . . . they . . . (*She cries. Marisol goes to her and covers her up with the fur coat. Marisol holds her.*)

Marisol: That can't happen.

Woman with Furs: A lot of things can't happen that are happening. Everyone I know's had terrible luck this year. Losing condos. Careers cut in half. Ending up on the street. I thought I'd be immune. I thought I'd be safe.

Marisol: This is going to sound crazy, but I think I know why this is happening.

Woman with Furs (*Looks at Marisol, suddenly very afraid*): No. No.

(*The Woman with Furs tries to get away from Marisol. Marisol stops her.*)

Marisol: It's angels, isn't it? It's the war.

Woman with Furs (*Panicking*): God is great! God is good! It didn't happen! It didn't happen! I dreamed it! I lied!

Marisol: It did! It happened to me!

Woman with Furs: I'm not going to talk about this! You're going to think I'm crazy too! You're going to tell the Citibank MasterCard people where I am so they can pick me up and torture me some more!

Marisol: I wouldn't!

Woman with Furs (*Grabs the golf club out of Marisol's hand*): I know what I'm going to do now. I'm going to turn you in. I'm going to tell the Citibank police you stole my plastic! They'll like me for that. They'll like me a lot. They'll restore my banking privileges! (*Starts swinging wildly at Marisol. Marisol dodges her.*)

Marisol: I am not an animal! I am not a barbarian! I don't fight at this level!

Woman with Furs (*Swinging*): Welcome to the new world order, babe!

(*The Man with Scar Tissue enters in a wheelchair. He's a homeless man in shredded, burnt rags. He wears a hood that covers his head and obscures his face. He wears sunglasses and gloves. His wheelchair is full of plastic garbage bags, clothes, books, newspapers, bottles, junk.*)

Man with Scar Tissue: It's getting so bad, a guy can't sleep under the stars anymore.

(*The Woman with Furs sees the Man with Scar Tissue and stops swinging.*)

Woman with Furs (*Indicating Marisol*): This brown piece of shit is mine! *I'm* going to turn her in! Not you!

Man with Scar Tissue: I was sleeping under the constellations one night and my whole life changed, took *seconds:* I had a life—then bingo, I *didn't* have a life . . . (*Moves toward the Woman with Furs*) Maybe you got it, huh? You got the thing I need . . .

Woman with Furs: Homelessness is against the law in this city. I'm going to have you two arrested! They'll like that. I'll get big points for that! I'll be revitalized!

(*The Woman with Furs runs off with the golf club. The Man with Scar Tissue looks at Marisol. He waves hello. She looks at him—wary but grateful—and tries to smile. She's instantly aware of his horrendous smell.*)

Marisol: She, she was trying to kill me . . . thank you . . .

Man with Scar Tissue: Used to be able to sleep under the moon *unmolested.* Moon was a shield. Catching all the bad karma before it fell to earth. All those crater holes in the moon? Those ain't rocks! That's bad karma crashing to the moon's surface!

Marisol (*Really shaken*): She thinks I belong out here, but I don't. I'm well educated . . . anyone can see that . . .

Man with Scar Tissue: Now the moon's gone. The shield's been lifted.

Shit falls on you randomly. Sleep outside, you're fucked. That's why I got this! Gonna *yank* the moon back! (*From inside his wheelchair, he pulls out a magnet. He aims his magnet to the sky and waits for the moon to appear.*)

Marisol: She's crazy, that's all! I have to go before she comes back. (*Marisol starts going back and forth, looking for south.*)

Man with Scar Tissue: Good thing I'm not planning to get married. What would a honeymoon be like now? Some stupid cardboard cutout dangling out your hotel window? What kind of inspiration is that? How's a guy supposed to get it up for *that*? (*Fondles himself, hoping to manufacture a hard-on, but nothing happens and he gives up*)

Marisol (*Noticing what he's doing*): I have to get to Brooklyn. I'm looking for my friend. She has red hair.

Man with Scar Tissue: And did you know the moon carries the souls of dead people up to Heaven? Uh-huh. The new moon is dark and empty and gets filled with new glowing souls—until it's a bright full moon— then it carries its silent burden to God . . .

Marisol: Do you know which way is south?!

(*Marisol continues to walk around and around the stage, looking hopelessly for any landmark that will tell her which way is south. The Man with Scar Tissue watches her, holding up his magnet.*)

Man with Scar Tissue: Give it up, princess. Time is crippled. Geography's deformed. You're permanently lost out here!

Marisol: Bullshit. Even if God is senile, He still cares. He doesn't play dice, you know. I read that.

Man with Scar Tissue: Shit, what century do *you* live in?

(*Marisol keeps running around the stage.*)

Marisol: June and I had plans. Gonna live together. Survive together. I gotta get her fixed! I gotta get Lenny buried!

(*The Man with Scar Tissue laughs and suddenly drops his magnet, then he jumps out of his wheelchair. He runs to Marisol, stopping her in her tracks. He looks fully at the shocked Marisol for the first time. He smiles, very pleased.*)

Man with Scar Tissue: You look pretty nice. You're kinda cute, in fact. What do you think this all means, us two, a man and woman, bumping into each other like this?

Marisol (*Wary*): I don't know. But thank you for helping me. Maybe my luck hasn't run out.

Man with Scar Tissue (*Laughs*): Oh, don't trust luck! Fastest way to die around here. Trust gun powder. Trust plutonium. Don't trust Divine intervention or you're fucked. My name is Elvis Presley, beautiful, what's yours?

Marisol (*Wary*): Marisol Perez.

Man with Scar Tissue (*Nearly jumps out of his rags*): *What?!!* No! Your name can't be that! Can't be Marisol Perez!

Marisol: It is. It has to be.

Man with Scar Tissue: You're confused! Or are the goddamn graves coughing up the dead?!

Marisol: I'm not dead! That was her! I'm . . . me!

Man with Scar Tissue: You can't prove it!

Marisol: I was born in the Bronx. But, but, I can't remember the street!

Man with Scar Tissue: A-ha! Dead!

Marisol (*A recitation, an effort*): Born 1966—lived on East Tremont—then Taylor Avenue—Grand Concourse—Mami died—Fordham—English major—Phi Beta Kappa—I went into science publishing—I'm a head copywriter—I make good money—I work with words—I'm clean . . . (*As she holds her head and closes her eyes, the Man with Scar Tissue starts going through his bag, pulling out old magazines and newspapers.*) . . . I lived in the Bronx . . . I commuted light-years to this other planet called . . . Manhattan! I learned new vocabularies . . . wore weird native dress . . . mastered arcane rituals . . . and amputated neat sections of my psyche, my cultural heritage . . . yeah, clean easy amputations . . . with no pain expressed at all—none!—but so much pain kept inside I almost choked on it . . . so far deep inside my Manhattan bosses and Manhattan friends and my broken Bronx consciousness never even suspected . . .

Man with Scar Tissue (*Reads from the* New York Post): "Memorial services for Marisol Perez were held this morning in Saint Patrick's Cathedral. The estimated fifty thousand mourners included the mayor of New York, the Bronx Borough president, the Guardian Angels, and the cast of the popular daytime soap opera 'As the World Turns' . . . "

Marisol: She wasn't me! I'm me! And I'm outta here!

(*Marisol starts to run off but is stopped as, far upstage in the dark, a Nazi Skinhead walks by, holding a can of gasoline, goose-stepping ominously toward a sleeping Homeless Person. Marisol runs back and hides behind the Man with Scar Tissue's wheelchair. The Skinhead doesn't see them.*

The Man sees the Skinhead and suddenly hides behind Marisol, shaking. He starts to whine and cry and moan.

The Homeless Person runs off. The Skinhead exits, chasing the Homeless Person. When the Skinhead is gone, the Man turns angrily to Marisol.)

Man with Scar Tissue: Who are you for real and why do you attract so much trouble?! I hope you don't let those Nazis come near me!

Marisol: I don't mean to—

Man with Scar Tissue (*Grabs Marisol*): What are you!? Are you protection? Are you benign? Or are you some kind of angel of death?

Marisol: I'm a good person.

Man with Scar Tissue: Then why don't you do something about those Nazis?! They're all over the place. I'm getting out of here—

(*The Man with Scar Tissue tries to leave. Marisol stops him.*)

Marisol: Don't leave me!

Man with Scar Tissue: Why? You're not alone, are you? You got your faith still intact. You still believe God is good. You still think you can glide through the world and not be part of it.

Marisol: I'm not a Nazi!

Man with Scar Tissue: I can't trust you. Ever since the angels went into open revolt, you can't trust your own mother . . . oops.

Marisol (*Looks at him*): What did you say? You too? Did angels talk to you too?

Man with Scar Tissue (*Worried*): No. Never mind. I don't know a thing. Just talking out my ass.

Marisol: You didn't dream it—

Man with Scar Tissue (*Scared*): I had enough punishment! I don't wanna get in the middle of some celestial Vietnam! I don't want any more angelic napalm dropped on me!

Marisol: But I saw one too—I did—*what do all these visitations mean?* (*She suddenly grabs the Man with Scar Tissue's hands—and he screams, pulls away, and cowers on the ground like a beaten dog.*)

Man with Scar Tissue: NOT MY HANDS! Don't touch my hands! (*He rips his gloves off. His hands are covered with burn scars. He blows on his boiling hands.*)

Marisol: Oh my God.

Man with Scar Tissue (*Nearly crying*): Heaven erupts but who pays the price? The fucking innocent do . . . !

Marisol: What happened to you?

Man with Scar Tissue (*Crying*): I was an air traffic controller, Marisol Perez. I had a life. Then I saw angels in the radar screen and I started to drink.

(*Marisol gets closer to the whimpering Man with Scar Tissue. She has yet to really see his face. Marisol reaches out to him and pulls the hood back and removes his sunglasses. The Man's face has been horribly burned. She tries not to gasp, but she can't help it.*)

Marisol: Ay Dios, ay Dios mio, ay Dios . . .

Man with Scar Tissue: You're looking for your friend . . . everyone here is looking for something . . . I'm looking for something too . . .

Marisol: What is it? Maybe I can help?

Man with Scar Tissue: I'm looking for my lost skin. Have you seen my lost skin? It was once very pretty. We were very close. I was really attached to it. (*He runs to the trash bin and starts looking through it.*)

Marisol: I haven't seen anything like that.

Man with Scar Tissue: It's got to be somewhere . . . it must be looking for me . . . it must be lonely too, don't you think . . . ?

Marisol: Look, I'm sorry I bothered you, I'm, I'm going to go now . . .

Man with Scar Tissue (*Looks at Marisol*): I was just sleeping under the stars. It was another night when I couldn't find shelter. The places I went to, I got beat up. They took my clothes. Urinated in my mouth. Fucking blankets they gave me were laced with DDT. I said, Fuck It. I took my shit outside and went up to some dickhead park in the Bronx . . .

Marisol (*Remembering*): Van Cortlandt Park?

Man with Scar Tissue: . . . just to be near some shriveled trees and alone and away from the massive noise, just for a little nap . . . my eyes closed . . . I vaguely remember the sound of goose-stepping teenagers from Staten Island with a can of gasoline, shouting orders in German . . .

Marisol (*Walks away from the Man with Scar Tissue*): June's waiting for me . . .

Man with Scar Tissue: A flash of light. I exploded outward. My bubbling skin divorced my suffering nerves and ran away, looking for some coolness, some paradise, some other body to embrace! (*Laughs bitterly*) Now I smell like barbecue! I could have eaten myself! I could have charged money for pieces of my broiled meat!

Marisol: Please stop. I get the picture.

(*The Man with Scar Tissue stops, looks at Marisol sadly. He motions to her that he needs help. She helps him with his gloves, sunglasses, hood.*)

Man with Scar Tissue: The angel was Japanese. Dressed in armor. Dressed in iron. Dressed to endure the fire of war. She had a scimitar.

Marisol (*Can't believe it, but wanting to*): She?

Man with Scar Tissue: Kissed me. I almost exploded. I kept hearing Jimi Hendrix in my middle ear as those lips, like two *brands*, nearly melted me. She was radiant. Raw.

Marisol and **Man with Scar Tissue:** Fulgent.

Man with Scar Tissue: She told me when angels are bored at night, they write your nightmares. She said the highest among the angels carry God's throne on their backs for eternity, singing, "Glory, glory, glory!" But her message was terrible and after she kissed me . . .

Marisol and **Man with Scar Tissue:** . . . I spit at her.

Man with Scar Tissue: Was that the right thing to do, Marisol?

Marisol: I thought it was . . . but I don't know.

(*Marisol looks gently at the Man with Scar Tissue. She kisses him softly. He smiles and pats her on the head like a puppy. He goes to his wheelchair and pulls out an old bottle of Kentucky bourbon. He smiles and offers the bottle to Marisol.*)

Marisol drinks greedily. The Man applauds her. She smiles as the hot liquid burns down her throat. She laughs long and loud: in this barren landscape, it's a beautiful sound.

As they both laugh, the Man motions that they should embrace. Marisol holds her breath and embraces him.)

Man with Scar Tissue (*Hopeful*): So? Feelin' horny? Can I hope?

Marisol (*Quickly lets him go and gives him back his bottle*): Let's not push it, okay Elvis?

Man with Scar Tissue (*Laughs. He goes to his wheelchair and prepares to hit the road again.*): Word on the street is, water no longer seeks its own level, there are fourteen inches to the foot, six days in the week, seven planets in the solar system, and the French are polite. I also hear the sun rises in the north and sets in the south. I think I saw the sun setting over there . . . instinct tells me south is over there . . .

Marisol (*Turns to face south*): Thank you.

(*The Skinhead crosses the stage again with the can of gasoline, chasing the frightened Homeless Person. Marisol and the Man with Scar Tissue hit the ground.*

The Homeless Person falls. The Skinhead pours the gasoline on the Homeless Person and lights a match. There's a scream as the Homeless Person burns to death. Marisol covers her ears so she can't hear.

The Skinhead exits. Marisol and the Man with Scar Tissue quickly get up. Marisol tries to run to the burnt Homeless Person. The Man stops her.)

Man with Scar Tissue: No! There's nothing you can do! Don't even look!

Marisol: Oh my God . . .

Man with Scar Tissue: I gotta get outta here. Look . . . if you see some extra skin laying around somewhere . . . pick it up for me, okay? I'll be exceedingly grateful. Bye. (*He gets back into his wheelchair.*)

Marisol: Why don't we stay together—protect each other?

Man with Scar Tissue: There is no protection. That Nazi is after me. He works for TRW. If I stay . . . you're gonna have torturers and death squads all over you.

Marisol (*Goes toward him*): I'm not afraid—

Man with Scar Tissue: No, I said! *Get away from me! Just get away from me!! Are you fucking CRAZY OR WHAT?* Just . . . just if you see my skin, beautiful . . . have some good sex with it and tell it to come home quick. (*He's gone.*) I'll always love you, Marisol!

(*Marisol is alone. More odd streaking lights rake the sky. Marisol hits the ground again and looks up, hoping that the barrage will end.*)

Marisol (*To herself*): South—that way—I'll go south that way, where the sun sets, to look for June until I hit Miami—then—I'll know I passed her.

(*The streaking lights stop. Marisol gets up. She takes a step, then another step. With each step the lights change as if she were entering a new part of the city or time has suddenly jumped forward. She finds some homeless person's old coat and puts it on.*)

I'm getting dirty . . . and my clothes smell bad. I'm getting dirty and my clothes smell bad . . . my fucking stomach's grumbling . . . (*Marisol runs up to the metal trash bin. She ducks behind it. She takes a piss. She finishes and comes out from behind the trash bin, relieved. Grabbing her empty stomach, Marisol tries to think through her predicament. To the gold crown.*) Okay, I just wanna go home. I just wanna live with June, want my boring nine-to-five back, my two-weeks-out-of-the-year vacation, my intellectual detachment, my ability to read about the misery of the world and not lose a moment out of my busy day. To believe you really knew what you were doing, God, please, if the sun would just come up! (*Beat. To herself.*) But what if the sun doesn't come up? And this is it? It's the deadline. I'm against the wall. I'm at the rim of the apocalypse . . . (*Marisol looks up and speaks to the Angel.*) Blessed guardian angel! Maybe you were right. God has stopped looking. We can't live life as if nothing's changed. To live in the sweet past. To look backward for our instructions. We have to reach up, beyond the debris, past the future, spit in the eye of the sun, make a fist, and say no, and say no, and say *no*, and say . . . (*Beat. Doubts. To herself.*) . . . no, what if she's wrong? (*She hurriedly gets on her knees to pray. Vicious, to the crown.*) Dear God, All Powerful, All Beautiful, what do I do now? How do I get out of this? Do I have to make a deal? Arrange payment and bail myself out? *What about it?!* I'll do anything! I'll spy for you. I'll steal for you. I'll decipher strange angelic codes and mine harbors and develop germ bombs and poison the angelic food supply. DEAR GOD, WHO DO I HAVE TO BETRAY TO GET OUT OF THIS FUCKING MESS?!

(*It starts to snow lightly. Marisol can't believe it. She holds out her hand.*)

Snow? It's eighty degrees!

(*We hear the sound of bombs, heavy artillery, very close. Marisol is suddenly, violently gripped by hunger pains. She grabs her stomach.*)

Oh God! (*Marisol scrambles to the trash bin and starts burrowing into it like an animal searching for food. She finally finds a paper bag. She tears it open. She finds a bunch of moldy French fries. She closes her eyes and prepares to eat them.*)

Lenny's Voice: Marisol, you don't want to eat that!

(*Marisol throws the food down.*)

Marisol (*To herself*): Lenny?

(*Lenny comes in pushing a battered baby carriage full of junk. Lenny is nine months' pregnant: huge belly, swollen breasts. Marisol is stunned by the transformation.*)

Holy shit.

Lenny: Don't eat anything in that pile, Marisol. It's lethal.

Marisol: You're alive and you're . . . bloated—

Lenny: Man who owned the restaurant on the other side of that wall put rat poison in the trash to discourage the homeless from picking through the pile. God bless the child that's got his own, huh? It's nice to see you again, Marisol.

(*It stops snowing. Staring at his stomach, Marisol goes over to Lenny.*)

Marisol (*Amazed*): I thought I killed you.

Lenny: Almost. But I forgive you. I forgive my sister, too.

Marisol: You've seen her?

Lenny: I haven't seen her, sorry. Hey, you want food? I have a little food. I'll prepare you some secret edible food.

Marisol (*Goes to Lenny, wide-eyed*): Okay . . . but . . . Lenny . . . you're immense . . . (*Marisol helps Lenny sit. He motions for her to sit next to him.*)

Lenny: I'm fucking enormous. Got the worst hemorrhoids. The smell of Chinese food makes me puke my guts.

Marisol (*Embarrassed*): I just don't know . . . what to think about this . . . and what would June say . . . ?

Lenny (*Chuckles*): I have something you're gonna like, Marisol. Took me great pains to get. Lots of weaseling around the black market, greasing palms, you know, giving blow jobs—*the things a parent will do for their fetus!*—until I got it . . . (*Lenny produces a bag. He opens it and reveals a scrawny little apple wrapped lovingly in layer after layer of delicate colored paper. Marisol can't believe what she sees.*)

Marisol: That's an apple. But that's extinct.

Lenny: Only if you believe the networks. Powers-that-be got the very last tree. It's in the Pentagon. In the center of the five-sided beast. (*Lenny bites the apple, relishing its flavor. He pats his stomach approvingly. Marisol hungrily watches him eat.*) I was on a terrible diet 'til I got knocked up. Eating cigarette butts, old milk cartons, cat food, raw shoelaces, roach motels. It's nice to be able to give my baby a few essential vitamins.

Marisol: You're really gonna be a mother?

Lenny: Baby's been kicking. It's got great aim. Always going for my bladder. I'm pissing every five minutes.

Marisol (*Tentative*): Can I feel? (*Marisol puts her hand on Lenny's belly. She feels movement and pulls her hand away.*)

Lenny: It's impossible to sleep. Lying on my back, I'm crushed. On my side, I can't breathe. The baby's heartbeat keeps me up at night. The beating is dreadful. Sounds like a bomb. I know when it goes, it's gonna go BIG.

Marisol (*Frightened, unsure*): Something's moving in there . . .

Lenny: When it's in a good mood it does backflips and my fucking kidneys end up in my throat. Did I tell you about my hemorrhoids? Here, eat. (*Lenny gives Marisol the apple. She bites into it—chews— then quickly spits it all out. Livid, Lenny takes the apple away from Marisol.*) Don't waste my FOOD, *you dumb shit!* (*Lenny starts picking up the bits of half-chewed apple spit out by Marisol and eats them greedily. Marisol continues to spit.*)

Marisol (*Angry*): It's just salt inside there . . . just *salt* . . .

Lenny: My baby's trying to build a brain! My baby needs all the minerals it can get!

Marisol: It's not an apple! It's not food!

Lenny: Get outta here if you're gonna be ungrateful! My baby and I don't need you! (*Lenny devours the apple and tries to keep from crying.*) There isn't a single food group in the world that isn't pure salt anymore! Where the fuck have you been?! (*He holds his stomach for comfort.*)

Marisol: This is your old bullshit, Lenny. That's a fucking pumpkin you got under your clothes. A big bundle of deceit and sexual CONFUSION. You're trying to *dislodge* me. Finally push me over the *edge*. Contradict *all* I know so I won't be able to say my own *name*. (*Marisol angrily pushes Lenny and he topples over, holding his stomach.*)

Lenny: There isn't much food left in the PENTAGON, you know!

Marisol: Oh, give me a break. When the sun comes up in the morning, all this will be gone! The city will come back! People will go back to work. You'll be a myth. A folk tale. (*Bitter*) Maybe you should stop pretending you're pregnant and find a job.

Lenny: *How can you say that when this is your baby?!*

Marisol: It's not my baby!

Lenny: For days and days all I did was think about you and think about you, and the more I thought about you the bigger I got! Of course it's yours!

Marisol: I don't know what you're saying!

Lenny: I shouldda had a fucking *abortion* . . .

Marisol (*Trying not to lose control*): I think you're a freak, Lenny. I'm supposed to know that men don't have babies. But I don't know that anymore, do I? If you're really pregnant, then we have to start at the beginning, don't we? Well I'm not ready to do that!

Lenny (*Gets to his feet, indignant*): I'm no freak. Every man should have this experience. There'd be fewer wars. *This* is power. *This* is energy. I guard my expanding womb greedily. I worship my new organs . . . the violent bloodstream sending food and oxygen . . . back and forth . . . between two hearts. One body. Two surging hearts! *That's* a revolution!

(*Lenny starts off. He stops in his tracks.*

He drops everything. He grabs his stomach. Pain knocks out his breathing.)

Marisol: Now what is it?

Lenny: Oh shit . . . I think it's time. I think this is it.

Marisol: Get outta here.

Lenny (*His pants are suddenly wet.*): My water's burst. Oh God, it can't be now . . .

Marisol: I'm telling you to stop this!

Lenny (*Panicking*): I'm not ready. Feel my breasts! They're empty! I can't let this baby be born yet! What if my body can't make enough milk to feed my baby?!

(*Lenny shrieks with pain and falls to his knees. Marisol helps him lie down. She kneels beside him.*)

Marisol: Okay, Lenny, breathe—breathe—breathe—

Lenny (*Incredible pain*): I'm breathing, you ASSHOLE, I'm breathing!

Marisol: Breathe more!

Lenny: Jesus! And I thought war was hell!

Marisol: Oh my God—oh Jesus . . .

Lenny: If I pull off this birth thing, *it'll be a miracle!*

Marisol: *Angel of God, please help him!*

(*Marisol quickly covers Lenny's abdomen with her coat. Lenny starts the final stage of labor. He bears down.*

Lenny lets out a final, cataclysmic scream.

The baby is born. Marisol "catches" the baby.

Marisol holds the silent baby in the coat, wrapping it tight. She examines the baby. Lenny's huge stomach has disappeared. He breathes hard. Short silence.

Lenny sits up slowly, wiping sweat from his face, happy the ordeal is over. All Lenny wants to do is hold his child. Marisol stands up holding the baby, looking at it a long time, a troubled look on her face.

Lenny holds out his arms for the baby. Marisol looks at Lenny and shakes her head, sadly, no. Lenny looks at Marisol, all hope drained from his face.)

Lenny: Dead?

Marisol: I'm sorry.

(*Marisol wraps the baby tighter. She gives Lenny his baby. Lenny takes the bundle, kisses it, holds back tears. Marisol looks at him.*)

Lenny (*Grim*): C'mon. There's something we have to do now.

(*Holding the baby, Lenny starts to walk around and around the stage. Marisol follows.*

They come to the downstage corner where the rosary-covered fire hydrant is. Special lighting on this area. Marisol looks down and notices little crucifixes scratched into the sidewalk in rows.

Dazzling, frenetic lights rip the air above Marisol and Lenny.)

Do you know where you are, Marisol?

(*Marisol shakes her head no.*)

You're in Brooklyn.

Marisol (*Empty*): Wow. I finally made it. I'm here.

Lenny: Everybody comes to this street eventually.

Marisol: Why?

Lenny: People are buried here. It looks like a sidewalk. But it's not. It's a tomb.

Marisol: For who?

Lenny: For babies. Angelitos. (*Lenny removes a slab of sidewalk concrete and start digging up the dirt beneath it. There's a tiny wooden box there.*) The city provides these coffins. There are numbers on them. The city knows how we live. (*Lenny gently places the baby's body in the box.*) These are babies born on the street. Little girls of the twilight hours who never felt warm blankets around their bodies. Never drank their mothers' holy milk. Little boys born with coke in their blood. This is where babies who die on the street are taken to rest. You never heard of it?

Marisol: Never.

Lenny (*Puts the box in the ground and covers it up with dirt*): Everyone who sleeps and begs in the open air knows this address. We come with flowers, with crucifixes, with offerings. The wind plays organ music. Hard concrete turns into gentle moss so the babies can decompose in grace. We all come here sooner or later to pay respects to the most fragile of the street people.

(Lenny replaces the concrete slab and scratches the name of the child into the concrete. He says a prayer. If there are other Homeless People onstage, they pick up the prayer and repeat it softly underneath Lenny.)

> Matthew, Mark, Luke, and John.
> Bless the bed that I lie on.
> Four corners to my bed.
> Four angels 'round my head.
> One to watch and one to pray.
> And two to bear your soul away.

(Lenny kisses the ground.)

'Night, little Marisol.

(Lenny lies on the ground and falls asleep. Exhausted, Marisol looks at the tiny cemetery. She reads the names scratched into the sidewalk.)

Marisol: Fermin Rivera . . . born March 14, died March 16 . . . José Amengual . . . born August 2, died August 2 . . . Delfina Perez . . . born December 23, died January 6 . . . Jonathan Sand . . . born July 1, died July 29 . . . Wilfredo Terron . . . dates unknown . . . no name . . . no name . . . no name . . .

(Marisol can't read anymore. She sits in the middle of the child cemetery, exhausted, not able to think, feel, or react anymore. For all she knows, this could be the end of the world.

Marisol lies on the street, in Lenny's arms, and falls asleep.

Upstage there's the sound of marching feet. The Skinhead enters and marches toward the sleeping Marisol and Lenny and stops. Only as the light comes up on the Skinhead do we realize it's June.)

Skinhead *(To herself, indicating Marisol)*: Look at this goddamn thing, this waste, this fucking parasite. God, I'm so sick of it. Sick of the eyesore. Sick of the diseases. Sick of the drugs. Sick of the homelessness. Sick of the border babies. Sick of the dark skin. Sick of that compassion thing! That's where it all started! When they put in that fucking compassion thing! *(Furious)* I mean, why can't they just go AWAY? I mean, okay, if you people want to kill yourselves, fine, do it: kill yourselves with your crack and your incest and your promiscuity and your homo anal intercourse . . . just leave me to take care of myself and my own. Leave me to my gardens. I'm good in my gardens. I'm good on my acres of green grass. God distributes green grass in just the right way! Take care of your own. Take care of your family. If everybody did that . . . I swear on my gold Citibank MasterCard . . . there wouldn't be any problems, anywhere, in the next millennium . . .

(*June looks down at Marisol. She unscrews the can of gasoline and starts pouring gasoline on Marisol and Lenny. Marisol wakes up. June strikes a match. Marisol jumps at June, grabbing her.*)

Marisol: Cut that shit out you fucking Nazi!

(*June tries to throw the match on Marisol.*)

June: Stay still so I can burn you!

(*Marisol grabs June and tries to push her away from Lenny. They're face to face for the first time.*)

What a day I'm having, huh?

Marisol (*Startled*): June?

June: I started out burning hobos and ended up torching half the city! The entire Upper West Side up in ashes!

Marisol (*Overjoyed*): Oh God, I found you.

June: You got anything for me?!

Marisol: I thought Lenny killed you—

June: You got nothing for me? Get outta my way, asshole!

Marisol: Don't you remember me?

June: You should see what I did! It's fire on a massive scale! Buildings melted all down! Consumed! Ashes of those evaporated dreams are all over the fucking place!

Marisol: June, it's Marisol. . . (*Marisol throws both arms around June, embraces her tightly, and kisses her. June tries to escape.*)

June: We could be picked up real fast by the police . . . they've built great big facilities for us . . . 'cause our numbers are swelling . . . (*Marisol tries to hold June. June resists. But the prolonged and violent contact with Marisol's body has started to awaken June's memory. She begins to sound a little like her old self.*) But they won't take me! I have a strategy now! I burn bag people! The troop likes that!

Marisol: No more! That's not you! (*Marisol throws the can of gasoline into the trash bin. She grabs June's hand and pulls June toward Lenny. June resists.*)

June: The Citicorps building was a great place to hide. A man would pull your teeth for free in Port Authority—

Marisol: Lenny's right here . . .

June: I hear the water in the Central Park reservoir is salty 'cause angels are falling outta the sky, Marisol . . .

Marisol (*Astonished*): You said my name. You said Marisol. (*Marisol joyfully embraces June and kisses her. That pushes June over the edge and she collapses. Marisol catches her and lays her gently on the ground. Marisol sits with June's head on her lap. This time June does not resist.*)

June (*Weak, rubbing her head*): I can't understand these nightmares I'm having . . .

Marisol (*Holds June. June and Lenny quietly start to cry.*): We survived. We survived, June. (*Marisol looks around her—at her two crippled, sobbing friends, at the distorted world—all too aware of the graveyard that has become the site of their reunion.*) For what? To do what? (*Marisol looks up at the crown—a long, still moment.*) Fuck you. Just *fuck you!*

(*Loud machine-gun fire rips the air. Marisol hits the ground and covers June and Lenny with her body.*)

June, Lenny . . . don't you guys worry . . . I have a clear vision for us. I know what I want to do.

(*The machine-gun firing stops. Marisol kisses her friends.*)

Listen to me. We're going to find the angels. And I'm going to ask them to touch your foreheads. To press their angelic fingers into your temples. Fire your minds with instant light. Blow up your bad dreams. And resurrect you. (*Marisol looks up at the crown.*) And then we're going to join them. Then we're going to fight with the angels. (*Marisol helps June and Lenny to their feet. June and Lenny see each other and embrace.*)

Lenny (*To June*): I'm sorry for everything I did . . .

June (*To Lenny, kissing him*): I'm sorry, too, Lenny . . .

(*As Marisol takes their hands to start their new journey, the Woman with Furs enters, unseen, behind them. She is completely still. She is holding an Uzi.*)

Marisol: What a time to be alive, huh? On one hand, we're nothing. We're dirt. On the other hand, we're the reason the universe was made.

(*The Woman with Furs loads the Uzi. Bombs are heard.*)

June: What's that noise?

Marisol: Right now, thousands upon millions of angels are dying on our behalf. Isn't that amazing? The silver cities of Heaven are burning for us. Attacks and counterattacks are ruining galaxies. The ripped-up planets are making travel impossible. And triumphant angels are taking over the television stations. All for us. All for me.

Woman with Furs (*Points the Uzi at Marisol, June, and Lenny*): Sorry, Marisol. We don't need revolution here. We can't have upheaval at the drop of a hat. No demonstrations here! No putting up pamphlets! No shoving daisies into the rifles of militiamen! No stopping tanks by standing in their way!

Marisol (*Turns to look at the Woman with Furs*): Unless you want to join us?

Woman with Furs: Traitors! Credit risks!

(*Marisol goes to the Woman with Furs and the Woman blasts Marisol, pumping hundreds of rounds into her. She dies instantly and falls to the ground. The Woman exits. There's a blackout. Suddenly, the stage is bathed in strange light. We hear the strange, indecipherable sounds of the angelic war. June and Lenny kneel where Marisol has fallen. Marisol is standing apart, alone, in her own light. Marisol's voice is slightly amplified.*)

Marisol: I'm killed instantly. Little blazing lead meteors enter my body. My blood cells ride those bullets into outer space. My soul surges up the oceans of the Milky Way at the speed of light. At the moment of death, I see the invisible war.

(*Beautiful music. The stage goes black, except for a light on Marisol.*)

Thousands of years of fighting pass in an instant. New and terrible forms of warfare, monstrous weapons, and unimagined strains of terror are created and destroyed in billionths of a second. Galaxies spring from a single drop of angel's sweat while hundreds of armies fight and die on the fingertips of children in the Bronx.

(*Light upstage reveals the Angel. She's dressed in a filthy, tattered uniform: the war has ravaged her. She also has huge magnificent* wings, her wings of war. She's got an Uzi. The Angel fires her Uzi into the air, at the invisible legions of God's loyal warriors. The terrible sounds of war. The angelic vision lasts only seconds. The stage once again goes to black. A spotlight on Marisol.)

Three hundred million million beautiful angels die in the first charge of the Final Battle. The oceans are salty with rebel blood. Angels drop like lightning from the dying sky. The rebels are in full retreat. There's chaos. There's blood and fire and ambulances, and Heaven's soldiers scream and fight and die in beautiful, beautiful light. It looks like the revolution is doomed . . .

(Light upstage reveals a single Homeless Person angrily throwing rocks at the sky. The Homeless Person is joined by Lenny and June. This vision lasts only seconds. The stage once again goes to black. A spotlight on Marisol.)

. . . then, as if one body, one mind, the innocent of the earth take to the streets with anything they can find—rocks, sticks, screams—and aim their displeasure at the senile sky and fire into the tattered wind on the side of the angels . . . billions of poor, of homeless, of peaceful, of silent, of angry . . . fighting and fighting as no species has ever fought before. Inspired by the earthly noise, the rebels advance!

(A small moon appears in the sky, far, far away.)

New ideas rip the Heavens. New powers are created. New miracles are signed into law. It's the first day of the new history . . .

(There are a few seconds of tremendous noise as the war hits its climax. Then silence. The Angel appears next to Marisol, wingless, unarmed, holding the gold crown in her hands. The Angel holds the crown out to the audience as Marisol looks at her.)

Oh God. What light. What possibilities. What hope.

(The Angel kisses Marisol. Bright, bright light begins to shine directly into the audience's eyes—for several seconds—and Marisol, the Angel, June, Lenny, and the Homeless People seem to be turned into light. Then all seem to disappear in the wild light of the new millennium— quick black out.)

END OF PLAY

The Gift

ALLAN HAVIS

The Gift received a staged reading at Playwrights Horizons in New York City on January 27, 1997. It was directed by William Foeller with the following cast: Ebony Booth as Libby; George Hall as MacAlister; Larry Pine as Butterworth; Felicia Dyer as Bibi; Charlie Huston as Oscar; John Gould Rubin as Vetter; and Mary Neufeld as Lyla/ Marilyn Kincaid.

The Gift was also directed by Christopher Hanna in a workshop at the Chautauqua Theatre Festival in New York, July 1996.

Cast of Characters

Libby, age 19, attractive black female college student

Bibi, age 19, attractive white female college student

Oscar, age 20, handsome white male college student

Butterworth, age 55, distinguished college president

MacAlister, age 60, blind, wealthy philanthropist

Bruce Vetter, age 45, charismatic college publicist

Lyla, age 35, Vetter's lively wife, librarian

Marilyn Kincaid, age 55, charismatic, willful professor

Setting

A California community bordering San Diego and Mt. Soledad; and a local college campus over three autumn months in the late 1990s.

Production Notes

The roles of Lyla and Kincaid may be double cast, and the same actor would supply the offstage voices of Butterworth's secretary, Doris, and Mom. An intermission may be added between scenes 14 and 15.

Author's Note

The Gift *was inspired by a series of embarrassments in the mid-1990s when super-rich Texan Lee Bass pledged twenty-five million dollars to Yale University. Due to a run of bad luck, revolving-door Yale presidencies, bureaucratic procrastination, and the meddling media, the university eventually declined the donation. During the course of his personal pledge, Bass was made to wait beyond his patience, which prompted him to raise the stakes: he demanded to handpick the faculty his pledge would support and to have Yale return to its focus on the Great Western Books at the expense of ethnic studies, feminism, alternative sexual lifestyles, and so on. Of course, it was the national press more than the campus infighting that had stirred this controversy far beyond proportion. Adding insult to injury, Yale quickly lost its endowment drive contest against Harvard. The charming Shavian epilogue was that another Texas alumnus—Bass's brother—wrote Yale a check for the same amount for building improvements and infrastructure. The check did not bounce.*

PROLOGUE

Mt. Soledad with a towering fifty-foot metal crucifix; the sound of low, persistent winds. Lights up over Libby.

Libby:
> Call the dogs off.
> Dammit!
> Vicious, seething,
> Barking beasts.
> Foaming graveyard bile.
> Call them off!
> Just want peace by the meadow
> In soft September heat
> Please, Mama
> Tell the bad boys to go home.
> Tell all the truants.
> All the lunatics.
> All the nose-pickers.
> All the jive hustler.
> All the false fathers.
> And gravel voiced Charley Tuna.

(Lights up over MacAlister, other side of stage)

MacAlister:
> With every successful enterprise,
> There's intuition.
> Of course,
> Mine usually evades me.
> Despite what I do.
> Or what is done to me.
> Please, I'm far from innocent.
> Given my sepia virtue,
> And predilection for control.
> True, there's the curious matter of luck.

Ladies' luck, God's luck
Dumb luck, my luck.
Best to hang around devious women
Get their unguarded thinking.
How to dress before a dance
How to feel before a first kiss
How to give from the heart.
All one fine feminine fandango.

(*MacAlister lingers as lights fade over Libby. His attention then turns to a slide projection of a giant Madonna statue.*)

SCENE 1

(*Office of the college president. Both men are standing in front of Butterworth's desk.*)

MacAlister: Happily married?

Butterworth: So my wife tells me. And you, sir?

MacAlister: Too many times, a repeat offender. (*Smiling*) Shirts freshly laundered?

Butterworth: Always.

MacAlister: I envy you.

Butterworth: Please don't. I'm so tired of starched jockey shorts. Have you made up your mind, Mr. MacAlister?

MacAlister: And if I said yes?

Butterworth: "Yes" is a wonderful word.

MacAlister: "Yes" is a *hungry* word.

Butterworth: There are some things a man can't hide.

MacAlister: Like the truth to an ironic rumor?

Butterworth: Or the rumor to an ironic truth?

MacAlister: Imagine an invaluable vault key down a bottomless well. A recurring dream, Butterworth. Lately, you look so melancholic.

Butterworth: Do I really? We've a virulent virus in our supercomputer eating our academic files. Now targeted by a Unabomber copycat,

Amway, the NEA, ABA, AMA, AAA, NAACP, ACLU, OSHA, two rabid bishops, three Nobel Luddites, four camouflage militias, and five gay ecology groups during our worst budgetary crisis this century.

MacAlister: Surely you exaggerate?

Butterworth (*Downs pill with water*): We're on the financial brink.

MacAlister: No stigma to bankruptcy. TWA, Dow, and my wife filed for protection. Fabled Orange County defaulted. And Bridgeport University in Connecticut found a savior with Moonie's Church.

Butterworth: Selling airport daisies buys an accredited college. God help us.

MacAlister: Flower power for the '90s. (*Pause*) My life goes back many years here. Lost my virginity above those horrible, vertiginous upper bunk dorm beds with ergonomic goal posts.

Butterworth: The bunk beds are gone.

MacAlister: A gesture toward safer sex or undisciplined bed wetters?

Butterworth: What exactly is your reservation about giving?

MacAlister: Your flagrant, ragtag faculty. The curriculum's gone to shit. Kids take notes with crayons or play Nintendo on their laptops. Departments hire idiot spouses just to spare the commute. Half your faculty wears T-shirts and cutoffs while singing the praises of multiculturalism. Abolish tenure. These scamp Ph.D. ninnies traipse right past the goddamn turnstile. In my business, we skin skunks and deadbeats.

Butterworth: The fur business is quite different from academe.

MacAlister: Is it? You clothe a young mind with a fashionable idea. I clothe a young body with an idea of fashion. What does your wife wear?

Butterworth: Chinchilla, three chilly nights each year.

MacAlister: And she loves rabbits during Easter? No woman really loves fake fur. (*Pause*) A big-hearted capitalist adopts a South Bronx sixth-grade class to cover college costs. A good deed buys world headlines. Does God notice? (*Pause*) I've mingled in campus cafés. Sat through classes. Reviewed the catalogs. One can tell the vigor has disappeared. Little substance is taught. Everyone couched lest they offend cultural diversity.

Butterworth: Call it intellectual etiquette.

MacAlister: What pabulum!

Butterworth: Otherwise it's pure anarchy.

MacAlister: Why wink at these frauds? You'll bind us to our hoaxes for life. I applaud Alan Sokal's brilliant publishing prank.

Butterworth: Yes, that rascal Sokal—stark echoes of Swift and Pope.

MacAlister: Postmodernism is such crap.

Butterworth: In other words, poo-poo on PoMo.

MacAlister: What the hell did you say?

Butterworth: Nothing.

MacAlister: Butterworth, let's talk several million dollars. Maybe more. To make a dent in the prevailing philosophy. Return to Western Civ. Don't fumble like Yale.

Butterworth: We don't have Yale's problem.

MacAlister: You will. The kids can cornrow their hair until Ziggy Marley's campus concert. Rastafarian hygiene's for the birds. I don't care what's in at Yale.

Butterworth: Yale's benefactor Lee Bass wanted to handpick the Yale faculty.

MacAlister: So?

Butterworth: A great university nearly prostituted itself to an eccentric Texas billionaire.

MacAlister: The undeniable charm of filthy rich Texans. (*Pause*) You recall Bernard Shaw on prostitution:

> "I can enjoy her while she's kind;
> But when she dances in the wind,
> And shakes the wings, and will not stay.
> I puff the prostitute away."

Butterworth: John Dryden. Shaw doesn't—

MacAlister: Rhyme. Every major institution whores itself, except perhaps the United Nations, where everyone gets screwed for nothing.

Butterworth: With Bass it crossed the line.

MacAlister: And the idiotic media made hash of it.

Butterworth: True. Perhaps you ought to put everything on the table.

MacAlister: Teaching the Bible as literature.

Butterworth: Yes?

MacAlister: Is that an endorsement of a religion or unadulterated agnosticism?

Butterworth: Neither.

MacAlister: What, then, is being taught?

Butterworth: The Good Book has contemporary merit.

MacAlister: Butterworth!

Butterworth: Literary and semiotic importance, irrespective of ontology or ecumenicity.

MacAlister: Old and New Testaments?

Butterworth: The canopy's awfully wide, Mr. MacAlister.

MacAlister: Aren't you a Christian?

Butterworth: Yes, a Lutheran with a respectable golf handicap.

MacAlister: And your catalog's renowned Busty Women of the Bible?

Butterworth: I haven't sat in on the course.

MacAlister: I have. The list of indignities to the weaker sex outshout the divinity of God.

Butterworth: Perhaps God approves . . . this year.

MacAlister: Your upper division seminar on Dr. Seuss's *Cat in the Hat*?

Butterworth: Is that Lacanian gem offered again?

MacAlister: A radical fem-psychoanalysis in two glorious semesters. Claiming Seuss reveals sacred texts as male hand-me-downs by a supernatural prick.

Butterworth: A *supernatural* prick?

MacAlister: Yes. As opposed to a *paranormal* prick hiding female functions. *(Pause)* What constitutes female functions?

Butterworth: Plumbing, progeny, pink margarita parties? *(Pause)* We pay a dear price for academic freedom.

MacAlister: *We* certainly do. (*Plays pocket recorder of Kincaid's lecture*) "The Mother-figure abandons the narrator and his sister to shovel snow. The Cat shows up. He eats . . . (*garbled*) . . . cake in the tub and leaves an indelible pink ring."

Butterworth: What sort of cake?

MacAlister: You're missing the point, Butterworth.

Butterworth: Indeed.

MacAlister (*Paraphrasing the lecture in a woman's voice*): "The kids are mortified. Kitty cleans the shit with Mama's white dress. When brother and sister speak up, the Cat removes the dress stain onto the wall. From the wall onto Papa's shoes." Etc. Etc.

Butterworth (*With likable charm*): A remarkable tale from the canon of great books. (*Pause*) Dr. Seuss lived nearby. The toast of La Jolla.

MacAlister (*Plays another section of the tape*): "Kitty doffs his hat to release a series of little bitty kittens who en masse rid the stain out of the home onto the snow outside. The moral problem compounds." (*Pause*) To Professor Kincaid, the Cat has violated religious laws, playing during worktime and desecrating the bathtub.

Butterworth: Desecrating the tub?

MacAlister: While the pink mess on the dress hints at menstrual taboos and lost virginity. The stain shows the hurt over Mama's absence. Not a thread of irony here.

Butterworth: Certainly not Dickensian. Are you religious, Mr. MacAlister? (*Silence*) I'll sit in on the class.

MacAlister: Please do. There are many "Kincaids" on campus.

Butterworth: My friend, there's just *one* Marilyn Kincaid. (*Pause*) A great college reflects pluralism and tolerance. Sometimes at the expense of common sense.

MacAlister: An understatement for the *Guinness Book of Records*.

Butterworth: I'll talk to my Board. We are your alma mater, bunk beds, warts, and all. But why not endow a few chairs in classics as part of your charitable trust?

MacAlister: I prefer prestidigitation. *Change the cockamamie curricula.*

(*Intercom buzzes*)

Butterworth: Yes, Doris?

Doris (*Offstage*): There's a mob of students outside.

Butterworth: Lovely. (*Pause*) The Rhododendron girl? Call Security. (*Sinks into chair*) Mr. MacAlister, please excuse me.

MacAlister (*Gives a prepared check*): I never tear up small checks. As Dr. Seuss dared to say at commencement, "Fake fur fleeces a fiery fool."

(*He exits.*)

Butterworth (*Reads check*): Dear Jesus . . .

SCENE 2

(*At a kitchen table, Libby and Bibi's apartment*)

Bibi: Libby? Are you done with dinner?

Libby: A closed book is never finished. An open mind never mends. No more fried tofu. It's coming out of my ears.

Bibi: TV?

Libby: No.

Bibi: We watched it last night.

Libby: Did we?

Bibi: Are you okay?

Libby: My skin's very dry.

Bibi: You've very dry skin.

Libby: Is there any lotion?

Bibi: I'll get some.

Libby: Smooth silky milk skin. (*Pause*) Bibi?

Bibi: What?

Libby: I can't see anyone. Lock the door.

Bibi: You're safe, honey. I'm here.

Libby: It'll happen again.

Bibi: No. Don't think that way. You got to finish out the term.

Libby: I can't decide.

Bibi: I understand.

Libby: Do you? (*Pause*) There's a money problem.

Bibi: I've the same problem.

Libby: How can I go back?

Bibi: Maybe the Dean can help out.

Libby: Get real. I've talked to that clown and every advisor. They blame me. Most of the frats do. They call me Tawana Bullshit Artist. Al Sharpton's next pawn. (*Both at window*) Everyone's so damn cavalier. Who's outside?

Bibi: Oscar.

Libby: Ducker?

Bibi: *Tucker.*

Libby: Oscar Mortimer Tucker, the Gnarly Zit Geek Greek.

Bibi: He isn't a geek.

Libby: Right, and Hillary Clinton's heterosexual. Body language doesn't lie.

Bibi: He came to your defense.

Libby: A little too late, don't you think?

Bibi: All men aren't bad.

Libby: A new bumper sticker: "All men aren't bad!" (*Pause*) Orphaned birds on our sill. See the fairy? And fat Aunt Jemina in spandex. Who are these people outside? (*Pause*) Bring me some hand lotion, please. And send Ducker-Tucker away.

(*After a few knocks, Oscar is let in by Bibi.*)

Oscar: Hi guys. I've shaved off my moustache. How do I look?

Libby (*Flip*): Like Leonardo DiCaprio in *The Beach.*

Oscar: I'd like to talk to Libby.

Bibi: I'll leave you two alone.

(*Exits. Awkward silence.*)

Oscar: You look better. I was really worried about you. I've lecture notes from our lit class.

Libby: Thanks.

Oscar: You know I obsess about you day and night. Can't sleep without pills. Kids are still talking about you. Protesting all over campus. You're kind of like a celebrity.

Libby: They can all go to hell. Please go.

Oscar: I just got here.

Libby: I know what you really want.

Oscar: What do I want?

Libby: That crappy Catholic word, "absolution."

Oscar: No.

Libby: I don't believe you.

Oscar: Look, I know you and Richard broke up all because of . . .

Libby: Get out, Oscar.

Oscar: He was getting real serious. He even wanted to marry you.

Libby: He never said boo to me.

Oscar: Richard's superstitious.

Libby: Right, like a vanishing Houdini. Richard dumped me a day after my birthday. My mother married at my age. And then my father turned into a ghost. That's my trauma.

Oscar: Would you see Richard again?

Libby: Who the fuck do you think you are?

Oscar: Richard's shy.

Libby: And my life's private. I can't believe he asked you to speak for him.

Oscar: Maybe he really loves you.

Libby: Not if he still wets his pants when trouble hits.

Oscar: This is tough on everyone. Get real, Libby.

Libby: There is no reality in California. (*Pause*) Just ask your good buddy Spenser and his bestial football squad. You pity me. You reek of it. It's in your eyes, your mouth, your blown hair.

Oscar: Yeah, maybe I do pity you.

Libby: I'm a Jerry Lewis telethon girl. And there's a racial thing too.

Oscar: Think so?

Libby (*Mocking*): Duh . . .

Oscar: I don't see race between us. At night you look like Whitney Houston. That's how pretty you are to me.

Libby: Did someone put you up to this? If not, you're the dumbest jerk on campus.

Oscar: Fuck you, Libby.

(*Exits*)

SCENE 3

(*President's campus office*)

Butterworth: He's that rich?

Vetter: Megabucks. We did a Dun and Bradstreet.

Butterworth: MacAlister left a fifty-thousand-dollar check.

Vetter: Not bad for starters.

Butterworth: Mac's like a cross between Atilla the Hun and Ross Perot, with a twist of Dana Carvey. This guy wants to weed out half the faculty.

Vetter: About time someone did.

Butterworth: And wants to shape the curricula. We'll lose our accreditation.

Vetter: No one has to know.

Butterworth: Stunts like that get more publicity than Clinton's Oval Office knee pads.

Vetter: It's your call. The last five donors all welched on their pledges.

Butterworth: The political climate is terrible right now. Some people want my head on a platter.

Vetter: I think so.

Butterworth: But I'm agile. I can balance money and principles. Is there any good news today?

Vetter (*Pause*): The three tenors *are* coming. (*Pause*) The Carreras, Domingo, Pavarotti Benefit.

Butterworth: Oh?

Vetter: One of the trustees is Pavarotti's surgeon. (*Pause*) Lipchitz. Face-lift, tummy tuck, penis enlargement. (*See pack of cigarettes on desk*) Sneaking cigarettes again?

Butterworth: Nerves. I'd gladly throw out all my Donna Summer records for another pack of Camels. What's in the news today?

Vetter: Madonna atop Mt. Soledad.

Butterworth: There's life after *Evita*? When is the metal cross coming down?

Vetter: Circuit Appeals punted. It's destined for the Supreme Court. (*Butterworth lights a cigarette, in spite of himself.*) This one's a Catholic statue—a genuine icon. Right next to the cross. From a distance she looks like *Attack of the Fifty-Foot Woman*. Nathan Juran's cult film.

Butterworth: Never saw it. Vermouth, Vetter? (*Butterworth pours himself a drink.*)

Vetter: No.

Butterworth: Who put up the statue? (*Sips drink. Flip.*) B'nai B'rith?

Vetter: Had to been "air-dropped" earlier in the week by a film studio. All steel girders. This is no papier-mâché piñata. And each day, a different old Hollywood face. Today, Joan Crawford. Starlets as saints.

Butterworth: The true countenance of modern Catholicism?

Vetter: Care to take a drive and get some air? Let's take a look. You loved Crawford's *Mommy Dearest*.

SCENE 4

(Vetter's home. Lyla is wrapped in several towels.)

Vetter: Lyla. I'm home early.

Lyla: There's no hot water!

Vetter: How about a kiss and then we'll make love?

Lyla: My feet are in Epsom salts.

Vetter: Wonderful.

Lyla: You're early.

Vetter: Get the operation.

Lyla: I hate surgery.

Vetter: Our HMO offers a choice of doctors.

Lyla: Our HMO's a first-aid kit with voicemail. You didn't want to buy the higher premiums, Bruce. The last surgery turned my toes into corn nachos. *(They kiss.)* The home security agent came by today.

Vetter: And?

Lyla: He went through the house, crossed-dressed as a very Irish Dennis Rodman. Monosyllabic to a fault. Five thousand dollars for basic installation.

Vetter: Not cheap.

Lyla: Fifty- or a hundred-dollar monthly contract. He knows we were robbed.

Vetter: What's the difference?

Lyla: Armed response.

Vetter: Fifty dollars more, we've the pleasure of a slaughtered thief?

Lyla: Either way they get there faster than Domino's pizza. *(Kittenish smile)* They've gone through the same year-long training as the police—except the last four weeks.

Vetter: What were the last four weeks?

Lyla: Civil liberties.

Vetter: Come on, let's go to bed.

Lyla: Hand me the towel. Butterworth called. Very upset. Another faculty member was found in flagrante delicto with an underage sophomore.

Vetter: Oh, Christ.

Lyla: Face it, darling. The school's going to hell.

Vetter: Not if I can help it.

Lyla (*High skepticism*): Yeah, with this new philanthropist?

Vetter: I've a good hunch about him.

Lyla: Like your hunch on beta videos twelve years ago? You've been in a salary freeze since the advent of e-mail. We're way behind in our bills.

Vetter: Lyla.

Lyla: And you can smell the poorhouse from here. You promised me, big fella.

Vetter: I'm sorry.

Lyla: A baby before the millennium.

Vetter: Sounds like a challenge grant. Lyla, I promise we'll pay off every bill by Christmas. And we'll use the thermometer method.

Lyla: For the bed or the bank? (*Sticks her tongue out*)

Vetter: Let's make love.

Lyla: Mother's in town.

Vetter: What?

Lyla: That's right.

Vetter: Yours or mine?

Lyla: I prefer yours.

Vetter: Since when?

Lyla: Our wedding in Barbados.

Vetter: Where is she?

Lyla: Sleeping in the bedroom.

Vetter: Just in from Baltimore?

Lyla: Neither of our mothers lives in Baltimore.

Vetter: Bethesda?

Lyla: She was on our doorstep with a mountain of luggage.

Vetter: I can't smoke when she's here.

Lyla: You can smoke in the yard. I thought you were going to quit?

Vetter: Any beers in the fridge?

Lyla: She drank them all.

Vetter: Jesus.

Lyla: She loves Corona.

Vetter: How long?

Lyla: Until her leg heals.

Vetter: What's wrong with her leg?

Lyla: Bowling accident. And so close to a perfect game. Nine consecutive strikes.

Vetter: Didn't she quit the senior pro tour?

Lyla: After racking up a hundred thousand dollars in winnings. More bucks than our combined salaries.

Vetter: A librarian and a publicist can't compete with bowlers, Lyla.

Lyla: You had a dandy offer from the Grand Foundation.

Vetter: The Rand Foundation. It was far from grand.

Lyla: Coward.

Vetter: Why do you hate the college? (*Phone rings*)

Lyla: Because they're all PC, narcissistic, backstabbing jerks.

Vetter (*Picks up phone*): Tell me what you *really* think, darling. (*Pause*) Hello? Mr. MacAlister?

Mom (*Offstage*): Is that you, Bruuuuuuuuuce?

Lyla: She's *your* parent, sweetheart. My mother only shampoos with beer.

SCENE 5

(Mt. Soledad. There is an image of a giant Madonna with Bette Davis's face next to a fifty-foot cross.)

Vetter: Mr. MacAlister? Bruce Vetter.

MacAlister: Hello, Vetter. How uncanny. A face that keeps changing, or so I'm told. Yesterday she was Crawford. Today, Bette Davis. Tomorrow I'm betting on Joan Blondell. Although I never understood Blondell's appeal.

Vetter: Her healthy irreverence.

MacAlister: Think it's a publicity prank?

Vetter: Only if Liz Taylor makes the cut.

MacAlister: Thank you for meeting me here. Despite how it looks to you, it feels like an inspired site. Might just set off a religious carnival.

Vetter: "A modern miracle."

MacAlister: What constitutes "a modern miracle"?

Vetter: Mormon underwriters?

MacAlister: My former wife was a Mormon. *(Pause)* If the courts acquiesce, this and the cross will be San Diego's best attraction, outdrawing SeaWorld and the Zoo. A thousand buses and concessions. Imagine if she were draped in flowing white sable?

Vetter: Bad for Bette. Good for the vandals.

MacAlister: Or Madonna moved to your campus?

Vetter: Our Catholic affiliation ended decades ago.

MacAlister: Catholic affiliation never really ends. On his death bed, Voltaire returned to the fold. Do you know why I called you?

Vetter: Butterworth mishandled your pledge?

MacAlister: Exactly. You can change that quickly. After all, it was you who reeled me in.

Vetter: I'll do my best.

MacAlister: You're a lapsed Catholic, Vetter?

Vetter: Yes.

MacAlister: When everything's completed, think about working for me. I'll double your salary and give you more paid holidays. I like lapsed Catholics. Their pain is adorable. You're cut from the same selfless cloth as that washerwoman, Oseola McCarty, who gave her life savings to USM. Childless, eighty-seven years old . . . an amazing bequest to black students.

Vetter: Heartrending.

MacAlister: Or dear centenarian Anne Scheiber who beat the stock market for Yeshiva University. Unassuming humble women, black and a Jew. While I'm just a corporate white male asshole fearing onomatopoeia. An opulent, obstreperous onanist. (*Pause*) Do you read the Bible, Vetter?

Vetter: In the better hotels.

MacAlister: Is there any book that has more authority?

Vetter: The new IRS Tax Code?

MacAlister: Touché. What if you were touched by a miracle?

Vetter: In this day and age?

MacAlister: But given one, would you change your beliefs?

Vetter: I don't have those kinds of beliefs.

MacAlister: What would you say in Jesus' time?

Vetter: A bulimic Roman is a good Roman.

MacAlister: I don't always get your humor, Vetter.

Vetter: My wife says the same.

MacAlister: I was poor and miserable for years. Nothing went my way. I had turned my back to Heaven. So God punished me. Where are my children? Where are your children? They shall inherit the earth. (*Pause*) Let's improve higher education and society. Are you with me?

Vetter: I'm with you.

MacAlister: Good. There are a dozen faculty members that must be dumped. You'd think that was worth ten million.

Vetter: Easily.

MacAlister: I'm looking for a quid pro quo.

Vetter: Should I quid or should I quo?

MacAlister: I quid, you quo. Tenure was a Bolshevik notion. And you know, of course, there are no more Bolsheviks. In Mexico, Trotsky was the first to get axed—right in the head.

Vetter: A page right out of history's barbaric barbering.

MacAlister: Here's a list of names. Get rid of these cocksuckers.

Vetter: I'm not authorized to do any such thing, Mr. MacAlister.

MacAlister: Vetter.

Vetter: We're sailing through so many controversies, one more will take down the entire ship.

MacAlister: I'm well aware how you finessed the Richardson pledge three years ago. You navigated that with ease. You're very good at this. Please don't disappoint me. Trump up some competency charges. Half of these scoundrels are close to retirement age. (*Folds paper list tightly inside Vetter's fist*) The black coed who was attacked . . .

Vetter: How do you know?

MacAlister: I'm chummy with the campus police. Libby?

Vetter: Libby Rhododendron.

MacAlister: That can't be her real name. Sounds like a La Jolla boutique with canaries and music boxes. I want to meet the girl.

Vetter: Butterworth wants the incident kept very quiet.

MacAlister: I understand. But I've a special feeling for her and want to set up a special scholarship.

Vetter: Fine.

MacAlister: She must finish her schooling. Please convey that to her. And look over that faculty list.

Vetter: I'll look it over.

MacAlister: Well, we've accomplished something today. Care to make a bet?

Vetter: A bet?

MacAlister: When this female colossus forfeits the mountain? (*Steps toward Vetter and slaps his shoulder*) I think the gal's here to stay at least a year. And I'll give you very decent odds. Ten thousand to one. One buck.

Vetter: Ten grand?

MacAlister: How can you go wrong?

(*Extends his hand. They shake.*)

SCENE 6

(*Libby's apartment. Libby is sitting awkwardly.*)

Butterworth: Libby, thank you for letting me visit. I trust you're feeling better. May I sit? (*He sits.*) You're shy when I come around. I want you to get to know me. I think about you every day.

Libby: Do you?

Butterworth: Every day. I see all kinds of students. I try to head a college ethically in these troubled times. When crimes go unreported and poor merit wins honor. There's no real defense against senseless crime today. Yet we must continue to trust others. I want your trust, Libby. I intend to earn it. (*Pause*) I've exciting news. An important donor has paid your full tuition. An extraordinary scholarship. Libby?

Libby: Thank you.

Butterworth: Four paid years. The award should give you peace of mind. "Peace of mind"—wonderful words. (*Pause*) When our endowment reaches a hundred million, I too will have peace of mind. And more deserving students will be assisted.

Libby: I'm not deserving.

Butterworth: On the contrary.

Libby: Who do I blame?

Butterworth: *Whom* do I blame? (*Pause*) Give us time to complete the investigation. We're combing through this extremely carefully. Justice will be served.

Libby: I truly doubt that.

Butterworth: Libby, what are your three favorite books?

Libby: What?

Butterworth: Mine are Cleaver's *Soul on Ice*, Wright's *Native Son*, and Friedan's *Feminine Mystique*. Evolution of ideas and empowerment to the—

Libby: Disfranchised.

Butterworth: Exactly. Power climbs and falls under a steady roll of conflict. Conflict regarding race, class, or sex. I'm reminded by the disturbing allegory in Mamet's college drama *Oleanna*.

Libby: I've seen the film.

Butterworth: Not a great film. It lacked balance and the right songs on its sound track. But the story generated debate.

Libby: You need two sides for a debate.

Butterworth: Perfectly so, two credible sides. Mamet gave his sympathy to the professor. Yet the student—

Libby: Was fucked up and confused.

Butterworth: Woefully so. And she grew marvelously into a malevolent Maoist man-hating monster. A willful decoy? An idiot savant? Mata Hari on roller blades?

Libby: What do you think?

Butterworth: It's more important to know what you think.

Libby (*Reluctantly*): She has a face. Somewhere. And a soul. I think the writer's a jerk.

Butterworth: An excellent comment, Libby. (*Pause*) When Mamet asked for a black to play the professor onstage in L.A., the theater balked.

Libby: What's the point?

Butterworth: Academic violence. Repressed animosities as in Freud's seminal *Civilization and Its Discontents*.

Libby: "Seminal" is such a male word.

Butterworth: Yes, indeed.

Libby: I'm getting a migraine.

Butterworth: Oh, dear. Then I won't stay long. (*Pause*) Libby . . . somehow you fell prey.

Libby: Prey?

Butterworth: To campus violence and public libel. I wish it were fiction.

Libby: My life is not a fiction.

Butterworth: I know that.

Libby: Do you? Black school groups want me like a political football. Campus whites just want to kick my ass. And your office treats this like a Sunday parking violation.

Butterworth: I've dispatched security escorts for you day and night. We've covered your medical bills, contacted your professors, and muzzled the press. We've a few leads, my child. But we'll apprehend the offenders.

Libby: And if it's Spenser and the others from football?

Butterworth: Football gets no special privileges here.

Libby: It was Spenser, Dr. Butterworth.

Butterworth: You said it was dark and you were hit from behind.

Libby: I remember now how he kept talking.

Butterworth: You recognized Spenser's voice?

Libby: I have my suspicions.

Butterworth: Then I'll interrogate him. (*Pause*) I've spoken to your roommate. She's worried about your mental health. You know, I've a daughter your age and equally troubled.

Libby: Is she scared to go out at night?

Butterworth: Yes.

Libby: There are evil people here.

Butterworth: And good people. Rich and poor. Black and white. A remarkable college devoted to truth, poise, and culture.

Libby: Poison culture. Toxic culture.

Butterworth: "Poise" is a more wonderful word. Embodying spiritual grace.

Libby: You're talking to yourself.

Butterworth: Forgive me. It would be nice to learn of your forgiveness.

Libby: My forgiveness?

Butterworth: "Forgiveness" is a wonderful word.

Libby: I can't forgive you or the school.

Butterworth: Let's try. We'd all sleep easier.

Libby: Sleep like a baby. "Baby" is a wonderful word.

SCENE 7

(*Mt. Soledad, evening*)

Vetter: Windy up here. Are you cold?

Lyla: Uh-huh. (*He offers his sweater. She accepts.*)

Vetter: You're angry at me.

Lyla: No.

Vetter: We used to make love every night.

Lyla: You brought me here on our first date.

Vetter: It was a difficult date.

Lyla: All blind dates are. You sounded like a shark over the phone. (*Pause*) But I fell in love with you. Over our first dinner, al dente, al fresco, à la mode.

Vetter: You never told me.

Lyla: It only occurred to me now.

Vetter: Oh?

Lyla: You're still very handsome. And your mouth has so much vulnerability. (*Pause*) Have you ever cheated?

Vetter: Never.

Lyla: Shocked that I ask?

Vetter: Yes.

Lyla: I imagine that other women are making moves on you, despite your occasional halo. You're away so many nights. And I don't know myself anymore. It's the strangest sensation. I don't want to lose you. (*She reaches for him. They kiss with feeling.*) I watch you sleep. Cradle you in my arms. Your spirit's gone somewhere.

Vetter: I think I'm fighting a depression, Lyla. Work-related. It will go away. I've had these things before. Don't be upset with me. (*Pause*)

Beautiful view of the ocean. The crowd's died down. They come here by the droves.

Lyla: The statue's hideous.

Vetter: Because we both left Catholicism.

Lyla: No loss on either side, Bruce.

Vetter: What if we can't have children?

Lyla: You ask the question a lot.

Vetter: Do I? (*Pause*) I know what you really want. You're not happy at work.

Lyla: More happy than you. A librarian doesn't take the job home. (*Pause*) I had lunch the other day with the provost's wife. The faculty can't fathom Butterworth's behavior. He's so caught up with the black coed.

Vetter: He suspects a few football kids but just won't act on it yet.

Lyla: Then he's a monster.

Vetter: Not a monster, Lyla. Just a coward with some virtues. For better or worse, I believe in the college.

Lyla: The provost's wife also talked about his dalliances.

Vetter: Pure hearsay.

Lyla: One or two boys that tend his garden?

Vetter: Totally laughable.

Lyla: I'm not laughing, Bruce. I'm fighting a depression too.

SCENE 8

(*Butterworth's office. As adversaries, they stay charming throughout the scene.*)

Kincaid: You wanted to see me?

Butterworth: Yes, Professor Kincaid. Thank you for coming in. Please sit. (*Motions to either chair*)

Kincaid: You spoke to my chairman.

Butterworth: The college is reviewing the new course offerings.

Kincaid: I see.

Butterworth: The Kirshner Report.

Kincaid: Wasn't Kirshner shipped to the Hoover Institute?

Butterworth: He came back, replenished with a hair weave.

Kincaid: I gather you made the appointment. Should I be worried?

Butterworth: Of course not.

Kincaid: It's not a witch-hunt?

Butterworth: Not in the least. This isn't the '50s.

Kincaid: There have been rumors.

Butterworth: When haven't there been rumors? You're back teaching Seuss's *Cat in the Hat*?

Kincaid: Among other books.

Butterworth: Under the rubric of Lacanian feminist psychoanalysis?

Kincaid: A very popular class.

Butterworth: Yes, wonderful numbers. Yet I found the syllabus . . . curious. Mind you, I'm an Italian medieval specialist removed from "the hit parade." Several onsite reviewers have taken issue with . . .

Kincaid:	**Butterworth:**
Please, stop right there.	. . . issue with . .

Kincaid: Dr. Butterworth.

Butterworth: In midsentence, I miss the trapeze.

Kincaid: The course has garnered extraordinary student evaluations.

Butterworth: So has Goldblum's New Age Cajun Cooking class. Your reading list lacks rigor, ardor, consistency.

Kincaid: You love those words.

Butterworth and Kincaid: Rigor, ardor, consistency.

Butterworth: Leave pop psychobabble and crackpot semiotics to our less-gifted junior faculty and stick with Aristotle and Kant. Of course, your chair agrees.

Kincaid: This is out of your jurisdiction.

Butterworth: I beg to differ.

Kincaid: You're picking a fight, Doctor.

Butterworth: Your courses impact our fund-raising efforts and—

Kincaid: I doubt that.

Butterworth: —accreditation. Then you're in a denial, my dear.

Kincaid: I'm our leading campus speaker on the national circuit and a frequent lecturer at Yale.

Butterworth: Indeed, I'm as mystified as the next person. The media has frequently cited Yale's disfranchised alumni. Their contributions falling like a biblical curse. So, after a decade of decline, Yale's redoubled Western studies. The lesson's quite clear. Unlike you and your cabal, I don't believe that Socrates was *necessarily* a hip black Athenian in a dashiki who supported, *wholeheartedly,* the first wave of third-world, precolonial radicalism.

Kincaid: You think you're cute.

Butterworth: I wish I were.

Kincaid: I'd prefer to take this up with the Committee on Education Policy.

Butterworth: By all means.

Kincaid: And I'm going to call an ad hoc committee on these sanctions.

Butterworth: Hand out leaflets and e-mail the entire campus on system relay.

Kincaid (*About to exit, faux tenderly*): Thank you for tipping your hand, *my dear.*

Butterworth: You only get one wake-up call here, Marilyn.

Kincaid: Is that a threat?

Butterworth: No, I'm starting a chic concierge service.

Kincaid: There's a tenet in our charter called "academic freedom."

Butterworth: There's also a preamble in praise of common sense. I've nothing against Dr. Seuss. He's brought distinction to children's lit. My kids grew up with him, and we still have a few of his tall hats. I also admire Gertrude Stein and the very musical John Cage. But the party's over. Your golden coach is now a pumpkin. This isn't The New School in Manhattan. You're not Camille Paglia and, happily, I'm not Marshall McCluhan. Good day, professor.

SCENE 9

(*Libby's apartment. Halloween.*)

Bibi: Going to the Halloween party?

Libby: I don't have a date.

Bibi: Be my date.

Libby: Don't have a costume.

Bibi: Screw it. We'll mousse up, throw on some housecoats and Day-Glo lipstick. There's a wired, albino reggae band from Salt Lake playing all night. Okay?

Libby: Do you think I'm attractive?

Bibi: Very.

Libby: How so?

Bibi: In the shower you're cuter than Vanessa Williams.

Libby: No one notices me like that anymore.

Bibi: Showers are private, Miss America, and baths take forever. You hog the bathroom.

Libby: I keep dreaming about my mother.

Bibi: Good or bad dreams?

Libby: I see her in rags washing my laundry. She stares at me but says nothing. Then I cry. There's a clothesline, wind blowing hard, sunny day. I hear her voice singing.

Bibi: You miss her.

Libby: I need her.

Bibi: My mother adores you.

Libby: I know.

Bibi: You can call her anytime. I mean that.

Libby: Thanks, Bibi.

Bibi (*Pause*): Butterworth came again today.

Libby: Trick or treat?

Bibi: He's trying really hard.

Libby: You spoke to him, didn't you?

Bibi: Briefly.

Libby: What did you say?

Bibi: Nothing really.

Libby: Don't betray me, Bibi. A lot of shit's going on and it's driving me crazy.

Bibi: What does Butterworth want that's so awful?

Libby: He wants me docile like a lamb for the price of a full scholarship.

Bibi: That's a lot of money.

Libby: It feels wrong. And I feel cheap. All the while he's obsessed with Dr. Seuss and the pink mess.

Bibi: Seuss from biochem?

Libby: *Cat in the Hat* Seuss.

Bibi: You're kidding?

Libby: A sick puppy. How did he ever get to be the president?

Bibi: Talk to a counselor.

Libby: I'm going to the police.

Bibi: And say what?

Libby: I was attacked and the fucking college sat on the news.

Bibi: Then what?

Libby: Then Butterworth breaks a sweat.

Bibi: Sometimes your memory's cloudy.

Libby: Bibi . . .

Bibi: First you said you were robbed. Then you said it was a rape. Later it was just racial hazing.

Libby: I was half-conscious.

Bibi: This hurts your credibility. Look, you were picked on at the top of the semester. I know it. You know it. But you acted out with these football shitheads. That didn't help things.

Libby: Are you doubting me?

Bibi: I'm not doubting you.

Libby: I didn't act out with these creeps.

Bibi: I'm sorry. I don't know what I'd do if I were you. No choice is easy. Maybe you have to go to the police.

Libby: I didn't act out, Bibi.

Bibi: But I know how the police are. You don't need to get slammed all over again if there's a half-assed investigation. Seek counseling. Get your story straight. Don't embellish a thing. Then talk to a good lawyer. Otherwise you're playing with fire.

SCENE 10

Butterworth's office

Vetter: It's in all the papers. Our shy little angel gave an exclusive to the *L.A. Times*.

Butterworth: I expected this.

Vetter: Are you taking their calls?

Butterworth: No. Absolutely no interviews. It's too premature. We don't want to make a faux pas.

Vetter: What about the five students?

Butterworth: They can't be named. It's still a campus matter.

Vetter: Harold . . .

Butterworth: One's under eighteen and his folks are big contributors. Besides, the allegations are totally contradictory.

Vetter: Have you spoken to the police?

Butterworth: Yes, they'll work with us when we're ready.

Vetter: You're just sticking your neck out again.

Butterworth: There's no other choice.

Vetter: Turn it over to the police now.

Doris (*Offstage, over the intercom*): Mr. MacAlister to see you.

Butterworth: Doris, not now.

Doris (*Offstage*): He insists.

Butterworth: Hell's bells. Send him in. (*To Vetter*) Stay. You loath surprises as much as I. (*MacAlister enters.*) Good afternoon.

MacAlister: Gentlemen. Such atrocious news over the radio. And I, for one, am appalled.

Vetter: We all are.

MacAlister: That girl is like a ticking time bomb. How difficult these incidents are. It's the talk of the town now. You need to act quickly, my friends, to counter this adverse publicity. I intend to do my part. Ten million dollars is a large, round number.

Vetter:	**Butterworth:**
Very round.	Very large.

MacAlister: And twenty five million?

Vetter:	**Butterworth:**
Very large!	Very round!

MacAlister: My lawyers like grand gestures. Perhaps they work on commission. Your college's a growing cesspool for scandal.

Butterworth: Compared to last week's Harvard dormitory murder?

MacAlister: Poor consolation. (*Pause*) Decisive action, gentlemen. Apropos your faculty problem. Rein in the troublemakers. For those who cannot adjust, boot them out. (*Places two checks on the desk*) One's signed. The other isn't. The smaller check will buy two dozen golden parachutes for the renegade profs.

Butterworth: Downsizing isn't that simple.

MacAlister: It is. There's fifty million on the table.

Butterworth/Vetter: Fifty million?

MacAlister: Look at the checks. Places this campus nationally and you're out of the woods.

Butterworth: What can I say?

Vetter: Unbelievable.

Butterworth: Too good to be true.

MacAlister: Perhaps. One last condition: these five sodomites must be punished.

Butterworth: Yes, with due process.

MacAlister: Skip the legal means.

Vetter: What are you suggesting?

MacAlister: Tough love. Corporal punishment.

Butterworth: Paddles and lashes?

MacAlister: Chains and hot coals. Singapore-style. Our courts are a farce.

Vetter (*Unsure of MacAlister's hyperbole*): We're not Singapore.

MacAlister: Why pretend to be Tahiti?

Butterworth: Mr. MacAlister . . .

MacAlister: Pay off some animal frat house to do it.

Butterworth: Mr. MacAlister . . .

MacAlister: An illicit extramural activity.

Vetter: And if none are guilty?

MacAlister: *Someone's* guilty.

Butterworth: This would never fly in the court.

Vetter: Or in the court of public opinion.

Butterworth: We'd be saddled with astronomical litigation.

MacAlister: I'll cover any liability. You'd be surprised what can be settled out of court.

Butterworth: Still, editorials would have a field day.

Vetter: Torture went out with the Dark Ages.

MacAlister: Vetter, this *is* the return of the Dark Ages.

Butterworth: Why are you so attached to this case?

MacAlister: I feel terribly for this girl.

Butterworth: We all do.

MacAlister: She deserves recompense. These young scum must suffer in a profound way. Not walk like the New York punks from St. John's.

Butterworth: St. John's kicked them out ten years ago.

MacAlister: While the Jamaican girl was humiliated for life? (*Pause*) Fifty million. On the table. The clock's ticking.

Butterworth: I need to meet with my board. I can't act alone.

MacAlister: You've twenty-four hours to have that second check signed. You know where to reach me.

SCENE 11

(*Libby's apartment*)

Vetter: I want to apologize. We were wrong to keep this from the police for so long.

Libby: It doesn't matter.

Vetter: But it does. Totally inexcusable. I don't sleep well at night. You must accept my apologies. (*Pause*) We're now taking big steps.

Libby: Not with me.

Vetter: Libby, we can't do anything without you.

Libby: I don't trust the college or the cops. I'm just another art student. My mind only on painting. I avoid sororities and everything that's bullshit. Don't want to pass for vanilla or chocolate in this Disney theme park. (*Pause*) I wish my mother were alive. I really do. You're different than Butterworth. I know you're trying to do right by me, but it's way too late. Please go.

(*Vetter starts to exit.*)

Libby: I know why Butterworth kept it quiet.

Vetter: Why?

Libby: He's close to one of the boys.

Vetter: What?

Libby: Very intimate.

Vetter: That's ludicrous.

Libby: I checked around. People thought Oscar was his nephew.

Vetter: What the hell are you saying?

Libby: Ask Butterball. You know the spin.

Vetter: There's no spin.

Libby: The male nudes in figure class? You know how kids are and love to brag. Oscar spent time with The Man. A fey cottontail toy. Wasn't the only boy to visit Buttermansion. Don't look dumbstruck.

Vetter: He's happily married.

Libby: Sure.

Vetter: Libby, let's forget we ever had this conversation.

Libby: Berendzen, the president of American University, resigned because he made obscene calls to young girls. Nothing's farfetched today. (*Pause*) I met with a lawyer.

Vetter: I want to believe your story. A star athlete like Spenser gets special protection at your expense.

Libby: The campus apologist . . . word perfect.

Vetter: I see it more from your point of view, and I don't care about my job. Like you, I carry a discernible injury.

Libby (*Opening the front door*): Go lick your sad-ass wounds.

SCENE 12

(*Campus café. Later that day.*)

Oscar: What is it?

Libby: Attitude.

Oscar: Mine?

Libby: I keep expecting you to tell the whole story. I know in my bones that you've horrible dreams each night.

Oscar: I do about you.

Libby: Come out with it.

Oscar: Why?

Libby: Sexual dreams?

Oscar: I can't say.

Libby: And if I told you I've those kinds of dreams about you?

Oscar: That would be weird. (*Pause*) You're mocking me, Libby.

Libby: Why would I? It would just piss you off.

Oscar: You're right. So knock it off.

Libby: I know you like a book.

Oscar: You hardly know me.

Libby: Thought you were independent. But you move with the sheep.

Oscar: I have a lot of different friends here.

Libby: I know.

Oscar: While you repulse half the men on campus.

Libby: Which half are you?

Oscar: You bait the wrong kind of guys. (*Pause*) Why don't you leave well enough alone? You got a full scholarship out of this. There was no actual rape. Everyone lucked out.

Libby: You don't like girls.

Oscar: I like girls.

Libby: Did you ever sleep with one?

Oscar: Yeah, right after high school. The back room of a Dunkin' Donuts.

Libby: You found the hole, Einstein?

Oscar: Flip off, Libby.

Libby: I'm sorry.

Oscar: I've been supportive to you through it all.

Libby: And I show no appreciation. Were you ever raped, Oscar?

Oscar: No.

Libby: Did anyone ever force you to go down on them?

Oscar: No.

Libby: It could happen to you. Someday. A cycle of fate. And I bet you'd see things differently. Maybe that's what you dream at night. It's on your face. I see it clearly. Your markings betray your history.

Oscar: That's true for you. There are markings on your face too.

Libby: You're right, Oscar. We have those bonds. Emotional scars from our same high school. (*Pause*) You're pre-med?

Oscar: Yeah.

Libby: So one day you'll be a responsible doctor.

Oscar: I hope. And I'm sorry about what happened. For the twentieth time. I know you were jumped. You had passed out. I was the first to leave. I called campus security. I asked the guys. No one saw anything. And your clothes stayed on.

Libby: What did you see?

Oscar: Nothing. There could've been a loiterer in the building.

Libby: With a guard and logbook at the entrance?

Oscar: People slip in and out.

Libby: Yeah, they sure do. Casper the ghost.

Oscar: I'm telling you the full truth. (*Pause*) I'd like to hold you right now.

Libby: Why?

Oscar: We'd trust one another again.

Libby: Doctor Feelgood?

Oscar: Libby. Please. (*He reaches for her in a long embrace.*) I got to go.

Libby: Are you gay, Oscar?

Oscar: No.

Libby: For Christ's sake.

Oscar: I got to go.

Libby: I'm not an idiot. Spill it. Saying so would make total sense.

Oscar: Okay, I'm bisexual.

Libby: You didn't touch me, but you watched. To be one of the guys. Right? Who started it?

Oscar: Talk to Spenser.

Libby: I will. But I want to hear it from you in plain English.

Oscar: Spenser was the last to leave. He'll get slammed before the end of the year. Someone close to him will talk.

Libby: I doubt it. I really doubt it. That's all you can say?

SCENE 13

(*Butterworth's office*)

Butterworth: I spoke to the board. They must have thought I was out of my mind. They were mortified.

Vetter: What did you expect?

Butterworth: The impossible. I'm not thinking rationally.

Vetter: I don't know what to say. The school's headed for a horrid reckoning.

Butterworth: Exactly my words to the board.

Vetter: Why not approach the boys' families, cushion the blow, transfer them to San Diego State with full tuition credits?

Butterworth: And if they balk?

Vetter: They'll be open to the idea rather than risk criminal prosecution.

Butterworth: It's not that simple, with the legal team they just picked up and discrepancies among the witnesses.

Vetter: Then summary expulsion. There's now enough evidence for a campus procedure according to counsel.

Butterworth: Academic due process takes months. Even with summary expulsion, MacAlister expects something more punishing.

Vetter: We'll stage a charade.

Butterworth: Vetter.

Vetter: Tussled by "Sigma Gamma Knuckle." We'll leak a report to the press about an off-campus attack on the football team and doctor up some bruised photos.

Butterworth: You've been drinking.

Vetter: A few martinis at lunch.

Butterworth: I'm tired of charades.

Vetter: Thousands of future students mean more than—

Butterworth: Five culpable freshman?

Vetter: Yes.

Butterworth: We can ease MacAlister's curricula demands while buying out some nettlesome faculty, but I must draw a line somewhere. I was up all night with my wife talking through every possible angle. If MacAlister has a genuine conscience, he'll meet us halfway.

Vetter: I talked with Libby yesterday.

Butterworth: More press interviews?

Vetter: Yes. She's lost her reticence. This is getting increasingly ugly.

Butterworth: Libby has a history of mood disorders. It's in her medical file.

Vetter: Harold, she claims to have information about a liaison between you and one of the boys.

Butterworth: A liaison?

Vetter: Yeah.

Butterworth: Get real.

Vetter: She sounded very assured and credible.

Butterworth: So did Squeaky Fromme and Linda Tripp.

Vetter: This girl is very, very angry at the school, and I think she won't stop until satisfied.

Butterworth: Vetter, we're talking about an exceptionally mixed-up young adult.

Vetter: You know the names that are tied to these allegations.

Butterworth: I don't. Do you?

Vetter: I don't want to know some things. I really don't.

Butterworth: The girl's out of her mind. Has this hit the press?

Vetter: Not yet. We've countered one libel suit last year on this accusation and a few crackpot stories on the Net. Now Libby's in the spotlight about to say very damning things.

Butterworth: This is not the end of the world.

Vetter: You said you were tired of charades.

Butterworth: You want to walk away from me?

Vetter: I didn't say that.

Butterworth: What are you saying?

Vetter: Where are we in terms of your character?

Butterworth: What do you want to hear?

Vetter: The truth, Harold. I feel like an attorney feigning ignorance.

Butterworth: You're really pissing me off.

Vetter: I'm sorry. Goddamn it. (*Pause*) What's your connection to Oscar Tucker?

Butterworth: Oscar Tucker?

Vetter: Yes.

Butterworth: Work-study landscaping my home. Care to check?

Vetter: Did you have any form of sexual intimacy with this student? Libby said Oscar's ready to come forward.

Butterworth: Christ Almighty.

Vetter: Whatever you say won't go beyond this office.

Butterworth: Get the hell out of here, Vetter!

SCENE 14

(*Kincaid's lecture with slides*)

Kincaid: American mythology strikes theorists from Derrida to Foucault as derivative, eclectic, perverse. While I can agree with the first two qualities—and strongly—it is the third that I find most fascinating and contentious. In the various icons we've covered this semester, there has been a strikingly bold, running motif. Namely, our country's exponential scale and vulgar fixations. Elephantiasis, a feature that captures our narcissistic imagination and our wide-angle lens, is definitively American. From Paul Bunyan to the imponderable Grand Canyon, we experience the New World's abundance, dominance, and mutated overgrowth. Through giant dimensions we embrace kitsch and perhaps God's perverse humor for this hemisphere. In lieu of traditional aesthetic values, kitsch reflects our unconscious irreverence, our affinity with the gutter, our profound, uncultured naïveté. To catch the eye, American art prefers pre-adolescent primary colors, unsubtle symbols, and mammoth monstrosities. We celebrate rap's baggy clothes, monster trucks, oversized SUVs, nomadic Winnebagos, and useless tonnage from the Price Club. Onscreen, lovable Hanks in *Big* and the retromythic *Forrest Gump*, Morenas in *Honey, I Blew Up the Kids*, DiCaprio's waterlogged *Titanic*, Crow in *Gladiator*, *X-Men* galore. Ever-expanding American ethos. (*Pause*) The extraordinary five-hundred-foot cross of *The Valley of the Fallen*, north of Madrid, was Franco's example of Spanish scale gone wrong. Scale gone Loony Tunes. More typically, as Americans, we think of Mount Rushmore, Wilt Chamberlain's ten thousand conquests and the ubiquitous Bob's Big Boy auctioned off at Sotheby's. Which brings us to the miraculous emergence of our fifty-foot fusion Madonna—Our Lady of Wax 'n' Surf. Inches taller and far more controversial than Mt. Soledad's world war veteran's cross. Crass, unforgettable, and—finally—in all her star spontaneity, glorious. A true sign of our Hollywood's Golden Age. At dawn, the sly-powdered bitch winks. The Tinsel Sphinx of California, claimed by no L.A. studio. I urge you to worship her in your own way as I do in mine. She is our holy, extemporaneous totem.

SCENE 15

(*Campus drawing class*)

MacAlister: Excuse me. Your line is quite fluent and lyrical. Brilliant, actually.

Libby: Uh-huh. (*Not looking up*)

MacAlister: So I am told. Color evades me along with spatial composition. But I do believe I can sense the moving line of your delicate hand. With the push of my outstretched finger. Your feel for portraiture is strong and full of feeling, young lady. I've talked to your art teachers. Name is Ian MacAlister.

Libby (*Looking up*): MacAlister?

MacAlister: The man behind your scholarship. You've missed several classes.

Libby: Yeah.

MacAlister: Under the circumstances, I can understand. Well, it's good that you're back taking classes.

Libby: How long have you been standing there?

MacAlister: Nearly twenty-one years.

Libby: I felt your eyes on me.

MacAlister: I wanted contact. I like this campus very much. Always have. Trees, fountains, wind chimes, elves. I was once a student here. I told the college that I wouldn't look for you, but my impulses got the better of me. You should know that. My shyness in your presence. A clumsy furrier who was rather mediocre at college.

Libby: What do you want from me?

MacAlister: I'm not sure. I want to answer truthfully, yet how can I? I've heard you on TV and radio. I'd like to take away your anger.

Libby: It's not for sale.

MacAlister: I didn't mean that. You can't buy a person.

Libby: Happens all the time.

MacAlister: Please tell me your life plans.

Libby: I have no plans.

MacAlister: Then tell me your dreams.

Libby: You're making me very uncomfortable. Maybe you ought to take back your scholarship.

MacAlister: That's how I felt at your age.

Libby: No one knows how I feel, Mr. MacAlister. (*Pause*) I don't want to stay in school. It's become a total circus. (*Returns to her drawing*)

MacAlister: I suppose it has. Perhaps it would be best to transfer to another college. Finish your degree. Know that—in our disconnectedness—you matter to me. Next year, things will return to normal. Mark my words.

Libby: Not after this latest round with the college administration.

MacAlister: You're probably right. (*Pause*) Guess my age. Come on. And then I'll leave you in peace.

Libby (*Not looking up*): Sixty?

MacAlister: More or less. Accept your scholarship.

Libby: I haven't earned it.

MacAlister: You have, young lady. You have. (*Presenting calling card*) Here's my number. Call me if ever . . . I won't betray you, and I will never come unannounced again.

SCENE 16

(*Butterworth's office, late at night*)

Butterworth: Years ago I had a crisis of personality. First, as a child, fearing my parents. I got caught watching something forbidden. The first blush of sin. (*Pause*) Later in life, as a college sophomore, I found sexual freedom, sophistication, power, and intellectual immortality. My best friends couldn't stand me, so great was my confidence. (*Pause*) But in middle age, despite my success, a stranger in the mirror addressed me. Mocked me. Few ever saw that side. Not even my wife. Only I knew the stranger thoroughly. I lost myself to him. And my wife's love. An ironic imposter. Fantasies of a young me in an old carriage. I refused the tyranny of my decay. (*Pause*) I began to crave the wrong people. Weak young adults. I took medication. Therapists sought out the demon. But I would not let them invade me. I kept the demon alive. How I despise myself so.

SCENE 17

(*Vetter's home*)

Lyla: Your mother was just arrested.

Vetter: What?

Lyla: Shoplifting. At Sears.

Vetter: Oh, God.

Lyla: The police are questioning her at the station. Shall I come with you?

Vetter: What did she steal?

Lyla: Liz Taylor's Poison. She tried to slip it into her leg cast and the bottle broke. When the store detective grabbed her, she stabbed him with a knitting needle.

Vetter: Oh, Christ!

Lyla: And some visiting Vatican nuns came under attack in the melee. It made the TV news.

Vetter: I thought you were going to keep an eye on her.

Lyla: She skipped out and stole my Volvo. We were out of Corona. It started with a her binge of diet pills, Ben & Jerry's Superfudge, and a loud rerun of "Roseanne" on cable.

Vetter: What if we just leave her there?

Lyla: In jail?

Vetter: For a few days.

Lyla: Bruce.

Vetter: A rehabilitation lesson.

Lyla: She's your mother.

Vetter: I know. Otherwise, she'll never learn. (*Pause*) We'll take my car. What's wrong?

Lyla: I heard from the doctor today.

Vetter: What's up?

Lyla: I'm pregnant.

Vetter: Pregnant?

Lyla: Uh-huh.

Vetter: Lyla?

Lyla: Are you in shock?

Vetter: Yes. (*Pause. Feeling mixed happiness.*) Pregnant?

Lyla: We've been trying for a long time.

Vetter: I know. But . . .

Lyla: How do you really feel?

Vetter: Tremendous happiness. (*Pause*) I guess infrequency is the key to fertility. (*Pause*) You look strange.

Lyla: Do I?

Vetter: You do. What's wrong?

Lyla: Nothing.

Vetter: Lyla.

Lyla: How do I start? (*Pause*) Sit down, Bruce.

Vetter: Oh, Jesus.

Lyla: It may not be yours.

Vetter: What?

Lyla: I'm not joking, darling. (*Silence*) I'm sorry.

Vetter: Lyla? You've just destroyed me.

Lyla: I'm sorry. Maybe you'll feel different over time.

Vetter: Are you nuts?

Lyla: No.

Vetter: Then I must be.

Lyla: You're not.

Vetter: But I must be very thick.

Lyla: We've both been distracted. You've been distant since last spring.

Vetter: Goddamn it. Who are you seeing?

Lyla: No one now.

Vetter: Who? (*Pause*) I have a right to know.

Lyla: It's over.

Vetter: I don't care. Who?

Lyla: Le May.

Vetter: Jack Le May? The dentist?

Lyla: It started with my last cleaning. You know his wife died a year ago last Christmas.

Vetter: Hit and run.

Lyla: Yes. I felt sorry for him.

Vetter: You've started a consolation service?

Lyla: Bruce, he means nothing to me.

Vetter: Jack Le May—Chula Vista's Man of the Year.

Lyla: You have to believe that. We had a few dinners together. I love you, Bruce. I need you. This was my one mistake ever.

Vetter: I don't know what the hell to do. (*Silence*) Honest to God.

Lyla: Please forgive me.

Vetter: What are the choices?

Lyla: I won't go to a clinic.

Vetter: You think I'm sterile.

Lyla: We've been trying for years. I just don't want to lose a child, darling. (*Pause*) I need your love, Bruce. Please understand. Be big of heart. (*Embracing him slowly. Pause.*) *I want this so badly.*

SCENE 18

(*MacAlister's lecture on fur at a local resort hotel*)

MacAlister: The new mood has touched more experienced hands. Karl Lagerfeld, Oscar de la Renta, Valentino, and Jerry Sorbara for Neiman Marcus. All dispensed with the metallic glitz and French ruffles of last year, with today's sporty Royal military coats and fur-trimmed jacket of laminated virgin wool. Even Arnold Scaasi cast aside his mastery of bonbon fashion in celebration of Calvinistic ebullience, most dazzlingly represented by a sleek pink leather coat with an ultraplush fur collar. Mr. de la Renta's furs also indicate that he still searches toward casual, feckless style. The rich metallics and jacquards have been replaced with a simple cow-brown belted fur; a loden-green, slim, ankle-length shearling; a cerise sheared peacoat; and a chaste, classic, honeydew, double-breasted, floor-scraping mink masterpiece.

SCENE 19

(Butterworth's office)

Butterworth: I'm glad you came in, Oscar. You've been on my mind all day. Please, sit. *(Oscar turns and bruises are seen along his profile.)* Good Heavens, what happened to you?

Oscar: I was jumped last night.

Butterworth: Are you all right? *(Rises from his desk chair to approach Oscar)*

Oscar: Some gorillas had some fun.

Butterworth: Robbery?

Oscar: No, a grudge paid back.

Butterworth: Dear Jesus! Did you a doctor? Did you report it? You need to. This is serious.

Oscar: I'll only get in more trouble. You can guess the connections to this.

Butterworth: I see. *(Pause)* Unbelievable. What's happening to this campus? *(Pause)* How are things at home?

Oscar: All right.

Butterworth: Has your father had his surgery?

Oscar: He's out of the hospital, triple bypass. He's on the upswing.

Butterworth: Good.

Oscar: I freak out at V.A. hospitals. The ammonia smell drives me up a wall. *(Pause)* I'm very unglued. Reporters are calling at all hours.

Butterworth: What do you say to them?

Oscar: Nothing.

Butterworth: Oscar, this is deeply uncomfortable. I hope you can find a way to wall off all their questions. *(Closer, about to touch Oscar, but stops)* Never in my wildest dreams would I imagine . . . never. I don't want you to get hurt. Such an innocent lamb. People simply misconstrue your visits.

Oscar: Do you?

Butterworth: No, I don't.

Oscar: And your feelings about me?

Butterworth: We've been through this before.

Oscar: Am I nothing in your eyes?

Butterworth: I never said that.

Oscar: Over champagne you said many things.

Butterworth: Then I'm truly sorry, it should have been Hawaiian Punch.

Oscar: What about your wife?

Butterworth: What?

Oscar: Does she know?

Butterworth: She knows nothing. What should she know?

Oscar: Maybe the truth?

Butterworth: You expect too much from me.

Oscar: What should I expect?

Butterworth: I'd be proud to have you for a son. You're a talent, Oscar.

Oscar: Thank you.

Butterworth: Please don't be flip.

Oscar: I never thought you were my father.

Butterworth: But you did. We enacted a ritual. Back to the Greeks. Such intimate ceremonies are intoxicating. We were drawn into a little dance. We gleaned something pure and magical, but now we must let go. That's how the Greeks conducted themselves. (*Pause*) I apologize from my heart, and I ask for privacy.

Oscar: I don't want apologies. I've lost my privacy. And I want my self-respect back.

Butterworth: I never stole it.

Oscar: You've cheapened me.

Butterworth: Nonsense. And don't look at me like that. How many times had I told you that we had to stop short, that it would be hard on both of us? You have your entire life ahead of you, Oscar, while I'm standing at the precipice. (*Pause*) I have to ask you to leave now.

Oscar: Why do you make conversation so crazy?

Butterworth: I've grown tired and despondent. I've stopped drinking, locked up the Swiss chocolates, and threw away your letters. I'm not a destructive person, Oscar. Never was. But I am an unlucky person. Moreover, I am not a homosexual. I still sleep with my wife. Don't sneer. You have me wrong. Your affection for me was sweet but at this point misguided. Discretion is the soul of good breeding.

Oscar: And you are the soul of discretion?

Butterworth: No, I'm a tragic figure in an untenable farce. Only I know the full extent of exploding contrivance. Antanas Mockus was the rector of Colombia's National University in Bogota. Some years ago he was confronted by a hectoring group of students and he simply dropped his pants and mooned them. He was pushed to resign, of course, but soon became the city's popular new mayor. That can never happen in America. Nor should it ever happen. (*Checking his watch*) What's important is to seek out Libby's assailant and resolve this crisis. It's grown way out of proportion. At the worse possible time. I can't press you for information that you cannot—or will not—divulge. I cannot be compromised by scurrilous ties to you or any other male student in the last ten years. That would be death. This isn't Athens. You're not Alcibiades. I'm not Socrates.

Oscar: But your mansion was Plato's Retreat, Harold.

Butterworth: You mustn't call me Harold. (*Pause*) Never again.

Oscar (*Sardonic*): I had admired your mad love for opera and the exotic garden flowers we planted behind your study. In L.A., your arm went around me during an invited dress rehearsal of *The Rape of Lucretia*. A Benjamin Britten sodomy? No. No. I was in bed with Big Butter. Burning buns and buggery. Sexing sexless Socrates and his famous dirty, noxious feet.

Butterworth: Oscar, aging men have fatal erotic weaknesses. A lesson as compelling as the birds and the bees.

Oscar: Since you decided to end it, I'll decide how to publicize it.

Butterworth (*Tongue-tied*): To continue this, really my boy, passion isn't . . .

Oscar and **Butterworth:** Probity.

Oscar: "Probity" is a wonderful word. Your public life is over, Harold.

Butterworth: I don't like your insinuations. I think I owe you some money. (*Takes out his wallet*)

Oscar: I don't want your filthy money.

Butterworth (*Looking out a window*): That didn't stop you before. Your dad's on disability.

Oscar: Fuck you!

Butterworth: What do you want?

Oscar: My virginity back. My goddamn innocence.

SCENE 20

(*Later that night in Butterworth's office. Loud disco music as Butterworth applies makeup on his face, shakes his hips, begins to dance alone. A door opens. The music stops. He freezes like a deer caught in headlights.*)

SCENE 21

(*The next day. Café.*)

MacAlister: Unbelievable.

Vetter: Absolutely.

MacAlister: I got the news in the middle of the night.

Vetter: It's enough to go on a drinking binge. There's no way to shield this from the press.

MacAlister: And he had a history of this sort of thing?

Vetter: Few knew.

MacAlister: How is his family?

Vetter: Holding up as well as can be expected.

MacAlister: Incredible. My heart goes out to them. No metaphor to such madness. No madness to such metaphor. (*Pause*) I'll work quickly through you, Vetter. Before the campus dispatches a new cretin my way.

Vetter: As you wish.

MacAlister: Butterworth's promises to me must be respected. Eight professors would be let go immediately.

Vetter: Of course.

MacAlister: Some promises were not in writing.

Vetter: I understand, sir.

MacAlister: Further, punishing all five students.

Vetter: No longer necessary. We know the lone assailant.

MacAlister: You do?

Vetter: One student stepped forward. To us, the crime's solved.

MacAlister: Do the police know?

Vetter: The circumstances are awkward. There's an audio of the testimony. Butterworth had a tape. Another tape's floating about. Equally problematic, the student spoke without the presence of an attorney. Our lawyers don't know how to proceed. Some frats roughed up the kid who squealed. Oscar Tucker, a freshman. Apparently, Butterworth knew the witness all along.

MacAlister: But kept it to himself?

Vetter: Expect Jesse Jackson or Louis Farrahkan any day on the heels of a campus race riot—triggered by a lewd football star. (*Pause*) It wasn't rape, thank God. But Spenser did undress her top for the sick sport of it. (*Pause*) Eventually this story will fade away and we can concentrate on your enormous charity. It would be a tribute to Butterworth's good name.

MacAlister: His name is damaged for life, Vetter.

Vetter: Schizophrenia isn't a sin today.

MacAlister: I suppose not.

Vetter: Thanks to your generosity, the college expects its focus to shift. Each semester a handful of professors will be pink-slipped or given ample retirement packages. And by closing one or two departments we've skirted the issue of tenure. A clean sweep.

MacAlister: I thank the trustees.

Vetter: And they thank you. (*Pause*) As to Libby leaving campus, we've tried to convince her otherwise.

MacAlister: I spoke to her. She wants to go to Cal Arts next semester. (*Pause*) How long will Butterworth be under observation?

Vetter: Fifteen days.

MacAlister: And then?

Vetter: He has a second home in Catalina. I suspect he'll convalesce there.

MacAlister: You seem demoralized.

Vetter: I pity his family. This is an impossible ordeal. His wife is shattered. (*Pause*) In a year, perhaps, he could return to teach a class or two, but his career is effectively over.

MacAlister: You've been very honest with me, Vetter.

Vetter: Thank you.

MacAlister: You must live for this school.

Vetter: I'll try to reduce my hours. I'm a very stupid man. I've neglected my wife for an entire year.

MacAlister: On the contrary. Your wife's indiscretion is quite understandable. I've tapped your phone. I always know more than I should. (*Pause*) I haven't been totally honest with you. I can't afford the risk.

Vetter: Mr. MacAlister . . .

MacAlister: Hear me out. I have sinned horribly, and I'm running out of time.

Vetter: I'm not a priest.

MacAlister: Shut up and listen. I've had my share of affairs, but there was one true love. Twenty years ago I was with an angel who had a beautiful baby. I was the father, of that I'm certain. A most clandestine romance. We were never seen in public. Just motels and that sort of thing. I wanted to marry her when I found the courage. The woman ran away despite my good intentions. I hired detectives. She made a practice of changing her name. Inspired by flowers and colorful shrubs. Years later she surfaced with our daughter. There was an attempt to reconcile. Again, race was the issue. (*Pause*) She ran away a second time. Then, last autumn, I was able to track them to San Diego, only to discover that she had died. Ovarian cancer. I was devastated. Yet my daughter was here in town, going to my alma mater. You see, her mother was black. (*Pause*) A rose is a rose is a . . .

Vetter: Rhododendron? (*Pause*) If all that's true, why attack multicultural studies?

MacAlister: I don't know. It panders to racial enclaves and academic ghettos.

Vetter: What about affirmative action?

MacAlister: Maybe we're all hypocrites. How do you favor one group over another in today's world? My child and I need a common, connecting culture. Isn't that plain enough? Ebonics is not a second American language.

Vetter: Are you certain she's yours?

MacAlister: I've hospital records and her birth certificate. Any lab can run tests on us. She's lighter than her mother. I have no doubts about this. Yet she will, believing her father died long ago.

Vetter: When will you tell her?

MacAlister: I thought I should get to know her first. Let a few days go by and break it to her indirectly. (*Pause*) Vetter, I want you to tell Libby the news.

Vetter: Me?

MacAlister: You can convey this more smoothly than I could. It's the least you can do as we conclude things. Agreed?

SCENE 22

(*President's office*)

Kincaid: Libby, I know the hell you went through. The police and the press can only do so much, and clearly the college has bungled everything since the attack six weeks ago. (*Pause*) You aren't alone. Women know these criminal things. With our eyes closed. We see each other in the dark. Under threat of a bestial world. We are quite injured. An irresistible case for Goddess worship and the end of paterfamilias. (*Pause*) Let's not forget this was also a racial attack. Exasperated by an indifferent team of white male administrators. We know that Butterworth kept things from view. But I'm stepping in. I'll smash the perpetrator. And I won't stop until I'm done. (*Pause*) I spoke with your roommate. She worries about your emotional health. Perhaps we should acknowledge this to the public. College students are fragile. I'll make this campus safer. There's a flame in my heart. I want women never to look back in fear. We are decendants of brave St. Joan. The Goddess is gazing at us. We need her. She is you and me and every child's mother. When we cry so, she is our mother in the sky. She is Mother Theresa and Florence Nightingale and Emma Goldman and a thousand other immortals. (*She turns Libby's chin.*) Please. Is there something else to tell me?

Libby: I've been to Mt. Soledad. The mystery Madonna's just a statue from Spielberg's Dreamworks Studio.

Kincaid: The Goddess is a metaphor, Libby. And metaphors can come from the most unlikely places. As the chair of this Executive Committee, I've read the police and campus files, the student affidavits. There are wild, incongruous reversals in your statement. Have you falsified anything?

Libby: No.

Kincaid: You're aware of the discrepancies?

Libby: What do you want from me?

Kincaid: The most compelling litigious truth. I want your complete account of Butterworth's obfuscation.

Libby: And in return?

Kincaid: You get Isis, Virginia Woolf, and Wonder Woman in one pair of stiletto shoes.

Libby: Why should I trust you over the next stick figure?

Kincaid: Because throughout her academic career Marilyn Kincaid has never disappointed a young woman in need.

SCENE 23

(*President's office*)

Kincaid: Nice to meet you finally, Mr. MacAlister, and to know that you made time for this meeting.

MacAlister: Nothing's more important to me.

Kincaid: Good.

MacAlister: Actually, I sat in on your lecture some time ago. *Cat in the Hat*?

Kincaid: I'm flattered. The events of late have taken us by storm. As you know, I'm on the Executive Committee.

MacAlister: Yes.

Kincaid: It's not an easy task.

MacAlister: Not at all.

Kincaid: The committee is aware of your large role in our Century Endowment Drive. Naturally, we don't want to drift and risk our good audience with you. Until we know who will head the university, as chair of this committee I've been appointed to oversee fund-raising and complete all unpaid pledges. (*Pause*) Bruce Vetter handed me your list of demands. I'd rather we start totally unfettered by past assumptions.

MacAlister: Our lives are built on past assumptions, Dr. Kincaid.

Kincaid: Then let's build a new habit of behavior and a creative new partnership. I want to serve your best interests, not just old assumptions.

MacAlister: In 1991, a female professor at Penn State said that Goya's *Naked Maja* in her classroom constituted sexual harassment. What is her assumption?

Kincaid: I don't quite understand.

MacAlister: You wrote on her behalf. The professor believed the painting—I quote—"prompted fantasies among her male students that made her workplace a pornographic territory"—unquote.

Kincaid: An *erotic* territory. I did not say "pornographic."

MacAlister: And in your piece from *The Atlantic Monthly:* "The crude violence released in highbrow *pornography* seen by heterosexist ideology linked with . . ."

Kincaid: You commit all my phrases to memory?

MacAlister: ". . . pictorial realism and raw naked seduction."

Kincaid: What is your point, Mr. MacAlister? (*Pause*) I gather you revere Goya.

MacAlister: When I had sight as a young man, his canvases enthralled me.

Kincaid: This isn't about Goya.

MacAlister: You continue to publish letters in support of that professor.

Kincaid: We're not focusing on Penn State. Reality resides here with our avalanche of debt. (*Pause*) I wasn't privileged to your discussions with Butterworth, but I realize your extreme goals. We'll find a happy medium.

MacAlister: Dr. Kincaid, there are no happy mediums.

Kincaid: Let's imagine there are. We need you to help us find them.

MacAlister: You have my list of names.

Kincaid: Those are *tenured* names. *My name* is on the list. *No one* will be let go.

MacAlister: Are you speaking for yourself or for the entire committee?

Kincaid: It doesn't matter.

MacAlister: Nothing is nobler than self-sacrifice.

Kincaid: Don't bully us, Mr. MacAlister.

MacAlister: I am not a bully.

Kincaid: You shall not shackle our way of being. That wouldn't be good for the university.

MacAlister: Who is the university?

Kincaid: The students. Staff. Faculty.

MacAlister: And what about Goya?

Kincaid: Please don't be absurd. Be aware that there's a motion by the board to make me president.

MacAlister: Who nominated you?

Kincaid: For your information, I was voted Professor of the Year in '88, '91, and '95.

MacAlister: Did you campaign on MTV?

Kincaid (*Amused*): Let me impress upon you some numbers. Less than 22 percent of American tenured faculty are women. Few are provosts or university heads. When seen by rank, women are paid 15 percent less than men. Half the names on your list are women.

MacAlister: The bone I pick is not a gender issue, professor. Simply pedagogical content. Butterworth gave me certain assurances.

Kincaid: Know that he racked up thousands of college dollars on 1-900 phone calls. (*Pause*) I'll make a deal with you, Mr. MacAlister. In a few years most of the names on your hit list will have left our faculty without coercion. I give you my word of honor on that. We welcome your financial support and will return the gesture without dismantling our entire academic foundation, which works quite well for now. (*Pause*) But I warn you that I, unlike Butterworth, will hold to certain unwavering principles. Do we have a deal?

SCENE 24

(*Campus café*)

Libby: You don't look so bad.

Oscar: It was three days ago.

Libby: Any stitches?

Oscar: No. Did you send those goons?

Libby: If I said I didn't you'd think I was the dumbest liar. If I did, just another vengeful bitch.

Oscar: So which is it?

Libby: I didn't have a thing to do with it, Oscar.

Oscar: Do you think I got what I deserved?

Libby: That's not for me to say.

Oscar: You should answer for some things.

Libby: I wish I never came to this campus. I wish I were twenty years older with a new identity. I wish there were no colors to race. I wish you had the balls to help me six weeks ago.

Oscar: We are the way the Good Lord made us.

Libby: Quite an original thought.

Oscar: I suppose not.

Libby: You could have been expelled.

Oscar: Accessory to a crime. Lucky me.

Libby: Were I your sister, would it all be different?

Oscar: I have three sisters. I don't need a fourth.

Libby: That's not what I asked.

Oscar: Okay, I'm an asshole. Guys like me spend years repenting for nothing permanent. Entire religions were created for us. We're like Switzerland during Hitler. We don't pay reparations if we're not fingered. But it doesn't matter now. Everything's out in the open.

Libby: You had a crush on Spenser.

Oscar: Yeah.

Libby: Spenser's the biggest shit on campus.

Oscar: But what a beautiful pinup. He kissed me once when he got drunk after the first home game. That was the start to everything. He thought you had seen us in the bedroom at the party.

Libby: I did.

Oscar: End of mystery.

Libby: And now you shoved Butterworth over the edge.

Oscar: We both gave him a good shove. Take credit for something.

Libby: I suppose we did. How you feel about it?

Oscar: Shame. He had a good side. He gave me a lot of money during a rough time. Revenge, the morning after, is not sweet. And you?

Libby: It's like slaying a parent and awakening to one almost worst.

Oscar: Kincaid?

Libby: Like the wicked witch from Oz. She's insufferable. (*Pause*) I actually miss Butterworth. I pity his family.

SCENE 25

(*Hospital room. Butterworth's in a robe, heavily medicated.*)

Kincaid: I didn't mean to wake you.

Butterworth: Just drifting.

Kincaid: The doctors won't allow me to stay long.

Butterworth: You cut your hair?

Kincaid: A recent styling.

Butterworth: Very flattering. Never too late for a make-over. (*Pause*) Dr. Ruth Simons was named president of Smith.

Kincaid: Yes, the first black to head an elite women's college.

Butterworth: Very good of Smith College.

Kincaid: It's generating excitement around academe.

Butterworth: I've tried to keep up with the newspapers, but they only give me *USA Today*.

Kincaid: You look healthier.

Butterworth: I'm off the heavy medication.

Kincaid: Good.

Butterworth: Haldol, I believe, now. Makes you walk like a zombie and pee like a Roman fountain.

Kincaid: Doctor Butterworth, has the board spoken to you?

Butterworth: No.

Kincaid: Well then . . .

Butterworth: My wife passed word. Congratulations.

Kincaid: Thank you.

Butterworth: You must be very happy.

Kincaid: Indeed I am. It'll be in tomorrow's paper.

Butterworth: Do value your privacy. Move off campus. Off to the mountains if you can.

Kincaid: Of course.

Butterworth: I was too accessible.

Kincaid: Perhaps you were. I need your thinking on MacAlister. We're close to closing the deal.

Butterworth: He can be a difficult S.O.B.

Kincaid: I know.

Butterworth: His demands are still workable. Yield to our attorneys. They're on top of it.

Kincaid: He's changed the terms so many times. We're at wit's end. I've gone over and over the lists. But what does MacAlister really want?

Butterworth: What everyone wants but God. To play God for a day.

Kincaid: He doesn't want a dialogue with me.

Butterworth: Vetter has rapport with MacAlister.

Kincaid: I know. MacAlister's final deadline is tomorrow. I'm prepared to dispense with his gift.

Butterworth: Both you and he know the school cannot afford that. (*Pause*) Do you want my honest view?

Kincaid: Please.

Butterworth: You must do everything you can to keep him on involved. If Mac is going to give fifty million, appoint him to the board.

Kincaid: Impossible.

Butterworth: Kincaid, it only occurred to me after the fact. Kick him upstairs and let the other board members work on him. In the meantime, multicultural studies is a nonstarter. Shelve these topics for now. Rescind tenure or dissolve a few departments after commissioning a blue-ribbon panel. That's what they did at the University of Minnesota. Reward early retirement with another acceleration. Drop affirmative action. Ban skateboards and body piercing on campus. You can return to business as usual after a few years when the red ink vanishes. Our creditors need immediate reassurances. Vetter's good with our big donors. Hold on to him. And presidential charm counts for a lot these days.

Kincaid: You think I've no charm? (*Pause*) I want you to persuade MacAlister to honor his pledge.

Butterworth: From my hospital room?

Kincaid: He wants to visit.

Butterworth: No.

Kincaid: Do it for the college. You'll have his sympathy.

Butterworth: There's no back to this cotton gown. My fat derriere is exposed. I'm truly sorry.

Kincaid: If you want me to protect your pension and . . .

Butterworth: Kincaid.

Kincaid: . . . reputation . . .

Butterworth: My reputation is damaged forever, and, thankfully, you can't touch my pension.

Kincaid: I implore you to help us. You still love the college with all your heart.

Butterworth: Yet I owe you no favors. If Mac wants to see me here, he's free to do so.

SCENE 26

(*Libby and Bibi's apartment. Libby is packing a suitcase.*)

Libby: I left a check on your dresser. That should cover food things and next month's rent.

Bibi: Libby, cut the nonsense.

Libby: I made up my mind.

Bibi: Does the D.A. know you're skipping out?

Libby: No one knows.

Bibi: This is so half-assed, after all the pretrial testimony.

Libby: I'm not going to court. I can't do this anymore. I hate all the attorneys and all the investigators. There's no privacy left. I'm not a basket case. Why did you talk so much about my behavior to all those people?

Bibi: Because of your deteriorating health.

Libby: I'm just fine.

Bibi: You don't sleep anymore. You're not eating well. All your clothes are piling up over the hamper.

Libby: It's like fucking spying on me.

Bibi: You're so damn paranoid. I care for you.

Libby: Why?

Bibi: I just do, dammit.

Libby: Maybe you . . . I don't know anymore. I don't have real friends. Do you know how shitty that feels? So many have dropped away. Now just you. And we were tighter months ago, before any of this crap began. We had our own language. It's gone. We used to confide in each other about everything. No more.

Bibi: Not true.

Libby: That's how it feels. Before you'd favor me over a new date most weekends. Now you have a new boyfriend and I'm alone.

Bibi: My mom thinks you might do better at another school. It's not a bad idea, given all that's gone down.

Libby: I don't want to be a runaway and a freak all my life. I can't think straight and I'm scarred. I thought I loved you yet I may never see you again.

Bibi: No matter what happens we'll stay close, Libby. I know that as fact. The important thing is to work with the D.A. and finish the court proceedings. Those boys have to go through this because you did.

Libby: I can't stand myself. (*Crying*) From the very beginning I've been trouble. (*Bibi holds her.*) I can't stand myself, Bibi.

Bibi: It's okay, baby. It's okay.

SCENE 27

(*President's office*)

Kincaid: Bruce, how do you keep pace?

Vetter: I don't sleep anymore.

Kincaid: I need eight hours' beauty sleep each night.

Vetter: A luxury.

Kincaid: Few luxuries are left. We've several unpleasant choices in front of us. Why don't you sit down. (*He sits.*) Not there. The other chair. (*He moves.*)

I'm very sorry about your marriage. I heard from the girls in the front office. Perhaps the separation will do you both a world of good. Or try marriage counseling? I've had two spectacular divorces. And my second husband died with a mistress in the French Alps a month after the settlement. You'll learn all about prenuptials now. It'll be tough. But we brace ourselves somehow. (*Pause*) I'm here for a full term. You do know that?

Vetter: I know.

Kincaid: And I want very much to send the right message. That should come as no shock. To the public at large and to our inner community. You're Butterworth's man. We can't expect anything else. You carried him far. I know you're loyal. Pragmatic. And often brilliant.

Vetter: "Brilliant"'s a wonderful word.

Kincaid: I've admired your noncombative style. Almost Zen-like.

Vetter: Thank you.

Kincaid: You listen and respect your audience. You bite your lower lip in a very empathic way. You rephrase things in very useful, witty turns and never show strain, even when attacked.

Vetter: But I do, Dr. Kincaid. I feel the strain right now.

Kincaid: Do you? Well, to the issue: a total overhaul is necessary, given the set of scandals. The swifter the better. And we must put the best spin on our changes. A whole new team is needed. More women, more people of color. Therefore, I prefer a woman at the helm of P.R.

Vetter: It's your call.

Kincaid: I suppose it is. You know how entitlement works.

Vetter: Apropos gender politics?

Kincaid: I don't believe in gender politics.

Vetter: What have you been teaching all these years?

Kincaid: Don't get me started, Bruce.

Vetter: No, go ahead. Please.

Kincaid: A stylish mix of feminist theory, with a dash of German philosophy. Everything from Susan Sontag to Nietzsche and Heidegger.

Vetter: German Existentialism or garden-variety supremacy?

Kincaid: Bruce, I'm not the villain here. I didn't sleep with an undergrad.

Vetter: I realize.

Kincaid: Nor do I support the political status quo. Too many professors and areas of study were slighted over the years. Butterworth allowed problems to simmer.

Vetter: Now it's your turn.

Kincaid: Thankfully, yes.

Vetter: You've a lot of ambition.

Kincaid: It will take a lot to realize our goals. Coffee? Decaf? (*He declines.*) Would you continue under Jane Hollander?

Vetter: No.

Kincaid: She tolerates you. Honestly. She admires your skills. You can keep your office just the way it is. Why not think it over?

Vetter: I don't like Hollander.

Kincaid: You know her well?

Vetter: She's incompetent, humorless, and an awful dresser. (*Pause*) I'll pack up.

Kincaid: You had this already played out in your mind.

Vetter: I did.

Kincaid: Bruce, I know about the Rand offer. It's a temporary position with a large pay cut in a pilot project. You'll be let go after a calendar year.

Vetter: What don't you know?

Kincaid: Can't you see that we should help each other?

Vetter: No.

Kincaid: You don't respect me, do you?

Vetter: I didn't say that.

Kincaid: You've said enough. You'll always be Butterworth's right hand.

Vetter: I need a new environment.

Kincaid: We could build a better, lasting institution and cleanse the stain. So much is riding on our transition. Don't be irresponsible. You've rapport with MacAlister and other donors.

Vetter: If that were true, you wouldn't be playing games. I'm not a kitchen appliance. You just don't care about inevitability.

Kincaid: I think you're being too literal, Bruce, and a bit too thin-skinned.

Vetter: Why not put Hollander under me?

Kincaid: You know the answer.

Vetter: I want to hear it from you.

Kincaid: Jane's a fresh feminine face.

Vetter: Her salary would surpass mine?

Kincaid: Your salary would rise with the new COLA index and anticipated bonus plan.

Vetter (*Laughing at himself*): Either you want me or not.

Kincaid: No matter what my problem is with MacAlister, I want you on a comfortable leash.

Vetter (*Rising from chair*): Didn't Nietzsche inspire the Nazis?

Kincaid: Pardon me?

Vetter: Wasn't Heidegger a member of the Third Reich?

Kincaid: No.

Vetter: I was led to believe he was.

Kincaid: He was rector of the University of Freiburg.

Vetter: Yet Heidegger injured Jewish careers.

Kincaid: Please.

Vetter: Wrote Nazi speeches. That sort of thing.

Kincaid: You're not Jewish, Bruce. Why play that card with me? This has nothing to do with Jews.

Vetter: I know.

Kincaid (*Smiling*): Even esteemed saints suffer blemishes. Cast no aspersions on my dear Heidegger.

Vetter: Well, Dr. Kincaid. I wish you success. Friday will be my final day.

(*Exits*)

SCENE 28

(*Vetter holding phone*)

Vetter: I had some time to think things over. I've been in Hell for days. You must know how much I love you. I'll die if you leave me, Lyla. I want you in my life. And I want the baby too. Please forgive me, darling. That's all I ask. (*Pause*) I love you more than anything else.

(*Begins to dial phone*)

SCENE 29

(*Restaurant*)

MacAlister: A very good table. Libby?

Libby: This is my friend Bibi.

MacAlister: Well then, lunch for four? Hello, Bibi.

Bibi: I don't want to intrude.

MacAlister: Please sit. Bibi, may I introduce Mr. Vetter?

(*They acknowledge one another.*)

Vetter: Bruce Vetter.

Bibi: Bibi Meyers.

MacAlister: Please sit everyone. (*They do.*) I hope you're hungry.

Libby: You said too many things over the phone.

MacAlister: There's time to cover everything.

Libby: How do you know my mother?

MacAlister: It's complicated.

Libby: Complicated?

MacAlister: Everything is. I knew your mother quite well. She had a special way of helping people come to terms with their weaknesses. And her sweet southern smile was the warmest expression under a summer sun. I could go on and on, but first I have to show you something beautiful. (*Removes glasses. Squints due to light sensitivity.*) I can see. I can see. I can see. (*Discomfort at the table. Puts glasses* *back on.*) Shapes and colors, all that I can make out at this point. A very fine start. I had returned to Mt. Soledad after midnight. Found myself in silent prayer. One could hear a whisper from the distant orbs. A glimpse of your mother. A bolt of light. My eyes were on fire. I burned inside. A miracle. After seventeen years. Would that your mother could rise again. To see her face alongside yours, no matter how blurred. (*Pause*) I felt your mother's warm, majestic hands. Upon my tired eyes. She hoisted me high up. Lighter than air. A floating feather. I fell back to earth. Dear God. You must go there. You will see my contrition. I am cleansed now. My heart is now pure. (*Gets up, hiding tears*) Excuse me please. (*Exits blindly*)

Libby: Who the hell is this guy?

Vetter (*Beside himself*): He and your mother go back a very long time. Romantically.

Libby: You're lying.

Bibi: Maybe the two of you need to talk this out.

(*Wants to exit, but Libby places a hand on her.*)

Libby: I want nothing to do with him.

Vetter: You're an heir to a fabulous fortune. He says that he's your father. He swears by it.

Libby: I don't want his love. I don't want his money. You can all get out of my life.

Vetter: He wants to be your father again.

Libby: I don't need a father. Not this sort of absentee father. You're a reckless S.O.B., Vetter.

(*She exits.*)

Vetter: So I am.

EPILOGUE

(*Mt. Soledad, with the image of the Madonna showing a classic face. The figure is cloaked in a full length mink.*)

Butterworth: A season of salt. Solitude. Undisturbed. Swordfish and shark. Unbound love. Lost. Unspoken. Such broken freedom. One less day in my heavy heart. At last, a forgiving God, a beautiful woman. (*Pause*) MacAlister?

MacAlister: Butterworth.

Butterworth: You see me?

MacAlister: A little, hazy. And I feel you.

Butterworth: Countless years have passed.

MacAlister: I was in your room yesterday.

Butterworth: Impossible.

MacAlister: Everything's possible.

Butterworth: I'm over my head.

MacAlister: It's understandable.

Butterworth: Your eyes?

MacAlister: They burn. I had a minute of sight.

Butterworth: Don't tell the authorities.

MacAlister: I won't.

Butterworth: I climbed down a rope of bed sheets. Fitted sheets. (*Pause*). Who is she today?

MacAlister: Carol Lombard?

Butterworth: God only knows. (*Butterworth takes his arm.*) Lena Horne was by far my favorite.

Butterworth: Here we are with our past. (*Pause*) How insidious I am.

MacAlister: Nonsense, my friend. Now you mustn't stay out too long. You'll die from exposure. (*Pause*) I've stopped the bequest.

Butterworth: Absolutely?

MacAlister: Not a cent will I give. Kincaid is appalling.

Butterworth: She has her principles.

MacAlister: So had Catherine the Great.

Butterworth: What will you do now?

MacAlister: Wait until Kincaid is dismissed. I give it a year.

Butterworth: Would you drive me back?

MacAlister: Of course. Your illness will dissipate.

Butterworth: God willing.

MacAlister: Come, it's getting chilly. (*Pause*) Take my hand. Please.

Butterworth: A person of no importance. (*Butterworth walks a step with MacAlister.*) Just a few coins in a torn pocket.

MacAlister: The perfect pilgrim. My car's just around the bend.

(*Libby, in a coat, steps into view and stands alone with her luggage. Butterworth turns away as MacAlister walks up to Libby.*)

You're so very angry with me.

Libby: Charley Tuna. The twisted gravel voice.

MacAlister: Charley Tuna. The nickname you gave me as a little girl. I'm so empty inside. I loved your mother so. You were the excitable little girl in a hundred remote motels. What a marathon for all of us. Know that I still love you and your mother.

Libby: You destroyed Mama.

MacAlister: I tried to find her many times. She needed to run from me.

Libby: If you can hurt her, you'll hurt me.

MacAlister: No. I'm a changed man. I give you my word. I've been through too much. (*Sincere tone. He extends an open palm, delicately.*) I will never hurt you again. You know these words are from my heart. In our dreams your mother has spoken to both of us with approval.

Libby (*She studies his face carefully and approaches.*): Your eyes are blue. How blue they are. Like a Bermuda sky.

(*She runs her fingers slowly across his face, from forehead to mouth. He gently touches her arm. They seem to have accepted one another. Peaceful silence.*)

END OF PLAY

Nixon's

Nixon

RUSSELL LEES

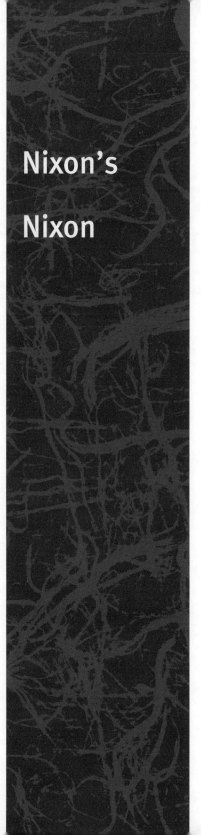

Nixon's Nixon received its premiere at
Manhattan Class Company (Robert LuPone
and Bernard Telsey, executive directors;
W. D. Cantler, associate director) in New
York City on September 29, 1995. The play
was subsequently produced at the
Westside Theatre in New York City on
March 5, 1996, by the Shubert Organiza-
tion, Capital Cities/ABC, Jujamcyn
Theaters, and Robert LuPone and Bernard
Telsey. It was directed by Jim Simpson;
administrative director, Lynne McCreary;
set and lighting designs by Kyle Chepulis;
costume design by Daniele Hollywood;
sound design by Mike Nolan; casting by
Bernard Telsey Casting; general manager,
Albert Poland; production supervisors,
Laura Kravets-Gautier and Ira Mont;
production stage manager, Erica Blum;
assistant stage managers, Ahri Birnbaum,
Bernadette McGay, and Corry Oullette. The
cast was as follows: Richard M. Nixon
portrayed by Gerry Bamman; Henry
Kissinger portrayed by Steve Mellor.

Cast of Characters

President Richard M. Nixon

Secretary of State Henry Kissinger

Setting

*August 7, 1974, 10:00 P.M., the
Lincoln Sitting Room in the
White House. This is President
Nixon's favorite room. He often
retires here to listen to classical
music or hold informal chats with
members of his family or staff.
It's a cozy retreat with a marble
fireplace, a writing table with
telephone, Victorian chairs, an
ottoman, a high-armed sofa, a
stereo with shelves of classical
albums, as well as nineteenth-
century prints of Lincoln with his
family.*

Production Note

*This play is a work of fiction. The
events depicted in this play are in
no way intended to represent
actual actions or opinions of
Richard M. Nixon or Henry
Kissinger.*

Author's Note

Americans are often told that we have no interest in history; that our nation is, in fact, predicated on forgetting the past and starting anew. In spite of this national quality, some twenty years after the resignation of Richard Nixon I found myself writing a play about him. There's something mesmerizing about the guy. You can't write about him without being funny. You can't write about him without being sad. His darkness and cynicism are in direct opposition to what we Americans like to think of as our national character; yet we doggedly elected him time and again, once in a landslide. Midway through the play, Nixon says, "I appeal to the Richard Nixon in everybody." I believe this to be true. I believe that in the cupboard of the national character there reside violence, paranoia, and secretive shame. Paradoxically, these can lead to astonishing achievements: despite and because of these qualities, Nixon made the world a safer place. A man of such contradiction, power, and self-hatred is, if nothing else, stage worthy. Beyond that, he is both a self-contained cautionary tale and a fascinating bundle of unacknowledged American traits.

My own interest in history, as is clear in the script, is fanciful. Nevertheless, it is a historical fact that the night before Richard Nixon announced his resignation from the presidency, he summoned Secretary of State Henry Kissinger to meet with him. What happened that storied evening has been the subject of conjecture and dispute ever since. This play gives my version.

(*At rise: President Nixon is listening to Tchaikovsky's* Fifth Symphony. *He conducts with passion using some rolled-up transcripts as a baton. The music is too loud, such that we can barely hear knocking at the door.*)

Kissinger: Mr. President? . . . Mr. President? (*He enters dressed in a tuxedo and raincoat, as if called away from a social occasion.*) Mr. President?

Nixon: Henry! Good to see you.

Kissinger: Mr. President?

Nixon: Sit. Sit, sit. How've you been, Henry? Long time no see.

Kissinger: This Mideast business—it's, I, I apologize.

Nixon: No. No, no. I'm not, it isn't, I'm not. It's good to see you.

Kissinger: Yes, sir.

Nixon: It's good you came.

Kissinger: Of course I came, sir. As I say, I've been busy, or I, in this difficult time. . . . Could we turn down the volume?

Nixon: Why?

Kissinger: It's a bit . . .

Nixon: A bit?

Kissinger: A bit . . .

Nixon: Oh. Yes, yes. Turn it down for God's sake. Can't hear yourself think. (*Sets down baton of papers, then is careful to turn them face down*)

Kissinger (*With concern*): How are you?

Nixon: I'm well. Really very well.

Kissinger: Good. I . . . as I say, it's a difficult time. . . . Well. Perhaps we should discuss what Ford might do.

Nixon: I'm light as a feather, almost giddy.

Kissinger: Yes. Good. I'm a little concerned about—

Nixon: Maybe it's the music. The spirit soars.

Kissinger: I worried you'd be depressed.

Nixon: Died penniless, you know. A pauper. Great man like that. Ended up in the shit can.

Kissinger: Tchaikovsky?

Nixon: Such are the vagaries of history.

Kissinger: Tchaikovsky died a wealthy man.

Nixon: Few men can control their own destiny, Henry. Only the truly great.

Kissinger: I'm glad you're taking this so philosophically.

(*Pause*)

Nixon: Taking what so philosophically?

Kissinger: The . . . Your . . . I understood you'd . . .

Nixon: Ron issued a schedule. You know that? A resignation schedule. Gave copies to Haig, Buchanan. I'm not supposed to know about it. I might react badly. It might influence my decision.

Kissinger: Mm. (*Pause*) So you haven't decided?

Nixon: 1958. Ike sends me on some functionary trip, some dull figurehead thing. South America. Caracas. July. Anti-American mobs surround the car. They're this far away from me, Henry. You're me. They're this far. Screaming. Pig-dog! Imperialist murderer! Stuff like that. Capitalist-piece-of-shit!! With bats, sticks, banging on the car. BAM! BAM! They want to rip my dick off and shove it down my throat.

Kissinger: Sir.

Nixon: So what do I do? What would you do, Doctor Kissinger? Ingratiate yourself with a quip? Negotiate your way out?

Kissinger: Mr. President.

Nixon: They're banging on the car! They're shattering the windows! Pig-shit!! Now, Henry, when confronting a mob, always do the unexpected. Me, I get out of the car. I get out of the car! Unexpected? They're stunned. Flabbergasted. A mass of dirty faces. Fierce bad teeth. I shake a couple of hands. How about that, Henry? I even shake a couple of hands. It's a campaign stop.

Kissinger: It's a wonderful story. I think, however, the lesson to be learned—

Nixon: Overnight, I'm a hero.

Kissinger:—is a lesson of courage, not recklessness.

Nixon: Courage. You're right. Courage. How did I win them over? Latin countries, courage is the thing. Balls. They love a guy with balls. *Cojones.* That's why you have so much trouble with them. In America it's a little different. Americans like fighters. Underdogs. The scrappier the better. That's me, now. Me. I'm the underdog. Everyone's deserted me. Now I'm the guy to root for. (*He goes into a kind of trance.*)

Kissinger: Mr. President?

Nixon: So? You see?

Kissinger: I don't see.

Nixon: I'm the guy to root for.

Kissinger: Root for? Root for to do what?

Nixon: I've always come back. Every time I've been counted out, I've come back. The governor's race. The Hiss thing. Even when Ike screwed me over.

Kissinger: This is not when Ike screwed you over.

Nixon: I've always come back.

Kissinger: Sir.

Nixon: Always.

Kissinger: This time . . .

Nixon: Haldeman, gone. Ehrlichman. My administration in shambles.

Kissinger: The Senate, it's been clear for some time, they simply aren't—

Nixon: . . . Colson, Mitchell . . .

Kissinger: —aren't going to rally behind you.

Nixon: Dean lying like a weasel. Goddamn. Mngh. Cocksucker.

Kissinger: Mr. President, will you listen? Impeachment is certain.

Nixon: I'm alone.

Kissinger: Impeachment and conviction.

Nixon: Impeachment? Conviction?! Know how many fat congressional butts I've . . . screw impeachment. Screw the Senators. Sheep. Candy-ass sheep. I get a groundswell, they'll follow like ducks.

Kissinger: Ducks? Ducks? Will you look around?

Nixon: Mnh!

Kissinger: Everyone's quit, fired, indicted. It's a tragedy. But you must, we all must come to terms with it.

Nixon: All my advisors, you're the only one. The only one who's escaped.

Kissinger: That's hardly—

Nixon: Even the wiretap thing, the press backed off. You threaten to resign, they collapse. Me, they're licking their chops.

Kissinger: I've suffered from the press. I'm sure they'd be overjoyed if I—

Nixon: No. It's true. You they still respect. Of course, they're Jews, most of them.

Kissinger: Sir, you don't think I've ever . . . Has someone said . . . ? I mean, I have good relations with the press. But I have never, never used that to hurt you.

Nixon: Somebody around here sold me out, you know.

Kissinger: I know.

Nixon: Was it you?

Kissinger: Mr. President, I've just explained—

Nixon: I didn't think so. But I wanted to hear it from you.

Kissinger: It would be crazy.

Nixon: Who was it?

Kissinger: I have no idea.

Nixon: It's somebody.

Kissinger: Yes, but who?

Nixon: You don't know?

Kissinger: Absolutely not.

Nixon: No idea?

Kissinger: None.

Nixon: Someday I'll find out. Things can't be kept secret forever you know.

Kissinger (*Pause*): Frankly, I figured it must be Haig.

Nixon: Haig?

Kissinger: Well. It makes sense—

Nixon: Haig?

Kissinger: He's the one who—

Nixon: The one man who's stood by me? The one man I can confide in?

Kissinger: But that's my point.

Nixon: I can't believe you just impugned General Alexander Haig.

Kissinger: It's merely speculation, based on—

Nixon: Because I listen to his advice.

Kissinger: I respect Haig. I absolutely respect Haig. He and I, we've . . . What's he say about me?

Nixon: What do you mean, "What's he say about me?"

Kissinger: It's just that in a bureaucracy it's tempting to . . . backstab. I've seen him do it to others.

Nixon: What does he say about me?

Kissinger: Haig? He's respectful. But he can . . . he likes to imitate people.

Nixon: I see.

Kissinger: No, but he's, generally . . . perfectly correct.

Nixon: Yes. Yes. Does *he* want me to resign? Probably does, but he won't come out and say so.

Kissinger: Mr. President, it's time to make the decision conclusively. This, this cloud hanging over you, it's—

Nixon: Cloud.

Kissinger: More than a cloud, yes. It's—

Nixon: We had our successes, we two. Not so long ago.

Kissinger: We did. And, if permitted, I will continue—

Nixon: China. Russia. Should be worth something.

Kissinger: The world is a safer place.

Nixon: Don't give me your platitudes. Haig. Haig, for one, has stood by me. Not like you. Compare what you've done for me to anybody, compare it to Julie. My family, *Julie*'s been the one, Pat and Tricia too, sure, but Julie's the one gave all those speeches. Went all over the place y'know. Hecklers and everything.

Kissinger: Yes.

Nixon: They booed her, you know. Sometimes.

Kissinger: I wondered how you—

Nixon: What?

Kissinger: —how you . . . were able to permit—

Nixon: How I let her do that?

Kissinger: She put herself in an awfully vulnerable position. (*Nixon thinks hard.*) I'm sorry, I . . .

Nixon: No. It's, um. (*He thinks hard some more then speaks abruptly.*) Think Brezhnev'll get along with Jerry like he did me?

Kissinger: So you *have* . . . You are going to, um, pass the baton.

Nixon: He won't.

Kissinger: Jerry? With Brezhnev? No. No, he won't.

Nixon: Leonid and I—

Kissinger: Yes . . . yes—

Nixon: He, he respects me.

Kissinger: Yes. Of course he did. Certainly.

Nixon: Yes, he does. He, for one, does. You be him.

Kissinger: Him?

Nixon: I'll be me.

Kissinger: . . .

Nixon: The Moscow summit.

Kissinger: Sir . . .

Nixon: Will you just be him? Jesus. Okay, I'll be him, you be me. Nixon! Good to meet you!

Kissinger: . . .

Nixon *(as Brezhnev):* Nixon! Good to meet you!

Kissinger: . . .

Nixon: For God's sake, do this one thing for me. Jesus-fuckin'-Christ! . . . (*As Brezhnev*) Nixon!

Kissinger *(as Nixon):* Premier Brezhnev. A great pleasure.

Nixon *(as Brezhnev):* Please, please call me Leonid. But this is historic! (*Grabs Kissinger and hugs him*) Yes. You are a strong man. A sturdy man.

Kissinger *(as Nixon):* You are a sturdy man as well.

Nixon *(as Brezhnev):* I feel we will accomplish much, my friend. We share a great deal.

Kissinger *(as Nixon):* Oh?

Nixon *(as Brezhnev):* We are simple men. Family men. Ah, but there . . . You love politics—your daughter marries a President's grandson. I love circuses, my daughter runs off with lion tamers, acrobats. We both love our daughters, but yours has brought you joy. Mine has brought me pain.

Kissinger *(as Nixon):* I've been lucky.

Nixon *(as Brezhnev):* You see. I've studied you closely. The KGB files, ah! again and again I've read them. I know you like I've known no lover. (*Big Soviet laugh. Kissinger checks his watch.*) We have both overcome adversity to become . . . what?

Kissinger: . . .

Nixon *(as Brezhnev):* Born to simple, working people we have succeeded in becoming—

Kissinger *(as Nixon):* Middle class. *(A look from Nixon)* The most powerful men in the world.

Nixon *(as Brezhnev):* Yes. Yes, you have it exactly. With intelligent minions to scamper about for us. But here we've been chatting and forgotten the primary thing. Vodka! First-quality Russian vodka! *(He gets a decanter of brandy.)* Will you please join me?

Kissinger *(as Nixon):* I believe I will.

Nixon *(as Brezhnev)* *(Pouring brandy):* So, Nixon. Tell me a bit about this Kissinger.

Kissinger *(as Nixon):* He . . . he and I have a . . .

Nixon *(as Brezhnev):* I get the feeling you're not very close.

Kissinger *(as Nixon):* . . . I suppose not . . . We discuss things. In depth. He's more than an advisor. Much, much more.

Nixon *(as Brezhnev):* Knowledgeable about history, I'm told.

Kissinger *(as Nixon):* Astonishingly knowledgeable.

Nixon *(as Brezhnev):* Tell me, Nixon, do you contemplate what the history books will make of you? Do you wonder about your place in history?

Kissinger *(as Nixon):* A statesman can't occupy himself—

Nixon *(as Brezhnev):* Of course you do. And it will be a glorious place, I'm certain. *(As himself)* This is wonderful. You be Brezhnev now. Just for a minute . . . Go ahead.

Kissinger *(as Brezhnev)* *(Drinks):* But Nixon, you must be careful. We have just this minute met and I already have advantage over you.

Nixon: You think so?

Kissinger *(as Brezhnev):* It's of little consequence. Each of us will gain and lose advantages in due course.

Nixon: What have you won here?

Kissinger *(as Brezhnev):* You are concerned with the history books. It's a weakness, Nixon. Me, I have no such concern.

Nixon: Very good.

Kissinger *(as Brezhnev):* This gives me leverage in our dealings.

Nixon: You're right.

Kissinger *(as Brezhnev):* And I shall use it, Nixon. I shall squeeze you until you're bloody.

Nixon: I'm certain you will.

Kissinger *(as Brezhnev)* *(Parody of big Soviet laugh):* Perhaps a little more Vodka.

Nixon: I have an advantage, too.

Kissinger *(as Brezhnev):* Yes?

Nixon: I have more nuclear submarines. 'Course, Kissinger nearly threw that away . . . Well? You did screw up on the submarines. But we got around it. We were out in uncharted territory. Mistakes were bound to happen, but we fudged 'em. That's our genius. History. That's where the big judgments are. You think history books're going to say, "He didn't do his homework on submarines?" No. It's boring. It's piddly-ass. "He got the first nuclear arms treaty!" That's good reading. Good history.

Kissinger: Mm.

Nixon: Which gets to the heart of it, doesn't it? What do you think, Henry? What'll they say about me in a hundred years?

Kissinger: You?

Nixon: What will be the verdict?

Kissinger: You . . . You'll be treated well enough, I'm sure. Yes. We've accomplished many remarkable things.

Nixon: You think so?

Kissinger: Oh, yes.

Nixon: I'll be well treated?

Kissinger: China alone.

Nixon: Mm.

Kissinger: Mm.

(Pause)

Nixon: They'll discount the piddly stuff.

Kissinger: Historians will look back bewildered.

Nixon: Jefferson had some funny business, didn't he?

Kissinger: I'm sure he did.

Nixon: He did all right. What about Lincoln, didn't he have some . . . ? No?

Kissinger: Lincoln, no.

Nixon: Crazy wife.

Kissinger: Yes, but—

Nixon: What about Grant? He as crummy as all that?

Kissinger: I think, yes, he was less than—

Nixon: What I mean is, the bad ones, were they that bad, or is it all press?

Kissinger: The bad ones. The good ones. What is important is the place you hold. History recognizes the trivial for just that.

Nixon: The big stuff'll stand the test of . . . yes.

Kissinger: But my point is that is only if our projects are carried to fruition.

Nixon: Our projects. The big-picture stuff. People don't understand.

Kissinger: For this, it's important that Ford understands how essential it is that I remain Secretary of State.

Nixon: And God knows what . . . All the rotten stuff we came up with here. Good Lord. That's what I'm worried about.

Kissinger: That . . . ?

Nixon: That every little thing'll come out.

Kissinger: Of course not.

Nixon: Because of the tapes, see. The tapes. They're making a big deal about 'em.

Kissinger: Well, yes.

Nixon: I must've listened to those damn tapes . . . it's enough to . . . God. "There's a cancer on the presidency." Jesus.

Kissinger: You shouldn't have gotten caught up in them. You neglected—

Nixon: You're on 'em, too, you know. There's bad tapes with you on there.

Kissinger: I suppose.

Nixon: There aren't any tapes of Lincoln saying bad stuff. He did. Any man . . . this office . . . has to consider all kinds of . . . but I'm the one everybody wants to hear the tapes. If I'm President, if I'm President in good standing, with no impeachment crap, I'm okay. The tapes are mine. I can throw away the crummy ones.

Kissinger: What conversations were . . . ? ·

Nixon: But now, the way things are, that's destroying evidence. If I'm under indictment, I can't, can't . . .

Kissinger: Exercise your prerogative.

Nixon: No, my hands're . . . you see?

Kissinger: It's a problem.

Nixon: They're my goddamn tapes.

Kissinger: Right.

Nixon: Like a diary. Like a presidential diary.

Kissinger: Which ones have negative things about me?

Nixon: Good God, which ones don't? Pakistan, Cuba, Chile for chrissakes, Christmas bombings. It's all through there.

Kissinger: That's on tape?

Nixon: . . .

Kissinger: Those conversations were taped?

Nixon: Don't you get it? Everything was.

Kissinger: But those were . . . I wasn't informed of . . . nobody has access to those.

Nixon: Access, no. Nobody has access. Of course not. You think I'm crazy?

Kissinger: They're locked up.

Nixon: You bet they're locked up.

Kissinger: They don't have any bearing on—

Nixon: No. You're safe for godsakes. Executive privilege up the wazoo.

Kissinger: No one has access.

Nixon: No one has access. No one has excess. Excrete, escape, exculpatory. Ex, ex, ex, ex-president. Historians?! What do they know?

(Pause)

Kissinger: I just want to be clear. No one can listen to those tapes.

Nixon: No. As long as they aren't subpoenaed . . .

Kissinger: And there's no reason for that.

Nixon: Right.

Kissinger: And there won't be.

Nixon: No. No, why should there?

Kissinger: Because it's separate.

Nixon: Right.

Kissinger: Good . . . Good.

Nixon: So as long as I keep them locked up, I'll be seen as, as . . .

Kissinger: Once you have . . . left office, your legacy in the field of foreign affairs, of course, will—

Nixon: Oh God, yes. Brezhnev was practically a brother. Not like those European sad sacks. Pompidou? My God. Sits around the Elysee Palace like a big cold turd. Willie Brandt. Germans are all Nazis. Don't understand why they pretend any different. The thing about history is it's a bunch of crock.

Kissinger: *My yes.* However, the best way to preserve your place is to gracefully—

Nixon: I mean look at Lincoln here. I mean yeah, there's a lot of . . . he wasn't . . . but underneath all that, *underneath,* he was a real guy. He sat in this goddamned chair. He sat here, and he ruled this country. As I have, Henry. Just a regular guy, caught in a very difficult . . . time.

Kissinger: Sir.

Nixon: Yes?

Kissinger: We have to talk about your decision.

Nixon: I'm all ears.

Kissinger: The country, our country has yet to heal from the war. And now we're plunged into this, this domestic crisis. Right or wrong. We're plunged into it and there's no solution that can bring all the camps together, that can unify this country once again. And, sir, if there's anything you've stood for it's the strength and unity of purpose of this nation.

(*Pause*)

Nixon: I grew up stacking groceries. I grew up spraying vegetables, picking spiders out of the bananas. My hands still stink of pesticide. Those were tough years.

Kissinger: In the present situation you've defended yourself well. You've defended yourself honorably. But it's dragged on too long. It's ripping apart the White House. It's ripping apart the country.

Nixon: Worked pumping gas. Worked mimeographing legal crap. Worked for everything I've ever had.

Kissinger: I really think the best thing for you personally, for your family, for Julie, for the nation, is for you to definitively step down and let me carry out our program.

Nixon: I didn't grow up on some aristocratic German estate.

Kissinger: You are, finally—

Nixon: Pampered and coddled like a Prussian prince.

Kissinger: I beg your pardon?

Nixon: Handed a meal ticket to the Ivy League.

Kissinger: My father was a schoolteacher. I went to college on the GI Bill.

Nixon: Don't play sob sister with me.

Kissinger: I owe a great deal to this country.

Nixon: My God, yes. A great debt of loyalty.

Kissinger: As a matter of fact.

Nixon: Well, we all do. I've always sought to . . . everything I've done, even my own interest, I've always sought first to honor . . . I've worked so . . . At night I go over . . . that's when. Fickle. The thing of it is, Henry, people elect you, they have high expectations. Christ, did they ever elect me! What a landslide! I appeal to the Richard Nixon in everybody. So they're all jam-packed full of hope and elation. They . . . there's no way to . . . They expect so much . . . and what happens is you're the leader, you're sure to . . . disappoint. So they want to get rid of you. Get some new . . . Even you want me to get out of the way. Of course you do. That brandy there? That's the brandy we toasted the China breakthrough with. Would you please? (*Kissinger pours brandies. They drink.*) We've toasted success in this room. Days gone by. Many, many triumphs.

Kissinger: Yes. This room holds fine memories for me.

Nixon: The protests, huh? We sat here. Thank God we had the brandy then. Will they put me in jail?

(*Pause*)

Kissinger: I can't imagine such a thing.

Nixon: They might. I might go to jail . . . So what. Huh, Henry? So what? This century's greatest political writing's been done in jail.

Kissinger: Yes, Castro. Lenin.

Nixon: I was thinking Sakharov and Gandhi.

Kissinger: Gandhi.

Nixon: The thing of it is, if I'm convicted, I lose my pension . . . I've looked into it. I lose my pension and Secret Service protection.

Kissinger: I, I really don't think you'll come to trial.

Nixon: Nope. I'd lose the uh . . . I mean in addition to the . . .

Kissinger: You. I really think.

Nixon: But who cares now? (*Pause*) Depends on Jerry.

Kissinger: I'm sure he'll—

Nixon: Have you heard any . . . ?

Kissinger: No.

Nixon: He's a good man.

Kissinger: He's a good and decent man.

Nixon: He'll . . . ?

Kissinger: He'll see that you're . . .

(*Pause*)

Nixon: Brought to this, what more could they do? What's left? I've been run over by a tank.

Kissinger: It's true.

Nixon: I'm the guy who came to the party and peed in the lemonade.

Kissinger: Now they're out to get you.

Nixon: They've gotten me.

Kissinger: Conspired against you.

Nixon: Picked me clean. Might as well strip myself naked.

Kissinger: Might as well.

Nixon: March down Pennsylvania Avenue.

Kissinger: With a band.

Nixon: Flopping all over the place.

Kissinger: A band and bunting.

Nixon: Baloop, baloop! And it all goes down the drain. China. Detente. Arms pacts. Vietnam. *That's* the . . .

Kissinger: It won't go down the drain if Ford keeps me on with full authority—

Nixon: We did the right thing there, Henry.

Kissinger: —full authority to. Where?

Nixon: Vietnam.

Kissinger: Oh. Yes.

Nixon: It was, it was a tough. Those cocksuckers! Thought they could . . . and the, the goddamn . . . We did the right . . . you won the goddamn prize for chrissake!

Kissinger: We—

Nixon: So, yes. I mean it was about boys, men slogging around in a jungle. My God, can you imagine? At night, in the mud, so far from home, all on your own. Your buddy's guts dripping from the trees. Enemies. Everywhere enemies.

Kissinger: Enemies there *and* here.

Nixon: Oh God. Jesus. God, Henry! My God. (*Pause*) You'd think it was a crime, what I did. You'd think getting us out was a crime. We were tearing our hair out.

Kissinger: The options were so . . .

Nixon: Boys died. Yes, boys died. You're President, that's part of the . . . Good God, look at the body count in the Civil War! Lots more than . . . and he's on Mount Rushmore.

Kissinger: You got us out.

Nixon: Henry, I said . . . I called you into my office, Henry, I said close the door.

Kissinger: Le Duc Tho won't budge. They're flaunting their disdain.

Nixon: Little faggot.

Kissinger: We need a credible threat.

Nixon: Tell 'em we'll, by God we'll . . .

Kissinger: They're sophisticated. They hector me about domestic opposition.

Nixon: You know how Ike won Korea? Do you know? He threatened nuclear—

Kissinger: Yes, but we—

Nixon: —he threatened nuclear . . . and they were in negotiating like somebody shoved an electric—

Kissinger: Eisenhower had nuclear dominance. We don't.

Nixon: Can't we threaten it?

Kissinger: The problem is we're fighting on two fronts. If we even mention nuclear—

Nixon: The beardos and weirdoes go berserk.

Kissinger: Right. We must avoid stirring up domestic opposition.

Nixon: We can't make our toughest threat.

Kissinger: One approach, how would we do this—

Nixon: We'd have to.

Kissinger: —is to convince the North somehow that we might go nuclear?

Nixon: Damn the consequences?

Kissinger: In a way. It's irrational, but we could convince them that you're, well, not rational . . .

Nixon: This is for the nuclear thing?

Kissinger: Yes. We convince them—

Nixon: I see.

Kissinger: —that the war's made you desperate—

Nixon: And maybe a little unhinged. Uh-huh.

Kissinger: Yes. They might believe you're willing to risk nuclear war with the Soviets.

Nixon: Whichever side wins, North Vietnam'd be a cinder.

Kissinger: Right.

Nixon: Right. Convince them I'm a little funny.

Kissinger: Right. But domestically . . .

Nixon: Domestically, we're screwed. We'd have to do it secret. I'd have to *secretly* be off my rocker.

Kissinger: How we'd manage that . . .

Nixon: We'd have to actually do something, I think.

Kissinger: I agree. We must take some action implying you're . . .

Nixon: Right. We can't, you know, write Ho Chi Minh a letter saying, "Nixon's a banana." We've got to get him to figure it out.

Kissinger: All right. How about this? The army's been after us about Cambodia. Well, what can we do? It's a neutral country. The Viet Cong aren't supposed to be there, but neither are we. We can't go after them. We can't just go and invade a neutral country.

Nixon: We can't?

Kissinger: It'd be expanding a war we want to end. *But* if we could get the V.C. headquarters hiding there, it'd cripple them. It's a vast jungle. We'd have to bomb the hell out of it. We'd have to follow up with ground troops.

Nixon: Bomb the hell out of it. And the peaceniks?

Kissinger: We'd keep it secret.

Nixon: The whole thing?

Kissinger: Yes.

Nixon: We'd bomb the bejesus out of Cambodia, send in ground troops, and keep the whole operation secret?

Kissinger: Right.

Nixon: This is good, Henry. This is very good.

Kissinger: We can't tell most of the army. We'll have to pick officers and units. We'll have to skip over several links in the chain of command.

Nixon: What about Sihanouk? He could screw us. I mean, we're bombing his country. He's bound to find out.

Kissinger: He's in a tricky position. The Viet Cong are in his jungle. He can't complain we're bombing them unless he admits they're there. I think he'll shut up and try to please everyone.

Nixon: Yes. What about . . . I suppose the Cambodians . . .

Kissinger: Those villages are completely isolated. Reports of destruction will be incoherent.

Nixon: Henry! This is a masterstroke. It's bold, daring, sweeping. It gets at those bastards without hurting us at home. Plus, it conveys to Hanoi they're dealing with someone capable of anything! It holds a subtle but distinct tinge of madness.

Kissinger: Thank you.

Nixon (*In present*): Ah. Might've worked. Eventually. Hadn't leaked out. (*Nixon pours another.*) Ike and I used to chat here. As much as we ever chatted.

Kissinger: When he wasn't golfing?

Nixon: He only won World War II for chrissake. And Korea. He was a father figure to me, a wonderful . . . he taught me goddamn fly-fishing . . . God, what he put me through in '52. I would've done . . . I worshiped . . . every two days I had to prove myself. Goddamn *cocksucker*. A drag on the ticket! Fuck him. I helped the ticket. I helped the ticket both times. I would've been President myself in '60, Kennedy hadn't've cheated. Kennedy. If he could, he'd've cheated his way into getting elected Pope. Smuggling Marilyn into the Vatican chambers. Hell, I'd make twice the Pope he would've. How 'bout that, Henry? Me, Pope? Jesus God, I'd grab the world by the tits and give it a whirl.

Kissinger: You'd make an excellent Pope.

Nixon: Because once you're elected, you're *it*. You're Pope till you die.

Kissinger: I don't think I'd have much chance at Pope.

Nixon: Anybody could pull it off . . . this goes back to the Kennedy thing . . . as long as you can act the part. I don't think Pope John really . . . I mean he's okay. Kennedy taught me something there. He was one great actor. Debates? I beat his balls off. Ask anybody. He acted his way to President.

Kissinger: You have to be an actor.

Nixon: God, yes. This job, you have to be. On the world stage and so on.

Kissinger: The press. To be properly duplicitous—

Nixon: You've got to portray . . . you've got to believe—

Kissinger: The true statesman, he's a chameleon. He shades his opinions, even facts, to draw in and seduce his opponents. Occasionally, I even convince myself.

Nixon: It's more than that, Henry. It's that . . . the burdens of the position. If you show your true self, you're standing there with your fly wide open. If you show your true self, your weaknesses are all . . .

Kissinger: You've got to wear the proper Greek mask.

Nixon: Yes.

Kissinger: You've got to be larger than life.

Nixon: That's it exactly. Because you've got to play the great man of state. You've got to play the wise leader, the brilliant schemer. The ruthless murderer. But with no backstage. There's no backstage. The mask gets stuck. You end up asking, "What color are my goddamn eyes?"

(*Long pause*)

Kissinger: You will certainly be remembered as a great man unjustly brought down.

Nixon: You think so?

Kissinger: You'll be remembered all the better for the tragedy of your fall.

Nixon: It is tragic.

Kissinger: Because you could have been one of the greats. Alexander, Caesar, Napoleon . . . Look how badly the British treated Churchill.

Nixon: Limey snots.

Kissinger: It is for me to carry on.

Nixon: Napoleon returned from exile, you know. After Russia, he was exiled to some island. He came back after a year or so with a few hundred men. The King of France sent an entire army to stop him. They form a line across the road, rifles at the ready. Bayonets trembling. He halts his troops, Henry. He halts them and walks alone to the front of the column. There he confronts soldiers who'd fought for him for years, now ready to shoot him down. "Men of France! You know who I am." Here he opens his greatcoat and stands before them. "Shoot if you must." One of the officers shouts, "Fire!"

Kissinger (*Pause*): Fire!

Nixon: Absolute silence. They throw down their muskets, run to embrace their Emperor. They carry him to Paris in triumph. Is that too much to ask?

Kissinger: Too much?

Nixon: Now you say Waterloo. Yes, Waterloo. But by coming back he got that chance. He almost won, he got that chance.

Kissinger: You're saying . . .

Nixon: I want my chance.

Kissinger: Your chance?

Nixon: I can fight this thing. It isn't over.

Kissinger: You'll be *impeached.*

Nixon: Yes, I know. I'll fight it out in the courts.

Kissinger: No.

Nixon: Pat's for it. My whole family's behind me. Julie, Tricia. Not David.

Kissinger: You had your chance. What're you trying to do, wreck us? Wreck everything we've done?

Nixon: I'm not gonna—

Kissinger: You are. Don't you understand? I can't do anything. I can't get an appointment with Dobrynin for godsakes. They're all waiting, the world over, waiting for your body to hit the floor. And here, in Washington? They don't even wait. They're gathering like smiling buzzards, gauging the spoils. Meanwhile, no one will talk to me. They know I can't make commitments until there's a new President. I can't continue my work.

Nixon: Too bad for you.

Kissinger: Too bad for me? If you're remembered, it'll be for what I did. And it's all coming apart. It's all going to shit because you won't get out of the way.

(*Long pause*)

I'm sorry.

Nixon: Who cares what the books say, if the guy on the street, the little guy in Peoria, if he thinks different? Historians. Fuzzy-headed clowns in tweed, jerking off in some library. The guy in the street! He thinks Nixon was a bum, then Nixon was a bum. Screw historians! How'm I gonna fix that, stewing in my own exiled juice? I can't. I'll go down in history a bum.

Kissinger: You could . . . you could write your memoirs . . . Perhaps it's a bit soon. Maybe we could set up some sort of consulting position with Jerry.

Nixon: I've thought about that.

Kissinger: We could . . . I don't know.

Nixon: It'll be tough to—

Kissinger: It is perhaps best to wait. Possibly after the '76 election. We could bring you in then.

Nixon: And then, *then* the soldiers will throw down their muskets.

Kissinger: You'll march into Congress and throw open your greatcoat.

Nixon: They'll cheer. They'll cheer me like they did in Amman. In Cairo. Like they did in Paris, Bonn, and London. Like Caracas. Nixon! Nixon! Nixon! They went wild. You got your share, too. Other times. Winning that Nobel thing. Acted like I was the doorman.

Kissinger: I was careful in my speech to—

Nixon: Nobody listens to that stuff. It's the headlines and the photo in the morning. But no, they loved me at the convention. They loved my State of the Union. Pretty pathetic, sit around here, listing the times I've been cheered. All I've done, I'm counting cheers.

Kissinger: We're all so fragile.

Nixon: But see, it's the cheers that . . . Did they really want me? That's what gets me. They seemed to want the hell outta me. If the Kennedys'd lived, would I have ever gotten elected?

Kissinger: That's quite an interesting question.

Nixon: Say Kennedy gets a second term in '64. Then Bobby in '68, maybe '72. Me in '76.

Kissinger: They'd have been stuck with Vietnam.

Nixon: You think they'd've won all those elections? No chance for me?

Kissinger: I'm saying if.

Nixon: I could've won. Damn near beat John in '60. Sometimes I wonder if I did win. Those damn Democrats, Christ! Illinois, people voted fifteen times. Dead people voted. Same thing in Texas, Missouri. I met with him, you know. After the election. Worried I'd contest it, demand a recount. I ever tell you about that meeting?

Kissinger: Ten, twenty times.

Nixon: He summons me like I'm . . . I walk in. He's sitting there, rich and presidential, like a cut of veal. I call him "Mr. President-Elect." "How the hell do you take Ohio?" he says. He expected to carry Ohio. I want to say, "I didn't steal it, buster." I sit down. I notice him glance at my shoes. My shoes! I swear, a little sneer came across his face. Then he says . . . you know what he says?

Kissinger *(as Kennedy):* The recent election, closely contested as it was, has left the country vulnerable.

Nixon: I have told you this.

Kissinger *(as Kennedy):* A divided America is a weakened America.

Nixon: My people tell me I should contest Illinois. They tell me I should contest Texas.

Kissinger *(as Kennedy):* The office of the President, Mr. Nixon, is the collective dream of a nation.

Nixon: My people think I have a case.

Kissinger *(as Kennedy):* But this is my point, Mr. Nixon. If you raised this hubbub, if you were to contest this or that state, the election is thrown into question. The collective dream would become troubled.

Nixon: I appreciate your position.

Kissinger *(as Kennedy):* Let's say you did. Let's suppose you raise this issue. Let us suppose, Mr. Nixon, you took those electoral votes from Illinois. What would you stand to gain? The election goes to the House of Representatives. I think you'll agree that the heavily Democratic House is likely to vote against you.

Nixon: I think that if I can show that I got more than 50 percent of the popular vote and that your party cheated during a presidential election, I think a lot of Congressmen would look awfully fair-minded by voting for me. Secondly, if I also carried Texas, which I think I did, I win the presidency outright and your House of Representatives can go fuck themselves.

Kissinger *(as Kennedy)* *(Pause):* Can I have someone bring you a drink, Mr. Nixon? Some lemonade?

Nixon: Thank you, no.

Kissinger *(as Kennedy):* I find it hard to believe that you, Mr. Nixon, would gamble the unity of your country for an outside chance at the presidency. You have experience in foreign affairs. You made sure no one forgot *that* during the election. Perhaps, in a few months, I could ask you to take a diplomatic assignment of some kind.

Nixon: He was trying to buy me off! Why not just offer me cash straight up?! You know what I should've done?

Kissinger: You did precisely—

Nixon: I should've said, "Grab hold of your pedigree, you sneering snob, 'cause by the time this is over, you'll look like the Prince of Thieves."

Kissinger: You did precisely the correct and honorable thing.

Nixon: Honorable? "Mr. President, I recognize you fully as President blah-blah-blah no intention of questioning blah-blah-bleah!" There is no honor in quitting, Henry. Ever.

Kissinger: On the contrary—

Nixon: You know what he said to me, after I'd yielded?

Kissinger: "Mr. Nixon, the President of the United States is grateful for the fine thing you've—"

Nixon: Ha! "Mr. Nixon, thank you for meeting with me. I think we can both agree, it's for the best you didn't quite make it."

Kissinger: Nevertheless.

Nixon: The one time I didn't fight hammer and claw to the bloody end, and I regretted it for the next eight years.

Kissinger: You were able to return at a more propitious time.

Nixon: There's no returning from this one.

Kissinger: But *I* will carry on.

Nixon: No comeback from total disgrace. Maybe things would've gone differently, I'd won in '60. Maybe I'd be all right now. (*Pause*) It's a ghostly city at night. Peopled by monuments to the dead and a few Secret Service men.

Kissinger: So. You understand that, in order to ensure—

Nixon: Yes. You don't have to hit me over the head.

Kissinger: But you agree.

Nixon: Agree to what?

Kissinger: Agree that—

Nixon: Agree I've got to ensure my legacy lives on somehow, some way. But what how? What way, Henry? What a fool I am! My legacy will live on in the person of you! Super K! Henry the Great! You will be the womb that carries my brainchild into the future. You, who I dredged out of obscurity, will nurse my fate at your bosom. You and your liberal coddling, starlet-schtupping, press-licking self! My protégé! My Machievelli with a belly.

Kissinger: I'm trying to protect your place in history.

Nixon: You're trying to protect *your* place in history.

Kissinger: It's the same.

Nixon: Oh, no. No. I'm well aware it's not the same.

Kissinger: Mr. Nixon. I have at all times remained loyal and have done whatever in my power—

Nixon: Have you?

Kissinger: Yes.

Nixon: Why, I better call Jerry this second. What if he gets it into his head that he's President? He might go mad with power. Hire Haig for State. Oh-ho. That's what this is about. You're worried Ford comes in here, he'll make a clean sweep. Haig's more his kind of guy. You came here to get me to convince Jerry to keep you. Jiminy-Christ, where's

his phone number? My last act as President should be to protect you—
the single one of my advisors who has never once made any attempt to
publicly defend me.

Kissinger: I have to protect my position as a political entity.

Nixon: Presidents may come and Presidents may go, but Henry
Kissinger—

Kissinger: I am trying to prop up a crumbling empire. Who has been
President? Who has been President these past months? You? Cocooned
in audio tape, intently listening to yourself, trying to discover an
inner, more honorable Nixon. Who's been President? I have. Working
to prevent Brezhnev, Castro, Sadat from taking advantage of your
feebleness. Me. I've had to cover your lapses and drunken absences.
Worse, your drunken presence.

Nixon: I am the President! You are Secretary of State. You owe me
respect. You owe me honor.

Kissinger: I owe you nothing. You think I'm self-interested? You self-
absorbed, self-pitying sap. (*Nixon throws his drink in Kissinger's face.
Pause.*) I'm . . . I . . . .

Nixon: You're not going?

Kissinger: Yes, I . . .

Nixon: No. Don't—

Kissinger: It's become . . . We've . . .

Nixon: No, no. Don't. I . . .

Kissinger: I'm sorry, Mr. President. The . . .

Nixon: Henry.

Kissinger: Perhaps in the morning.

Nixon: Don't go, Henry. Don't leave me. Please. (*Pause. Kissinger
moves to the brandy.*) Oh yes. Drinks, by all means. Freshen mine.
Freshen mine right up. We'll . . . I'm . . . the stress.

Kissinger: Yes. Me, too.

Nixon: I, uh, a drink, yes. You're right about the drinking, but good
God you'd have to be a monster to . . . this job . . . without a snort, how
could I ever?

Kissinger: Ford's not really thinking about Haig, is he?

Nixon: Haig?

Kissinger: He couldn't. It's ludicrous.

Nixon: Mm.

Kissinger: Preposterous.

Nixon: Of course.

Kissinger: He'd be crazy.

Nixon: When I drink with Bebe, we . . . on the *Sequoia*. Sailing the Potomac. It gets nostalgic sometimes. Cherished memories. He's got some doozies. Me too. I have so many. So many good memories.

Kissinger: Mmm.

Nixon: That's why I drink with Bebe. We usually get raucous. That's why I don't drink with Pat, by-the-by. My God. Still, I've got a lot of good memories. No regrets.

Kissinger: Mm.

Nixon: No, I don't think Ford's thinking of Haig.

Kissinger: It would be crazy. I do think you should talk to him.

Nixon: Talk to Ford.

Kissinger: Yes.

Nixon: About you.

Kissinger: Make it clear what would be lost if—

Nixon: Henry, please. Let that go for now. One memory. Growing up. Used to sing this hymn. (*Sings*) "A mighty Fortress is our God." You know it? Oh. Of course not. Sing it with me anyway.

Kissinger: I never sing.

Nixon: Just this once. It's a hymn. A mighty fortress is our God. Go ahead, just that much. It won't kill you.

Nixon and **Kissinger** (*Sing*): "A mighty fortress is our God."

Nixon: Then, um, "A something deep and something." (*Falters*) Can't remember it. (*Pause*) What about you? You must have some something. Growing up in Dusseldorf or wherever.

Kissinger: Furth.

Nixon: Fleeing the Nazis and all that stuff.

Kissinger: I suppose I do.

Nixon: Tell one to me. I don't know much about you really. Tell me a nice memory.

Kissinger: Well, when we moved to New York—

Nixon: From Germany.

Kissinger: —Yes, we fled the . . . as you said. I was twelve. I was exploring our neighborhood . . . I was exploring Washington Heights and got a little lost. I looked up and saw four blond-haired boys coming toward me. I stopped. Should I cross the street or just turn and run? Then I remembered I was in America. They passed me, talking and laughing. I was in America, I was safe.

Nixon: You've never told me that story.

Kissinger: No.

Nixon: I'm touched. It's touching.

Kissinger: I've come such a distance. Sometimes I stare in the mirror. What's happening behind those eyes? I'm astonished. Mystified. I like it.

Nixon: I don't stare in the mirror much. I did on the way up. I did at the height of my . . . At the height, I'd talk to myself in the mirror. "You sly dog," I'd say. "You never thought you'd get this far." And we'd share a secret smile. But then I fell. I fell like Satan tossed from Heaven.

Kissinger: It's the great American story: Requited Ambition. The son of a grocer and an immigrant boy rise to the highest levels of power, change the world.

Nixon: I suppose. If it'd ended a few months sooner: Happy Ending.

Kissinger: A happy story, you keep it going, becomes a tragedy. Tragedy becomes farce.

Nixon: I set myself up. Ambitious people like us, Henry, once we reach our goal, we should just blow our brains out.

Kissinger: So you get elected, you kill yourself. You miss Moscow, China, the Arms Pact, all of it.

Nixon: There's the catch. You don't know when to kill yourself until it's too late. By the time you figure it out, the moment has passed . . .

Here's a memory for us both. Meeting Chairman Mao! Gongs sounding, throngs cheering. Zhou being inscrutable all over the place.

Kissinger: That was a moment.

Nixon: Mao. I've never . . . honestly, Henry.

Kissinger: Mao. Mao was—

Nixon: He . . .

Kissinger: Yes.

Nixon: I've met a lot of great men.

Kissinger: I agree.

Nixon: He . . .

Kissinger: He had an aura.

Nixon: That's it exactly. An aura. You, in his presence, you *felt* . . .

Kissinger: I could see how he lead 800 million in revolution.

Nixon: Oh, yes.

Kissinger: The presence.

Nixon: He did that, the uh, very long hike.

Kissinger: The Long March.

Nixon: My God. I think of myself as a world leader, but . . . Be him for me.

Kissinger: Mr. President, it's late. It's been a difficult—

Nixon: Just be him. Like you did Brezhnev.

Kissinger: —evening.

Nixon: The Imperial City. Big statues of jade and rosewood. Dragons on the bedposts. Okay. We're led to the Great Hall. Opulence, Henry. Opulence. Thousands of years of opulence. Carpets thick as thieves. Doors two stories high. And there he sits. "Chairman Mao. The honor of your presence is overwhelming." Then my interpreter says, "Fen Mao shen syin chr he mu gwan lyang!" And Mao says . . .

Kissinger *(as Mao):* We are—

Nixon: No. You have to do the Chinese. Mao talks in Chinese.

Kissinger *(as Mao):* Womén hèn gàusyìng nén yu womén mei gwó de péng you jyàn myàn.

Nixon: No. We're not capturing . . . it's . . . Let's try it again. See if you can get . . . you know. Okay. I enter.

(Drunkenly game, Kissinger becomes Mao. He speaks Chinese as some kind of outsize Samurai warrior. For his part, Nixon mimes his words as best he can with superfluous hand gestures.)

Chairman Mao. The honor of your presence is overwhelming.

Kissinger *(as Mao):* Womén hèn gàusyìng nén yu womén mei gwó de péng you jyàn myàn.

Nixon: We feel this meeting is the first step in a long and harmonious exchange between our two lands.

Kissinger *(as Mao):* Wo shr lín yáng, ni ye shr lín yáng.

Nixon: Yes. Or rather, you are the dragon, we are the tiger. But the dragon and the tiger can run together.

Kissinger *(as Mao):* Lyang gwó jr jèn je yin èu túng de jèn jr li lyàn.

Nixon: I have traveled far. I have traveled far to learn from the mouth of the honored Chairman Mao.

Kissinger *(as Mao):* You are yet young, Nixon. You too will make your Long March. You too will make the Long March from Nixon to yourself.

Nixon: Will I survive this March?

Kissinger *(as Mao):* Many of my friends died on the March. But they died with honor.

Nixon: Boy was he right. It's much longer than I ever suspected. How will it end? Banished from the kingdom of power! Wandering some hellish golf course, waiting to die. Bathed in glory then flung out on the asphalt tarmac of obscurity. So you see?

Kissinger: Yes . . . See what?

Nixon: I've got to stay on. I've got to complete my charge. Finish the March.

Kissinger: I don't see. I don't see at all.

Nixon: You've got to help me.

Kissinger: What are you saying?

Nixon: It's bigger than all of us.

Kissinger: It's . . . have you been listening?

Nixon: America loves a fighter.

Kissinger: America's . . . you've got to . . .

Nixon: It's clear. It's so clear.

Kissinger: Clear?

Nixon: Once you give up power, it's gone. You're out, finished. As long as I'm in power, I've got a chance. I've got somewhere to fight from.

Kissinger: Fight for what? Everything's gone to hell.

Nixon: Better a ruler in Hell, Henry, than a servant in Heaven. If I've learned anything, I've learned that.

Kissinger: Look . . . Wait . . . No . . . Our last visit to Russia . . . you and Brezhnev, out at his *dacha*.

Nixon: With the hunting.

Kissinger: Yes. And after. He spoke to you. Alone.

Nixon: He wanted . . . just he and I. He wanted to—

Kissinger: I know what he wanted to say.

Nixon: —he wanted to tell me—

Kissinger (*as Brehznev*): Nixon! I knew you would make a hunter. I knew it.

Nixon: He didn't say anything like that.

Kissinger (*as Brehznev*): Truthfully, I almost never catch anything. So today is not so different. It's the hunt itself I love. The actual killing—peah.

Nixon (*Enters into game*): We almost . . . I damn near got that one.

Kissinger (*as Brehznev*): We Soviets, Nixon, we love the outdoors. A country so vast, so unconquerable. It is sublime. I'm sorry about your troubles.

Nixon: Oh, it's, um . . . I'll easily overcome the . . .

Kissinger (*as Brehznev*): I so love it out here, away from the corridors of power. Everything such a tawny green. Did I ever tell you what happened with Svoboda? Oh, Nixon, what a story! So. '68. Prague.

Spring. Our tanks roll in, BAM, movement crushed. We take Dubček into custody. Bring him to the Kremlin. Czechoslovakia's left in turmoil. We don't know what to do about the whole thing. You crush a national movement, now what? I schedule a chat with Svoboda, hoping to work something out. You know. You know him?

Nixon: I know the name.

Kissinger *(as Brehznev):* Went from apricot farmer to soldier to President of the Republic of Czechoslovakia. A true believer in the rights of the common man. Drink. He comes to the Kremlin. To discuss. We sit, very civilized. Much like you and I now. I know what I want, I'm holding all the cards. I look across the table, complacent in my fat power. "Svoboda," I say, tapping his file, "from here on out you do just as I decide." And here, Nixon, here, Ludvik Svoboda, a two-bit functionary from Eastern Europe, throws his Lenin medal to the table, reaches to his pocket, and suddenly is holding a revolver.

Nixon: In the Kremlin?

Kissinger *(as Brehznev):* But Svoboda didn't want to shoot me. This man, he presses the barrel of the gun to his own neck. *(Kissinger points his finger toward Nixon's neck.)* "Release my friend Dubček, or I scatter my brains."

Nixon: "Release my friend Dubček, or I scatter my brains."

Kissinger *(as Brehznev):* You see Nixon, I can't call his bluff. I can't. He kills himself, who will believe it? No one. The world will think we murdered him. The world will think we murdered Ludvik Svoboda in cold blood in the Kremlin.

Nixon: What happened?

Kissinger *(as Brehznev):* I gave him Dubček. Otherwise it's public relations disaster.

Nixon: Ludvik Svoboda. I had no idea.

Kissinger *(as Brehznev):* Many heroic acts go unheralded. They are still heroic. When I looked into Svoboda's eyes, eyes green as this field, I knew he meant it. I knew I'd met a man who placed his convictions far above his own person.

Nixon: You think I should resign.

Kissinger *(as Brehznev):* One day a scientist will write the equations of politics. Power equals Force times Time. We'd like the personal to be a factor in the equation, but ultimately it is no factor. Khrushchev was a friend, a mentor, a father to me. But my love for him was not enough to counter the great forces of history. So I ousted him. Now the equations of politics are turned against you, my beloved Nixon.

Nixon: Force times Time.

Kissinger (*as Brehznev*): It will be painful. I know that. I've seen what loss of power can do. But then again, how many chances does one have to perform a heroic act? A selfless act that serves one's nation?

Nixon: Very impressive, Henry. Had me going. "Tawny green fields." "Heroic act." Yes, nicely done. When you came in, you know what I was hoping? I was hoping for the smallest of things . . . I was hoping you'd try to talk me out of resigning. Just one little attempt, one little gesture, out of . . . respect? But no. Brandy?

Kissinger: It's getting late.

Nixon: I got these yesterday. You might be interested. Transcripts.

Kissinger: Of . . . ?

Nixon: J. Edgar never took the tap off. He took all the others off, but not yours.

Kissinger: Transcripts of my . . . ?

Nixon: Read what you said.

Kissinger (*As he reads*): These are . . . this is . . . taken completely out of context. But this, I didn't say anything . . . Oh. Oh. Part of staff camaraderie is to ridicule you. I had to ingratiate myself. You know how it's played.

Nixon: Do I?

Kissinger: You're getting sidetracked with irrelevancies.

Nixon: You're missing a larger point here. About the transcripts.

Kissinger: I didn't mean any of this.

Nixon: Look at that one.

Kissinger (*Reads*): This was recorded?

Nixon: . . .

Kissinger: This was recorded?!

Nixon: . . .

Kissinger: This . . . You've . . . Where're the tapes?

Nixon: That's it, Henry. That's just it. You see, in the tapes, the subpoenaed tapes, I talk about these. Haldeman and I, it's discussed. The tap on you.

Kissinger: But they have nothing to do with your whole mess.

Nixon: Yeah, but somebody thinks they might, they'll want to hear 'em. I go meddling with 'em, say erase a few minutes, well, as we know, everybody screams bloody murder.

Kissinger: The Bureau's got them?

Nixon: It does.

Kissinger: So no one can get to them. So Gray can fix this.

Nixon: Gray? Gray doesn't know me from Grover Cleveland.

Kissinger: But he can fix it.

Nixon: Why, Henry? I don't know the guy. It's not like when J. Edgar was alive. I can't just call up FBI and say whatever. There's no percentage in it for him. I'm out.

Kissinger: But this gets out . . . This gets out . . . This is highly confidential government business.

Nixon: You're right.

Kissinger: This is not for the public to know.

Nixon: Yes. I see.

Kissinger: IT WOULD BE A CRIME.

Nixon: Your work—

Kissinger: DOESN'T HE UNDERSTAND?

Nixon: —it would—

Kissinger: WHAT DOES HE . . . HE . . . I'm . . . You've got to talk to him.

Nixon: I have.

Kissinger: Again. You've . . . Don't you see, it's *our* reputation. Our place in the books.

Nixon (*Wanders to the record player*): He won't see reason. He's adamant.

Kissinger: No. No, no. We've got to. There's got to be some . . . How can we do this?

Nixon: Henry. If I'm President, if the impeachment thing goes away, then it's okay. If I'm President, Gray comes through. I've got to be President.

Kissinger: "If the impeachment thing goes away?" What on earth can make that happen?

Nixon: You're the genius.

Kissinger: You can't stay President. It's impossible.

Nixon: Perhaps some Ravel. *Rhapsodie Espagnole*?

Kissinger: Somewhere, stuffed in Hoover's old mattress, is a spool of brown tape that can *tarnish* . . . irredeemably . . .

Nixon: You.

Kissinger: Yes.

Nixon: And what the fuck are you going to do about it? Now look here, Henry. I pulled you off the Harvard shit pile, I gave you power you never dreamed of, I made you a world figure. Now, here, at this historic moment, at least you can fight for me. And for you. I'm President, those tapes disappear.

Kissinger: One must base one's decisions on basic principles. In the case of reputation, one must not imperil actual power—

Nixon: There's a real possibility Ford might choose Haig.

Kissinger: Haig?

Nixon: If you were Ford, you'd want to show you're your own man.

Kissinger: Ford might choose Haig?

Nixon: Al's probably lobbying right this minute.

Kissinger: You're saying keeping you in power—

Nixon: Keeps *you* in power.

Kissinger: And if you're in power, you'll fight to prevent the tapes from getting out.

Nixon: How do we do it?

Kissinger: The tapes will remain—

Nixon: *Yes.* How do we do it?

Kissinger: To block impeachment in the Senate you need thirty-four votes, and you've got . . . ?

Nixon: Ten.

Kissinger: Ten?!

Nixon: Six.

Kissinger: Six?! You need twenty-eight Senators?

Nixon: They change their minds in herds. Even Goldwater for chrissakes. Judas priest.

Kissinger: Has the FBI got stuff on twenty-eight Senators?

Nixon: That stuff's no good.

Kissinger: Of course it's no good, but can you use it?

Nixon: They could beat it. Claim political motivation. Which, let's face it . . .

Kissinger: It's hopeless. You'd need an international crisis.

Nixon: That's what I was thinking.

Kissinger: . . . You were thinking you'd need an international crisis?

Nixon: Don't you think so? Look at it. It's my only hope.

Kissinger: But . . . It's, it's too obvious for one thing.

Nixon: We'll do it subtlely.

Kissinger: You're being forced to resign so you provoke a crisis.

Nixon: *I* don't provoke a crisis.

Kissinger: What? *I* provoke a crisis?

Nixon: Don't you get it? Brezhnev, Zhou, Hussein, they're our friends. They're our base of support.

Kissinger: You want them to provoke a crisis?

Nixon: One of them.

Kissinger: Well, which one?

Nixon: Dammit, are you going to work with me on this? How many international crises have you and I dealt with? What's one more?

Kissinger: Say we try it. How would it work?

Nixon: All right. You'd go to, say, Israel and say, "Golda, here's the deal."

Kissinger: Madame Prime Minister, here's the deal.

Nixon: Then you—

Kissinger: No . . . "Madame Prime Minister, here's the deal."

Nixon: What?

Kissinger: What's she say?

(Pause)

Nixon *(as Golda Meir):* What deal?

Kissinger: President Nixon has been a good friend to you.

Nixon *(as Golda Meir):* What do you want?

Kissinger: The President is in grave difficulty. We feel that if certain . . . tensions latent in the Middle East situation were to become more apparent, the American Congress might better appreciate President Nixon's worth.

Nixon *(as Golda Meir):* You want me to start a war to save Nixon?

Kissinger: We don't want you to risk anything of the sort. We just want to point out, in view of the President's great friendship and support of Israel, that if you were planning any provocative action vis-à-vis any of your neighbors, perhaps your timetable could be moved up. That's all.

Nixon *(as Golda Meir):* What kind of Jew are you?

Kissinger: I don't think Israel's the one to go to.

Nixon: No. A flare-up in the Mideast isn't going to do it anyway. People've gotten used to it.

Kissinger: We could get Brezhnev to attack somebody small. But . . .

Nixon: The reactions on both sides . . .

Kissinger: Not much margin for error. We need something . . . it would be good if it didn't directly involve the U.S. That way, if it gets out of control, you know, who cares?

Nixon: Right. Right. But it'll have to be pretty big. We've got to think big. *(They think.)* How 'bout . . . no. No, that's stupid.

Kissinger: We talk to the CIA, we talk to . . . (*Hesitates*)

Nixon: Colby?

Kissinger: No. We talk to . . . We're not being recorded now, are we?

Nixon: You think I'm trying to destroy us?

Kissinger: We talk to . . . the appropriate person.

Nixon: I'm with you.

Kissinger: And we say, "Do such-and-such at such-and-such a place."

Nixon: Secretly.

Kissinger: Secretly, yes.

Nixon: And such-and-such is some—

Kissinger: I have it.

Nixon: —some very dire—

Kissinger: All we need, this is perfect, is some very provocative act along the Chinese-Soviet border.

Nixon: Yes.

Kissinger: Something, um . . .

Nixon: A provincial mayor gets assassinated kind of thing.

Kissinger: Right.

Nixon: Right.

Kissinger: It looks like the Russians are behind it.

Nixon: Exactly.

Kissinger: China reacts, Brezhnev threatens escalation—

Nixon: Back and forth. Up and up.

Kissinger: We tell both sides what's going to happen.

Nixon: Then, sonofagun, it does.

Kissinger: They each think we're with them.

Nixon: We play 'em like banjos.

Kissinger: Everybody's tense. This conflict, so far away, so uncontrollable. Apt to grow exponentially. A real chance of global nuclear exchange.

Nixon: A world on the brink.

Kissinger: Who can prevent world war? Who has the Power and Prestige and *Trust* of the Soviet Union and China? Who?

Nixon: Me.

Kissinger: The one man on the *globe* who can reconcile all parties. The one man who can restore peace.

Nixon: Me.

Kissinger: Bungled cover-ups will seem so paltry. Inconsequential. The Congress, the courts will be embarrassed to pursue such trivia.

Nixon: Me.

Kissinger: So, it plays out kind of, um . . . (*As if responding to reporters on the Capitol steps*) "I, I really can't speculate on what the President will say this evening. I do know he's been in contact with several world leaders. I've shared my thoughts with him, but no, he's kept us all in the dark about what he'll be saying tonight."

Nixon: "My fellow Americans." What am I, LBJ? "Fellow citizens." No. "Loyal subjects?"

Kissinger: Fellow Americans.

Nixon: "Fellow Americans, a world in crisis finds no easy solutions. Many of you tonight are deeply troubled by the tensions in northern China. You fear that events are spinning beyond control and feel the shadow of nuclear war approaching." That's good.

Kissinger: Shadow of war's good. You need more "here it is."

Nixon: Um . . . "Even more troubling is the fact that this crisis comes at a time when my own Presidency is under attack here at home."

Kissinger: Good.

Nixon: "I suffer no delusions about the extent to which my personal plight has divided this nation. But, citizens of America, I am yet President of the United States."

Kissinger: Excellent. Then you get in "spoken at length with Brezhnev, Zhou-en-Lai, who've requested your personal involvement."

Nixon: Right. And then, "Secretary of State Kissinger," something, "also believes . . ." Um . . .

Kissinger: . . . the strength of your friendship with both countries is required for and so on.

Nixon: Yes. Exactly. Then I end it on a, um, you know . . .

Kissinger: "But to do this, I'll need your support. The support of each of you . . ."

Nixon: . . . "no matter your opinion of me personally, I ask you to reach into your hearts and to afford me . . ."

Kissinger: . . . "a brief space of time to devote myself unflaggingly to the crisis in Manchuria."

Nixon: "In return for your forbearance, beyond my gratitude I pledge that once the crisis has passed, once the crisis has passed . . . I will resign."

(They are surprised.)

Kissinger: My God.

Nixon: "And the United States of America can turn to healing itself."

Kissinger: That's it! You resign then.

Nixon: Christ, I'm a genius.

Kissinger: You save the world, then one final gracious bow.

Nixon: What court would pursue me?

Kissinger: A few weeks of empty legalities, then it's forgotten.

Nixon: I'm off. Scot-free.

Kissinger: The resignation becomes a heroic act.

Nixon: The great warrior quitting the field.

Kissinger: After my role in such a thing, Ford could never let me go.

Nixon: "Men of France!"

Kissinger: Nothing could stand in my way.

Nixon: All right, Henry. We've got the scenario. How do we set it going?

Kissinger: Like we said.

Nixon: Some dinky assassination in Irkutsk's not going to make Middle America pee its pants.

Kissinger: Well . . .

Nixon: We need something with bravado. Pizzazz.

Kissinger: Sure.

Nixon: You think Ike did things by half-measures?

Kissinger: So what do we need?

Nixon: Burning villages! Rape, pillage.

Kissinger: We can't just do that. We've got to . . . maybe air-drop, I don't know.

Nixon: Bad chemicals or something.

Kissinger: Yes. Or why not just . . . bombs?

Nixon: Bombs?

Kissinger: We've always been good at—

Nixon: We don't even have to drop any. We put a plane up there with Soviet markings. The Chinese shoot it down. Slam! Everybody's on red alert.

Kissinger: *Then* an assassination.

Nixon: Then an assassination. Right.

Kissinger: The press starts talking Archduke Ferdinand.

Nixon: Maybe an incident in Berlin as well.

Kissinger: The imagination runs riot.

Nixon: Bam! Bam!

Kissinger: We time the incidents according to the press.

Nixon: Provincial mayors dropping like flies.

Kissinger: If it comes to it, we detonate a small one somewhere.

Nixon: Let 'em know they've crossed me. Let 'em know they've pushed me too far. Cities crumble. Nations catch fire.

Kissinger: They'll never recover.

Nixon: Then let 'em impeach me. Let the hippies and the Harvard judges and the pinko Congressmen and the fag reporters impeach me with the world on fire.

Kissinger: Destruction. Destruction everywhere.

Nixon: Bombs from the sky. Kablooie!

Kissinger: Novosibirsk.

Nixon: Bombs from the sky. Kablooie!

Kissinger: Shanghai.

Nixon: Bombs from the sky. Kablooie!

Kissinger: Mozambique.

Nixon: Kablooie!

Kissinger: Brisbane.

Nixon: Kablooie!

Kissinger: Hong Kong.

Nixon: Kablooie!

Kissinger: London!

Nixon: Bombers blacken the skies. People think the sun's going down.

Kissinger: Then the bombs fall.

Nixon: They fall like leaves. Like hailstones.

Kissinger: Like ashes.

Nixon: Bombs fall like night. A night of fire. A snow of embers.

Kissinger: Rice farmers harvest little bits of their friends.

Nixon: People everywhere open their mouths, but their tongues lie dead of shock.

Kissinger: And then, you step in!

Nixon: "Fellow Americans."

Kissinger: Order is restored. You're a hero.

Nixon (*Picks up phone*): Get me Brezhnev. No, let's not let him in on it. Get me the CIA.

Kissinger: Let me talk to them.

Nixon: Yeah. Who is this? Blow the fuckers up.

Kissinger (*Grabs phone*): Blow them up. Whoever. Whatever. Whenever.

Nixon (*Grabs phone*): Start with small fuckers, then blow up bigger and bigger fuckers.

Kissinger (*Grabs phone*): Those're the orders, pal. From the top.

Nixon: The very, very top. The President of the United States. (*Hangs up*)

(*Somber. Time passes. Nixon gazes out front.*)

It's lovely, isn't it?

Kissinger: The . . . ?

Nixon: If you didn't know it was real, you'd think it was phony. You'd think it was a painting. What's that way out there, Henry? Some famous pass? Some famous mountain? Towering above the land of the great Khan. This wall has kept away enemies for twenty-three hundred years. What is it out there, Henry? What do you see?

(*Pause*)

Kissinger: I see the plains of Tun-shen stretching out to the Gobi.

Nixon: Imagine the power.

Kissinger: Yes.

Nixon: It must've felt good to give that command. "Build a wall." That's all you'd have to say. Next day, *this*'d be begun. How long is it?

Kissinger: Fourteen hundred miles.

Nixon: Feel this. The dust of dynasties. If I were the Emperor Huang-Ti, those years ago, I'd build this wall. I'd build this wall so strong, none would dream of attacking me. I would build this wall and my kingdom would be secure.

Kissinger: It's late, sir. We should head back.

Nixon: At this moment, standing here, gazing over the plains of Tun-shen, right at this precise moment, I'm the most powerful man ever. For just this . . . moment. (*Nixon has returned to the present.*) How many did we kill, Henry?

Kissinger: When's this?

Nixon: You know. Over all. How many? In Vietnam, say. Since I'm President.

Kissinger: Fifty-five thousand.

Nixon: No. Since I became President.

Kissinger: Oh. Twenty-one thousand.

Nixon: How many Viet Cong?

Kissinger: Two hundred eighty thousand.

Nixon: North Vietnamese army?

Kissinger: One hundred twenty thousand.

Nixon: South Vietnamese army?

Kissinger: One hundred forty thousand.

Nixon: Civilians?

Kissinger: One hundred eighty thousand.

Nixon: The Cambodian bombings?

Kissinger: Eighteen thousand.

Nixon: And in Laos?

Kissinger: Laos? About twenty thousand.

Nixon: Chile?

Kissinger: But these aren't—

Nixon: Chile?

Kissinger: Twelve thousand.

Nixon: About eight hundred thousand so far. Eight hundred thousand and one, counting Allende. Then there's Kent State. Eight hundred thousand and five.

Kissinger: Mr. President.

Nixon: Eight hundred thousand and five all together. Eight hundred thousand and five dead on my watch.

Kissinger: A world leader makes decisions.

Nixon: Still. Eight hundred thousand dead. Kablooie. Now I resign? Now I spend the rest of my days wading in a swimming pool of blood? There're times. Muh. In the army they've got it easy. Someone leaves a gun in a drawer. I don't have a gun.

Kissinger: Sir, you've got to—

Nixon: Oh, dear God, I need your help. I feel like I should be asking forgiveness, but I don't feel like I've done anything wrong. They gave me so much power, why are they surprised I used it? And where were You? Where the fuck have You been? Here I am, on my *knees.* Just to get You to help me realize that sometimes the courageous thing isn't to struggle on. Sometimes, it takes more courage, more honor to, to throw in the towel. Can't You help me realize that? But then what, Henry? Then I'll need Him more than ever. You see, I can make the speeches. I can thank people and say, you know, the things that have to be said. I can do that. But after, I've got to climb the ramp into the helicopter. To take me away. Climb those metal stairs fighting the roar of the engines. One step after another. Nothing but a handrail. And then, at the top, I'll have to turn to the crowd. I'll have to say good-bye with dignity. Good-bye to all my power. Good-bye to all my joy. Good-bye to all my pain. Good-bye to all I've ever been. How on God's green earth will I be able to do it?

Kissinger: Sir. Sir.

Nixon: I need You to let me know it'll be all right, if I can just make it up that ramp. Please. Just let me know that. If I can just . . .

Kissinger: Sir. It'll be okay.

Nixon: God. Why won't You let me know it'll be all right? Goddammit, why won't You just tell me that?

Kissinger: It'll be all right. (*Kissinger touches him on the arm. Nixon pulls away in fury.*)

Nixon: Sorry, Henry. I'm . . . I . . .

Kissinger: It's . . . Sir.

Nixon: I didn't mean for . . .

Kissinger: I should be leaving.

Nixon: It's the strain. The . . . It's unbearable. It's a miracle.

Kissinger: You've withstood. Considering . . .

Nixon: I'll need a speech. A resignation speech to the nation. I suppose the boys in the back've already written something.

Kissinger: An outline. Just in case.

Nixon: Also a good-bye to the staff. I'll write that. To all those who've . . . stuck by . . .

Kissinger: Of course.

Nixon: All those who've . . . in the face of so much . . . Especially Julie, Henry. She's been such a soldier.

Kissinger: Yes. Yes, I know.

Nixon: I wish I could . . . There're some things I wish I could say to her. All she's done. Gone through. I just don't know if I . . . I should say, Julie, I let you down. I let you make all those speeches. All over hell's half-acre, telling everybody what a good man I am. I let you tell people I hadn't done things. When you were a little girl . . . Four, five? After I gave the Checkers speech, just after, I came home, I thought it was a dud, I thought my career was over. I was angry, I snapped at Pat, everyone trying to tell me it'd gone so well. I came into the house and slammed the door and there you were with Checkers in your arms. You looked up at me with the biggest smile. "Daddy! You said Checkers on TV!" I thought my heart would . . . break. (*Pause*) Julie. I did do things. I did. And if I let you go saying over and over that I hadn't . . . it's just that nobody ever showed me that much love before. (*Pause*) I didn't know how to tell you that your dad was a bum. I was afraid you'd lose all respect for your old man. That was something I couldn't . . . Julie. Could you. Could you tell me . . .

Kissinger (*as Julie*): Father. I've always respected you. I'll always love you.

Nixon: All right. Now what'll I tell those bastards? Friends. Dear, dear, friends. We think that when someone dear to us leaves, we think when we lose an election, we think that when we suffer a defeat, that all has ended.

Kissinger: Mr. President.

(*Slow fade-in of helicopter noise*)

Nixon: Not true. It is only a beginning, always. The young must know it, the old must know it. It must always sustain us, because the greatness comes not when things go always good for you—

Kissinger: Mr. President.

Nixon: —but greatness comes and you are really tested when you take some knocks, some disappointments, when sadness comes.

Kissinger: What about the tapes, Mr. President?

(*Add underlying grating drone to helicopter*)

Nixon: Because only if you have been in the deepest valley can you ever know how magnificent it is to be on the highest mountain.

(*Nixon seems to be ascending the steps to the helicopter.*)

Kissinger: Can you keep the tapes!? Mr. President! Come back! The tapes!

(*But Kissinger is lost in darkness and his continued pleas are swallowed by the roar of the engine.*

Noise swells to a deafening level.

Richard Nixon, standing atop the stairs, turns and determinedly gives his final wave, complete with rueful, forced smile/frown.

Blackout. Cut sound.)

END OF PLAY

7 Blowjobs

MAC WELLMAN

7 Blowjobs received its premiere at the
Sledgehammer Theatre in San Diego,
California, on October 13, 1991. It was
produced by Ethan Feerst, directed by
Scott Feldsher, set design by Robert Brill,
lighting design by Ashley York Kennedy,
costume design by Lisa Noelle Stone, and
sound design by Pea Hicks. The cast
included Susan Gelman as Dot, Walter
Murray as Messenger/BobBob Junior,
Bruce McKnezie as Bruce/Bob Junior,
Sandra L'Italien as Eileen, and Douglas
Jacobs as Senator Bob.

Cast of Characters

*Dot, a receptionist in the office of
the Senator on the Hill*

*Eileen, the Senator's Administra-
tive Assistant*

*Bruce, the Senator's Legislative
Assistant*

*Tom, a television evangelist of
some note*

Bob, the Senator himself

Bob Junior, the Senator's son

*BobBob Junior, an idea of
surveillance*

Express Mail Delivery Person

Setting

*The Old Senate Office Building
during late afternoon and evening*

Production Note

*When an asterisk (*) appears in
the text, it means that the next
speech begins at that point and
that the two speeches overlap.*

Author's Note

The author would like to thank the following for their generous support: The New York Foundation for the Arts, The John Simon Guggenheim Foundation, and the National Endowment for the Arts. He would also like to thank the Bellagio Study and Conference Center of the Rockefeller Foundation and the staff at the Villa Serbelloni, where this play was written.

7 Blowjobs *is dedicated—like* Sincerity Forever *before it—to those supreme clowns of our sad time, Jesse Helms and Donald Wildmon; and also to Representative Dana Rohrabacher and the Reverend Pat Robertson, because they have shown such an abiding interest in my work. These Gents (God help them!) comprise the Four Harebrained Horsemen of our Contemporary Cornball Apocalypse.*

ACT 1

SCENE 1

(*The Senator's office on Capitol Hill. A not-so-busy receptionist—Dot—is seated primly behind a desk. She smiles. She stops smiling. A furry blackout.*)

SCENE 2

(*The Senator's office on Capital Hill. A busy receptionist— Dot—is dealing with a busy phone.*)

Dot: Hello. Senator X's office. Hello,
Nothing of value inside, please.
Please don't steal our stuff . . .

(*Pause*)

Yes. No. Maybe.

(*She hangs up.*

Pause. Phone rings.)

Hello. Senator X's office. Hello,
Nothing of value inside, please.
Please don't steal our stuff . . .

(*Pause*)

Yes. No. Maybe.

(*She hangs up.*

Pause. Phone rings.)

Hello. Senator X's office. Hello,
Nothing of value inside, please.
Please don't steal our stuff . . .

(*Pause*)

Yes. No. Maybe.

(*She hangs up.*
Pause. Phone rings.
There is a knock at the door.)

Phone. Door. At the same time, wow.

(*She tries to decide which.*
She goes to the door.
The Delivery Person enters.
Phone rings. She smiles.)

Hello. Senator X's office.

(*The phone rings.*
She answers the phone.)

Hello, please.

Delivery Person: Package for the Senator.

Dot (*To phone*): Hello, please.

Delivery Person: Sign here.

(*She signs.*)

Dot (*To phone*): Yes, hello, please.

Delivery Person: Thanks, lady.

(*He puts down the package.*)

Dot (*To phone*): Yes, hello, please.

(*He goes out. Pause.*
She hangs up the phone.
She looks over the package.)

Maybe. Maybe not . . .

(*She shakes the package.*
She listens to the package.
Pause.)

Maybe I should. No.

(*Phone rings*)

Hello. Senator X's office. Hello, nothing of value inside, please. Please don't steal our stuff . . .

(*Pause*)

Yes. No. Maybe.

(*Pause*)

I said: Yes No Maybe . . .

(*Pause*)

Yes, no, maybe: he is obsquatulated.

(*Pause*)

YES NO MAYBE.

(*Hangs up. Pause.*)

Maybe I should. No . . .

(*Pause*)

Yes.

(*She opens it.
The package contains photos.
She looks at them.*)

Eek!

(*She faints. Hits the deck.
Blackout.*)

SCENE 3

(*The same, only a little later. Dot's back at the phone.
Bruce, the Senator's L.A., and Eileen, his A.A., are examining the contents of the package.*)

Eileen: What do you make of it, Bruce?

Bruce: The real thing.

Eileen: Serious . . . stuff . . .

Bruce: In basic English, I would say. The real thing. Serious stuff.

Dot: What do you mean? Cripes! It's hypoallergenic. I'm ill on account of it. Cripes!

Eileen: Bag it, Dot.

Dot: Cripes, you guys.

Eileen: Okay, Dot. Just bag it.

(*Phone rings*)

Dot: Hello. Senator X's office. Hello, nothing of value inside, please. Please don't steal our stuff.

(*Pause*)

Yes. No. Maybe.

Eileen: The photographs decked Dot, Bruce. She fell down on account of them.

Bruce: Eileen, at best she's not up to much. Eileen, why does she do this thing? Why does she do this thing of "Hello. Senator X's office. Nothing of value inside, please"? Senator X is not Senator Bob's name and this other stuff, crazy!

Dot: Bruce, I do this "Hello. Senator X's office. Nothing of value inside, please" thing at the request of Surveillance, who is afraid for Senator Bob's life after he said the speech Eileen wrote for him about the Arabs being an insect.

(*To the phone*)

No, not you. Yes no maybe.

(*Hangs up*)

Bruce, you crossed my wires.

Eileen: She's got feelings, Bruce.

Bruce: Eileen, at best she's not up to much. Especially, if these photos* decked her.

Eileen: Okay, bag it, Bruce. I've got feelings, you've got feelings, Everybody's got feelings that deck them. It's normal to be decked by one of them when they are . . . like this . . .* Okay, Bruce? So just bag it.

Dot: The pictures aren't normal but it didn't deck me, Eileen. I fell over on account of lunch hour having come and gone and no lunch. Cripes, Bruce!

Bruce: Sorry. Sorry. I was . . . trying . . . okay?

(*Pause*)

Dot: But they sure aren't normal. Cripes!

Eileen: Bag it, Dot, okay?

(*Pause*)

Maybe they are a FACT of some . . . maybe they are an evidence . . .

Dot: Maybe it's a dilemma.

Bruce: Could be. They are personal.

Eileen: Quite. I would say so.

(*They look long and hard.*)

Bruce: Are those people doing that?

Eileen: They are not cows and pigs, Bruce.

Bruce: I was being euphuistic, Eileen.

Eileen: You're a scholar, Bruce.

(*Dot joins them.
They look long and hard.*)

Dot: Maybe it's a dilemma. These two ones here. He's got to make a choice. Somehow. He has to.

Eileen: Why do you say that?

Dot: Look at that, there.

Bruce: True . . . Urgent . . .

Eileen: And this arm here . . . Whose?

Dot: Is that a face, Eileen? Whose . . .

(*A long pause*)

Eileen: Wow. Look at that one.

Bruce: Which?

Dot: That one there.

Eileen: Wow. Is that one real?

Bruce: Very funny, Eileen. Ha ha.

Eileen: I was not making light of it. I was just of a mind. Two actually, if this is what a person means when they are contorted, so to speak. As, uh, in the case of having sex, you know . . . Bag it, Bruce.

Bruce (*Pointing*): You would call that, that?

(*Phone rings*)

Eileen: No, I would not call that, that. Did I call that an instance of that? No.

Dot: Hello. Senator X's office. Hello, nothing of value inside, please. Please don't steal our stuff.

(*Pause*)

Yes. No. Maybe.

(Palming the phone)

Is he in today, ever? Senator Bob?

Eileen: Bag it, Dot.

Dot: You're getting heavy-lidded from looking at that.

Eileen: We are not looking at that. We are just . . . ah . . .*

(They look long and hard.)

That's unusual, that.

Dot: No, not you. Hello? Hung up.

(She hangs up.)

Bruce: That?

Eileen: No. That.

Bruce: I don't think so.

Eileen: I know what you mean to say. You mean to say you've had experience with that, with one such as that. Bag it, Bruce.

Bruce: I was not saying that. I was saying something else.

Eileen: You were making a claim. Ha!

Bruce: I was not* making a claim.

Eileen: He was making a claim, Dot.

Dot: He is always making claims, Eileen.

(All look hard.)

Cripes.

Eileen: Why are they on a chair like that. With no clothes on?

Bruce: Eileen, please. Can you not
please use your imagination?
This is a possible evidence.
You are agitated. Please,
Eileen, do not become agitated
because you know how you get
and how the boss feels about
getting that way, when you do.

Eileen: Bag it, Bruce.

(*They look. Dot goes
back to her desk. Pause.*)

Bruce: Anyway, that is not an arm.

No, I would not say it is

an arm.

(*Pause*)

Eileen: What are you saying, Bruce?

(*Dot laughs.*)

Bag it, Dot.

(*Pause. Eileen looks hard.*)

That is not that, Bruce.
That is something else, because
the light is not so bright
in the photo. It's a somewhat
dark place where they are,
clearly, so a big mistake is
possible. I think it's a . . .
No. Maybe a . . . piece of clothing.

Dot: Bob will want to know what it
is, and why you are taking so
long at . . . it . . . This is . . .
maybe an important stuff.

Bruce: He is not *Bob*, Dot. He is,
you will recall, a Senator.*
Hence the name is Senator Bob.

Dot: It's the real thing,* Eileen.

Eileen: Oh, shut up, Bruce. You are
an exasperating person, really!

Bruce: Eileen, don't look at more.
You're starting to get . . .
you know . . . wiggly . . .

Eileen: Bag it, Bruce. I am not.

Bruce: Women get wiggly when they look
at the real thing. We men do
not, having been hardened by
the war experience and hardship.
Growing up in law school and
the rest. Money, responsibilities.
It's awful. I don't know how we
put up with the pressure, but we
do. At least some of us do, if
we are not stabbed in the back
by our women, and those on the
left and in the opposition party,
those who want us not to succeed.
It's true, all of it, I swear,
Eileen. You are a sweet kid,
but you don't know how bad
a place the world is, having
been a girl at some, I bet,
Ivy League place, where they
are permissive about stuff,
about people who do that (*He points.*)
and that and THAT! CAN
YOU BELIEVE THAT!? THAT
A MAN WOULD DO THAT? A
FULL-GROWN MAN DOING THAT . . .
Your background is too
nice for understanding of
how gross and disgusting
people can be. I think you are
a liberal underneath your
clothes and underwear, all
women are. Even Dot, who is
more low than we, but has the
privilege of working on this*
staff. Even when it is awful

work it is exciting. But I
know, I went to Bob Jones
University and I know how
people get twisted by false
gods, and how a life of crime
awaits all those who . . . get
weak and . . . experiment with
drugs . . . atheism . . . And
the real thing . . . that, I mean
. . . and THAT . . . I mean, will
you get a load of . . . *THAT*!
. . . Eileen, for Pete's sake.

Dot (*Aside*): I think I will change. I think
I will not let this bother me.
I think I will use this as an
instance to my true, life purpose.

Eileen: That is not *that,* Bruce, so
just bag it. That is the . . .
radiator, and not an active
participant . . . So just bag it,
Bruce, because where do you get
off saying those things? Drugs
are not on my resume. Atheism
is not on my resume. Have you
looked at my resume, Bruce?
You are a silly goose, Bruce.
So just bag it.

(*They look long and hard.*)

Dot: Maybe it's a dilemma. These
two ones here. He's got to make
a choice. Somehow. He has to.

Eileen: Why do you say that?

Dot: Look at that, there.

Eileen: True . . . Urgent . . .
Wow. Look at that one.

Bruce: Which?

Dot: That one there.

Eileen: Wow. Is that one real?

Bruce: Very funny, Eileen. Ha ha.

(*Bruce pointing*)

You would call that, that?

(*Phone rings*)

Eileen: No, I would not call that, that. Did I call that an instance of that? No.

Dot: Hello. Senator X's office. Hello, nothing of value inside, please. Please don't steal our stuff.

(*Pause*)

Yes. No. Maybe.

(*Palming the phone*)

Is he in today? Senator Bob?

Eileen: Bag it, Dot. That's unusual, that.

Dot: Bag you, Eileen.

No, not you. Hello? Hung up.

(*She hangs up.*)

Bruce: That? Are you asking is that an instance of that?

Eileen: No. That.

Bruce: I don't think so. I was not saying that. I was saying something else.

Eileen: You were making a claim. Ha!

Bruce: I was not* making a claim.

Eileen: He was making a claim, Dot.

Dot: He is always making claims, Eileen.

(*All look hard.*)

Cripes.

Eileen: Why are they on a chair
like that. With no clothes on?

(*They look long and hard.*)

Dot: I was shocked by those photos.
I do not see either of you,
cripes, being so shocked as I.
I think you like those things
they are doing, like that, the
animals. I think you both
want to look at that stuff
too much not to be . . . cripes!
Suspicious. And when the
Senator gets back I plan
to ask him for a raise, I
did not come to the Hill to
be exposed to a moral vice
as with this experience, cripes!
All seven photos remind me
of what you're not supposed
to think, each one worse
than the other, and you both
pretend to be Christians, cripes!
I am truly shocked by this . . . (*Points*)
Not to mention *that* . . . sick.
I've never thought of bending
over . . . like that . . . And wow,
you sure are lapping it up, ha.

Eileen: Bag it, Dot. This is work.
Documentation of evidence.

Bruce: I feel unstable, wow.

(*He sits.*)

Eileen: What's wrong, Bruce, did
the putty-tat from Puscaloosa
poop his panties? You putz . . .
The real stuff got to you,
I can see, all seven, each
one worse than the other.

Wow, what a man! What
a tough-minded Young
Republican! No American
Enterprise Institute for you,
wussums. No, the real stuff
gives you the wiggles too.
Brucey better take his crackers
and milk and curl up for his
little nap on his little blankie.
Wow! What a man! What
a tough-minded Young
Republican. No American
Heritage Foundation for you,
wussums. No. The real thing's
got you a little dizzy, huh?
Brucey better take his crackers
and milk and curl up on his
little blankie for his little nap.

(*Pause*)

Bruce: I felt unstable for a moment
is all. Wow.

Dot: You sure are lapping it up,
both of you, cripes.

Eileen: Bag it, Dot.

(*Pause.*

She and Bruce look.)

Do you think that is what
it actually looks like? Or,
how else do you explain
what it really is, if that's
not right? I mean, well,
if what we are seeing is
photos—of stuff—say . . .

Dot: The real thing, I would say.

Eileen: But maybe doctored . . . maybe . . .

Bruce: They sure look healthy to me,
Eileen. Ha ha.

Eileen: Very funny, Bruce. You are
a wit. Dot, Bruce is a wit.
Bag it, Bruce.

(*Pause*)

Bruce: The photos may be doctored
to emphasize that and that,
for instance, though . . . *why*
is beyond me . . . why they
would need to emphasize
that anymore than . . . that . . .
is unclear to me. Perhaps, in
the light of day we can see
a clear evidence of tampering,
perhaps at the lab. Do we have
access to a lab of some sort,
Dot, do we?

(*Phone rings*)

Dot: Hello. Senator X's office. Hello,
nothing of value inside, please.
Please don't steal our stuff.

(*Pause*)*

Yes. No. Maybe.

(*Hangs up*)

Eileen: Dot is circumscribed, Bruce.
So don't bother her. But yes,
we do have a lab, but it is
not Congress's. The lab, I mean.
Congress does not have a lab
for this, but Surveillance does,
and that is the Surveillance
that watches out for stuff
just like this, bad stuff,
meant to injure the mind
and screw up public morals.
We need to be wary, because
stuff meant to injure the
soul exists aplenty, and people
too. People who do this . . .
And this . . . And this . . .

and this one . . . wow . . .
I did not see that one.

Bruce: That one, that was on
the bottom, being the worst.

Eileen: That one is clearly the worst.
I did not think bodies did
that. Bodies do not have
things like that, on them.
Look, Dot, look. Look at
that thing there, there.

Dot: Wow.

Bruce: That one is clearly the most . . .
worst . . . But that thing is
not a part of that body,
no, Eileen, it's much worse.
Because, see that body
over there, that one? With
the hair on, see it? There?

Eileen: There? No . . . that could not
possibly belong to that, it
couldn't fit, on her, oh my.

Bruce: That part is not a part that
is *on* anything, it is a part
that is normally inside, it's
not meant to be seen. See?

Eileen: If it's not meant to be seen,
that part, then I have never
seen one, nope. I would
know if I had, and so . . .
Dot, take a look at this thing,
here.

Dot: Where? That one? Which?

Eileen: No, this part here. It's not
what we think it is, maybe . . .
Sweet Jesus, I hope for their
sake it is not what it looks
like, because that would make
me ill. I knew some parts are

capable of bending and being
bent, stretched and wiggled
in ways that suggest . . . all
kinds of stuff . . . stuff that decent
people try not to think about,
but the human anatomy, Dot,
how can it be so . . . unstable,
as to do that to itself, and say,
hey, I'm normal. I'm okay,
and just having a fine time, but
Sweet Jesus, I hope for their
sake it is not what it looks
like because, they never told
us about this or that, at the
Dartmouth Review, when we
tore down the ugly shanties
of those colored people who . . .
you mean to say, Bruce, do
you mean to say, that part
there is normal that is normal
only when it is inside that
other part way over there!?
oh no, I can't believe that . . .
That is not how nature is
supposed to be. They never said
that that could be bent or flexed
like that, at the *Dartmouth Review*
when we tore down the shanties
of the colored people, of the Indians,
and of the other liberals. Because
that part is not normal, that
part should not be distended
to such an extent that it flares
out like that. It might pop.
It might pop and burst and
the stuff inside, why! it would
trickle down the sides here, and
God, that part is not where
God intended, when he placed
it, modestly, where it is, back
inside, nestled like a little
pink wildflower. Inside,
nestled like a little, pink

wildflower on the woodsy . . . thing,
there. In the soft, woodsy part.

Dot: It's not what you think, it's
not that, it's something else,
so calm down, Eileen. It's
only a picture.* A picture can't
torture and rape you . . . a picture . . .

Eileen: A picture can too torture and
rape your mind, Dot, I mean
can't you imagine that, being
bent and wiggled and so
forth, and stretched and so
forth . . . like that . . . I mean,
look at that look on her face, the
pain, the intense anguish of the
poor thing. A picture can do
these things, I know it, and
so do you, which is why you
are here, and not down the hall
working for Senator so-and-so
who represents a state where
that kind of behavior is all
too common, Dot. A picture
can too torture and hopelessly
maim the insides of you,
and can destroy the outside
of the inside part of you
like that poor girl there, that
Bruce is looking at, and not
helping me to argue the point
because that photo, like the
one before, and the one before
and the one before, and the
one before, and especially the
one before that, and the one
we saw first that now seems
tame—almost innocent, one
might say, by comparison—
have turned his brain to mush.
Look at Bruce, Dot, look at
his eyes, how empty and ill
they are, like an animal who

has seen too much of human
life ever to be an animal again.
They never, never told us about
the look in those eyes, at the
Dartmouth Review when we
were tearing down the shanties
of the colored people, and the
other people, Indians and the
rest. I feel tortured and maimed
by the impact of these pictures
upon the inside of my brain.
So just bag it, Bruce and
you too, Dot, bag you, I
mean, bag it. Really, bag it!

Dot: Eileen, Eileen. Calm down,
Eileen, it's only a picture.
A picture cannot torture and
maim your heart. A picture
is a picture, Eileen. It
can't do that (*Points*), or that . . .
If you want to be destroyed
by a picture, a picture
will destroy you, like
Bruce here, but Bruce is
sick anyway, Eileen. We
both have seen how sick
Bruce is, at office parties,
Eileen. It's a fact. Cripes,
so don't get so worked
up. I have seen all this
before, back in Oil City,
Pennsylvania, we had this (*Points*)
and this and even that,
even though it was not so
swollen as that, and I
never saw such clear
photos of the whole thing,
and so many participants, all
in one room, at it, Eileen.
I knew such things happened
because it was a fact they
were not talked about, and

you can be sure that when an
activity is not being talked
about, it is going on. It is
definitely going on when it
is not being talked about,
because, Eileen, you go figure:
if you were an activity . . . like
that . . . or that . . . or even that
astonishing part there. That
one. And someone decent, say,
from the church, or an elderly
person in a position of power,
or a person in your family you
are supposed to look up to
for advice in troubled times. . . .
Times like these, Eileen, times
like the ones the Senator has
talked about in the speeches
you have written for him,
and in the restrictive legislation
Bruce there—will you get a
load of whacko Bruce there!
Wow! What a sickey! What
a sex fiend's look in those
eyes, Eileen. Bruce, are
you drooling? Bruce is
drooling, Eileen, look at
the drool on his sleeve, oh
God, I hope it's drool, oh
please, God, let it be drool . . .
and Eileen, the point is . . . I . . .
was trying to say before Bruce
here, Bruce began to drool . . .
that if you were an activity (*Points*)
. . . like that . . . or that . . . or even that . . .
that astonishing part there . . .
that one you said should be
more normal . . . if you were
such an activity, and a
person came up to you, even
a good person like the Senator
or the Reverend, a good decent
person who talks on the TV

about God and stuff and
how you should behave and
observe God's rules and listen
to the speeches you write for
the Senator and support the
restrictive legislation that
is drafted in this office, by
Bruce—sick, sad Bruce;
at least when he is not
drooling over dirty pictures—
would you not, being that
healthy, unspeakable act
simply reply: GO TO HELL!
MIND YOUR OWN BEESWAX
BECAUSE I AM HAVING A
GOOD TIME, THANK YOU!

(*Pause*)

MIND YOUR OWN BEESWAX
BECAUSE I AM HAVING A
GOOD TIME, THANK YOU!
GO TO HELL! GOOD-BYE!

(*The Senator enters unseen.*)

Bruce: Dot, shut up. Eileen, shut up.
I am not a pervert, I am a
man who does his job. I
am examining these photos
because of them being sent
to the Senator, by a delivery
person, and therefore they
are evidence of a smear . . .
Yes, Eileen, I am capable
of seeing through these photos . . .
even this one . . . which I confess
is strong stuff. This one
is more than the real thing. This one
is abnormal, even by the sick
standards of the sex-obsessed,
subnormal person who took it,
and all the rest because, this
photo cannot harm you, it
cannot make you sick

if you are not sick already,
but if you are sick already
it can make you . . . more
sick than before. That is true, and
I resent that crack, Dot,
about me and my drool, Dot.
That was unfair. I was
doing my job of work here,
while you and Eileen stood
and yelled at each other
and then yelled at me. I
do not call yelling at
my colleagues "work", no,
but maybe I'm old-fashioned
and not "with it" as you
"hip" people say, as you "hip"
people say at your clubs
and discos, and at your
Dartmouth College when I
did not come from no damn
high-class Eastern Liberal
Establishment family but
was always working on my paper
route, Eileen, while you played.
Eileen, while you partied and
played I was lower middle-class,
Eileen, and that hurts, Eileen,
that hurts because of not
being allowed to the country
club dances, where girls like
you wore white gloves and
are debutantes and do stuff
like "coming out" and stuff.
I know what that stuff
is, all that debutante stuff,
and how you all go on to
Dartmouth College with
all the other rich kids and
pretend to be conservative!
Yes, pretend, Eileen, pretend!
Because I went to Bob Jones
University which is where you
go if you are the real thing,

Eileen, conservative, Eileen.
I know what that stuff
is, all that debutante stuff:
you wear white gloves and
are debutante and do stuff
like "coming out" and stuff.
But Dot and me, we know,
because we have to work for
our daily bread, not like you,
Eileen, because Dot and me
know you're faking it
when you write those speeches
for the Senator, yes, Eileen,
your heart's not in it, Eileen.
Face it, you're an imitation.

Eileen: Bag it, Bruce, just go bag it.
Bruce. Because I bet you know
what that is . . . and that . . .
And that you've done that
with this and that, I just bet!
Because I know you rich
kids have access to good
drugs and stuff, and do
all the things that are in
these seven photos, yes,
I am not an idiot, Eileen.
Because all rich kids know
what that is . . . and that . . .
And that that thing there,
which is supposed to be
over there, on that one, is
the source of indescribable
joy if it has been over there
like that, in a sick and
twisted way, even if that
rich kid joy is loathsome
and morally reprehensible
and unAmerican and so
forth and so on, and I
bet these people here, these
sick and depraved people
in these photos, are friends of

yours, from Dartmouth
College, where you claim
you worked on the *Dartmouth
Review*, where you claim
you did patriotic activities
like pulling down the shanties
of the colored people, and the
Indians, and the liberals,
while all the time, Eileen,
you were up to no good,
doing stuff like this . . .
and that . . . and that . . .
and even this one here, wow.
This one sure got to me, wow.

(*All see the Senator
and fall silent. Pause.*)

Senator: What in the name of Sam Hill
has happened around here? You
all look like you got poison
ivy on the back of your eyeballs.

(*Pause*)

Bruce: These came in the mail* today, Senator.

Dot: They certainly did not come in the
mail. They were expressed here . . .
Cripes, Bruce!

Senator: What were expressed here today?

Eileen: These. Take a look. You'd
better sit down before you
take a look.

Bruce: That would be wise, Senator.

Dot: I did not sit down before I
took a look at them, only I
fell down. Then I got adjusted
and now I feel fine, but
these two, you would not
BELIEVE how these two have
been carrying on. I mean,
it's only a picture, and both

of 'em're having a fit, yup
a regular conniption,* like
you never saw a thing such
as what people have between
their legs before, cripes!

Eileen: Bag it, Dot.

(*He sits wearily.*)

Senator: Okay, okay. Show me.

(*Bruce eyes Eileen.
Eileen eyes Dot.
Dot eyes Bruce.
Bruce shows them to the
Senator. Pause.*)

Eileen: I would advise deep breathing
if you feel faint, Senator.

(*Pause*)

Senator: What kind of film would you say
it is? This here? Fast or slow . . .
I'm a bit of an amateur photographer myself.

Bruce (*Pointing*): What is that, there, would you say?

Senator: What is what?

Bruce: That. There.

Senator: That?

Bruce: Yes. That.

Senator: Well, I dunno. Let me look.

(*Pause*)

Bruce: That is a blowjob.

Senator: That is not a blowjob. That is the Pope.

(*He's got it upside down.
Bruce helps him get it right. Pause.*)

Bruce: That is a blowjob, Senator.
We've got about seven of 'em
here. In this office. Someone
sent us seven photos of this

blowjob-type behavior,
and we're deeply concerned.

Senator: I still say that's the Pope.

Dot: It does look like the Pope—with no clothes.

Senator: I need my reading glasses, where
in hell are my reading glasses?
I always leave my reading
glasses by the ant-farm. Whose
idea was it, by God, who the
hell moved the ant farm? I
can't do no reading without
the ant farm, I mean the reading
glasses I make a point of
leaving next to, or on top
of, the goddamn ant farm.

Eileen: There they are, sir, in the ant farm.
With ants all over them.

(*All look. Pause.*)

Dot: Boy, do they ever swarm when
they swarm. Cripes. Do you suppose
they are making a meal of your
reading glasses?

Senator: Hell. (*Picks them out*)
Go clean these off. (*To Eileen*)
Who sent these photos, Bruce.

Bruce: I . . . We don't know . . . sir.

(*An autocratic pause*)

Senator: You did not bother to ascertain,
Bruce, who sent them? You did
not do this, Bruce? I cannot
believe it. . . .

(*He sighs deeply.*)

Dot, who sent them?

Dot (*She digs through the trash.*):

Well, now, let's see . . . It's gotta
be here . . . in the wastepaper . . .

Senator: What a bunch! What a royal bunch!

Dot: I think it was Senator So-and-So. The guy from down the hall . . .

Eileen: See, Senator? Look. See? That thing there. And that one too . . .

Senator: Oh me, oh my. That is a blowjob . . .* Wow!

Eileen: No, Senator, that's not the blowjob. That is a borzoi dog that is chained to the banister. You can see, it's a split-level den of iniquity, this den of iniquity is . . . But the, ah, the blowjob is over here, by the ah, potted plant. Now, this blowjob is a mild case compared with this one there. This one decked Dot, isn't this the one that decked you, Dot?

(*Bruce rolls his eyes as Dot pipes up.*)

Bag it, Bruce.

Dot: Eileen, what a thing to say. I have seen worse than that back in Oil City, Pennsylvania. What got to me was that there . . . that fuzzy area,* no, it's not on this one it's on the other one, that . . .

Eileen: Believe me, Senator, this one decked Dot. She was out cold. And Bruce here . . . sick Brucey . . . why, he got all, you know, wiggly, and this after saying how we women get wiggly when we see stuff like that . . . and that . . . and that. Well, just look at Bruce and tell me who the wiggly one is. Bruce there is drooling again, see, and that kind of

abject drooling is as close to
the state of being incurably
wiggly as you can get, yes.
And then there is this one . . .
and this one, and that
one . . . and that . . . and
then this really scary one . . .

Senator: Oh me, oh my.

Eileen: But for my money, this one
is the worst: see it, there?
Because we had a discussion,
Dot and me, and Bruce too,
this was before he got wiggly
when his drooling was under
control, or at least he was
better capable of controlling it.

Senator: Oh my God, will you get a
load of that. Is that, that?

Eileen: Yes, Senator, that is that . . .
And what's worse, Dot and
I surmise that this thing here,
is the thing that is normally
inside here, but—pardon
my French—it got stretched
way out to here by their . . . ah,
exertions. Now, I certainly
wouldn't know, but I do
know that that there is not
supposed to go all the way
there. It is against the law
of nature for a human thing
to be distended like that, all
flared out and in full view,
And that look on her face . . .

Bruce: That is not a look on her
face, that is a look on
his face. Face facts, Eileen.

Eileen: Bag it, Bruce.

Dot: Cripes, Eileen, it's only a picture.

Senator: Dot, that is a picture of an
unnatural act. That is an act
we knew about when I was
growing up, back in Mad Wolf,
but we did not have a name
for. Bruce, are you alright?
Bruce is not alright, Eileen,
get him a glass of water.

Eileen (*Aside*): Dot is the secretary, I am the
Administrative Assistant, why
must I get Bruce the glass of
water, it really bothers me . . .
really, really, really, really . . .

Senator: Dot and Eileen would not be
familiar with a kind of act
of that sort, and I did not
know the name of that act myself,
although I knew it occurred
to people who were not right
in the heads, but the name of
it, I did not want to know
because the name of it was
forbidden. It was unAmerican,
and leads to saggy eyelids,
and if you say to an act
like that . . . calm down, boy,
you are not acting right,
why it will sneer at you
and say: GO TO HELL!
MIND YOUR OWN BEESWAX
BECAUSE I AM HAVING A
FINE OLD TIME,* THANK YOU!

Dot: That's just what I said, sir.
That's exactly* what I said.

Eileen: She said no such thing, Dot
is such an errant exaggerator.
Don't take a word serious, sir.

Dot: Is too, is too, is too, is too . . .

Eileen: BAG IT, DOT.

(*Pause*)

Senator: Cool down, Eileen.

(*Pause*)

And get him out of here.

(*Bruce comes to.*)

All I know is a monster case
of blowjob like that means one
of two things: smear or surveillance . . .
We've got to find out which. Dot . . .

Dot: Yes, sir?

Senator: Call the Reverend and find me the
file we have on Senator So-and-So . . .
our surveillance on his surveillance . . .

Dot: Yes, sir.

Senator: Eileen, help Bruce clean out his desk.

Eileen: Yes, sir.

Bruce: I'm fired?

Senator: Yes, Bruce, fired.

Bruce: But why? WHY?

Dot: But Senator So-and-So died day
before yesterday, sir. You sent
flowers to the widow, sir.

Senator: Flowers to the widow. Indeed I did.

Bruce: But sir, why?

Eileen: Bag it, Bruce.

Senator: Get that pervert out of here, Eileen.*
A blowjob like that's got to be
the tip of the iceberg. Either
smear or surveillance. Good Lord (*Looking*)
would you get a load of that?

Eileen (*Aside*): Dot is the secretary, I am the
Administrative Assistant, why
must I help Bruce clean out his

desk, it really bothers me . . .*
really, really, really, really . . .

Bruce: But why, sir?

Senator: Because you are not right
in the head, Bruce.

ACT 2

(*The same. Eileen. The Senator and Reverend Tom. The
photos are on the table. It is night.*)

Eileen: This is it, Reverend Tom, this is it.
Dot says this is it, this is the
fatal blowjob, the blowjob in question.

Tom: It looks like a pekinese to me.

Senator: You're looking at the wrong part, Tom.
That's the part with the incriminating
thing on its whatsis, the thing out
there, wiggly, that part there.

(*All look hard and long.*)

Tom: No, that cannot be that, that really
cannot be that. Way over there.
Christ in a Christmas tree! I
mean, that defies describing, it
being all the way over there, how
in the name of saltpeter could it get
all stretched out like that . . . wow,
I mean, I seen some things and
you would be amazed what you see
in the God business, because it
sure as hell is a business and it
therefore ought to be run as one, but
the soul—even the precious purity
of the Christian soul, even in
its infrequent state of being
saved, this human soul . . .
is attached to a human body . . .
by a thing, by a thing like

that . . . and there's the rub,
and that rub is where the
trouble starts . . . because
if you rub a thing like that,
a thing like this thing here, (*Points*)
up jumps the devil and the
devil is a creature of rubbing,
touching, stretching and all the
damned contortions the human
body is heir to. It don't matter
what you do about it, you
are in a fallen state and . . .
to look upon a scene like . . .
that one . . . there . . . and that, wow . . .

(*He has to sit down.*)

Eileen: That one is the one that did in
Bruce. That one, and the way
that thing there is. You see the
face between the other parts,
the leer there, on that face . . .
That did in Bruce, Bruce
started to drool at that . . .
That did not have that
effect on me, * though I am
no prissy-type person, but
now this other one, I bet
you didn't see this one, did
you? this one here, this one
did something not right
to me in my head—part . . .
so I refused to look at it,
except for a little peek
every now and then just
to see if it's still there and
if it still has that powerful
effect on me so that my
knees knock and my head
swims and I dare not think
what else is going on, else-
ways and nowhere, where
it shouldn't ought to do.

Tom: Eileen, you are a picture of
what a soul ought to do
to be saved: Not to look at
the devil's work is the mark the
Good Lord leaves on the water,
Eileen. The mark the Good Lord
leaves on the water of life,
Eileen. You will be saved . . .
I believe you will, because . . .
you can resist the cloven
hoof on the forehead of your . . .
wom . . . wom . . . womanliness . . .

Senator: As for that Bruce fuck . . .
The dumb fuck was no damn
fucking good at all . . .

(*Pause*)

As for that Bruce fuck . . .
The dumb fuck was no damn
fucking good. Nobody who ever
didn't go to no goddamn fucking
Bob Jones University was ever
worth an ounce of weasel shit
in the Good Lord's silver spoon.
Tom, he had a pronounced
sado-momo-statistical drive,
and the leanings of this drive
could be observed in the Men's
Room, where he would look
at your pecker, if you were
not careful. That's right: look
right at your pecker. Everybody
who ever went to Bob Jones
University is a fairy and
you ask how I know, I
know: he played tennis.
People who play tennis: fags.
Your typical Bob Jones–type
University-type student: fag.
And that's the fucking truth.

(*Pause*)

I like my flacks Ivy League.
Ivy League flacks may be
faggy, but they know how to
network. Bob Jones University
flacks are fags and don't know
network from netsuke *and* they
are sado-momo-statistical on
top of that, and on top of
that they don't talk good, like
Eileen. Eileen, talk.
Talk some of that good
Ivy League talk for Tom.
Go on, don't be shy.

(*She smiles.*)

Go on . . .

Eileen: I'd be delighted to . . .

Senator: See, Tom, see. That's what
I call high-toned talk. That
kinda talk I like because
that kinda talk is the coin
of the realm when it comes
to networking, ain't it so?

(*Eileen looks embarrassed.*)

She's the modest type, but it's true. So . . .

(*Pause*)

Dot said these photos came from
down the hall. Senator Dick . . .
Dick So-and-So. From the upstate
of his state. The glacial part.
Two days ago he died. Fell
on the floor. Bam. Dead.
It was a monster apoplexy, I hear.
That is what it was I heard:
apoplexy—was it not, Eileen?

Eileen: That's what it was that you
heard, Senator.* At least,
that's what Dot said . . .

Senator: So the question is was it
a case of these photographs
being an instance of him, ah
directing an act of smear
at us, ah, me, my person, or
is it an act of his Surveillance
on the lookout for a something
he thought I ought to know
before he up and kicked off,
like that, bam, on the floor, dead.

(*Pause*)

So it's smear or surveillance
the way I see it. But which . . .

Eileen: That's obviously the way we
all look at it, here, sir.

Senator: Tom, it's an attack on public
morality. And that means you.

Tom: If it's an instance of something
we ought to go public with, we
ought to go public with it
then. But this Senator Dick,
wasn't he one of us, Bob?
I used to get a check from him.
I used to pray with him, at
the Holiday Inn at Beltsville.
Good Christian gentleman, Bob.
And his wife, Maybelle, a fine
Christian lady, a little hard
of hearing and not a looker . . .

Senator: Not a looker is mild, Tom. She's
got a face like a Poland-China hog.

Tom: But Bob, Senator Dick was a fine* man.

Senator: A fag, Tom.

Tom: No, not Dick.

Senator: Senator Dick So-and-So: faggot.

(*Pause*)

It's true, Reverend Tom.

Tom: Indeed, the works of the
Devil exceed the number
of digits in the mind of
an IBM superfast computer.
Praised be the name of the
Lord, Jesus Christ, amen.

Senator: Leastways, that's what I suspect.
He was another pecker-watcher.
He was a confirmed pecker-watcher.

Eileen: But our Surveillance tells us
his Surveillance was busy not
with watching us, but was
busy with watching Bob Junior.

(*Pause*)

Tom: Bob Junior. Who's Bob Junior?

Senator: Tom, you know Bob Junior.

Eileen: You must know Bob Junior.

Senator: My son, Bob.

Tom: Can't recall I do.

(*Pause.*
She looks at the photos.)

Senator: Eileen, stop thinking that thought.

Eileen: I was not thinking that thought.

Tom: What was that? You folks'd
leave a poor man of God to
guess what color the inside
of a polecat's asshole is,* ah . . .

Eileen: Beg your pardon, Reverend?

Senator: Eileen, call Bob Junior.

Eileen: Now, sir? It's ten o'clock.

Senator: Call and tell him to get
his butt here pronto.

Eileen: Okay.

(*She dials.*)

Tom: Now, now, Bob. This don't
smack of no damn smear. Why,
Dick was one of us, our party,
our God, our men's club.
Just because he served in the
other service, and not the
one we are both veterans of
and lived upstate somewhere,
there, of his corruptive state
where people act funny and
are likely to be Jews, colored,
or émigrés from the Pakistani
restaurants of New York City,
and had a slight limp and
a somewhat unnoticeable
speech-impediment owing
to a piece of shrapnel in his
head from the last good war
this country had don't mean moosedick.

Senator: Like hell it don't mean moosedick.
He cheats at poker and is a dyed-
in-the-wool pecker-looker-at-er.
Take it from me: Senator Dick: fag.

Eileen: But the Reverend has a point, Senator.
Why would Senator Dick want to
smear you. It's not a reasonable
supposition. You were close friends.

Senator: That's where Bob Junior comes in, I'm afraid.

(*Bob Junior enters.*)

Eileen: Hi Bob Junior.

Bob Junior: Hi. I'm Bob.

Eileen: I'm Eileen. Remember? From the hog roast?

Bob Junior: Oh yeah. Hi.

(*Pause*)

Hi, Dad.

Senator: Bob Junior this is Tom. Tom, Bob Junior.

Tom: Hello, Bob Junior.

Senator: Don't just stand there like a moron jackoff!
Tom here is deacon of the Television
Church of the Tachistical Wonder
of Jesus Christ, Autodidact. Ain't
it that, Tom? A real TV church.

Tom: Something like that, yes.

(*Pause*)

Eileen: Sit down, Bob Junior.

(*She hands the photos to
the Senator. Pause. He
hands them to Bob Junior.*)

Senator: Bob Junior. Is that you?

Bob Junior: That? No. That is a borzoi.

Senator: Not that, fool. That.

Bob Junior: That thing, there?

Eileen: No, Bob Junior, the Senator means that.
There.

Bob Junior: No, that's not me.

Senator: That looks like me. I mean you.

Bob Junior: That doesn't look like me.

Senator: Bob Junior, come clean. If that's you
just say so. It's okay. But if that's
you, I'll kill you, boy. So come clean,
for your mother's sake.

(*Pause. BobBob Junior enters.
All look a bit puzzled as BobBob
Junior is identical to Bob Junior.*)

BobBob Junior, this is Tom. Tom, BobBob Junior.

Bob Junior: But Dad, that's not me.

Tom: Hello, BobBob Junior.
Bob Junior, are you sure?

Senator: Don't just stand there like a moron jackoff!
Tom here is deacon of the Television
Church of the Tachistical Wonder

of Jesus Christ, Autodidact. Ain't
it that, Tom? A real TV Church.

Eileen: Bob Junior, it's a very vital concern of ours
having to do with a national security matter.

Tom: Something like that, yes.

(*Pause*)

Bob Junior: Eileen, it's not me.

Eileen: Sit down, BobBob Junior.

(*Hands him photos*)

I believe you, Bob Junior.

Senator: BobBob Junior. Is that you?

(*Pause*)

I don't believe you, Bob Junior.

BobBob Junior: That? No. That is a borzoi.

Bob Junior: I know you don't believe
me, Dad. You never believe
me, Dad.

Senator (*To BobBob Junior*): Not that, fool. That.

Tom: The boy's got a point, Bob.
This here, the thing in question
attached to the offending part
over here . . . the part you, Eileen . . .

BobBob Junior: That thing, there?

Eileen: That's the part that decked Dot.

(*Pause*)

No, BobBob Junior, the Senator means
that. There.

Tom: That part only looks that way because
it is not what it looks like . . .

BobBob Junior: No, that's not me.

Senator: What are you driving at, Tom?

(Pause. To BobBob Junior.)

That looks like me. I mean you.

Tom: That thing there is not a blowjob, it's a borzoi.

BobBob Junior: That doesn't look like me.

Senator: Let me see.

(All look hard.)

Hot damn, you may be right. But that does too look like Bob Junior, don't it?

(Pause. To BobBob Junior.)

BobBob Junior, come clean. If that's you just say so. It's okay. But if that's you, I'll kill you, boy. So come clean, for your mother's sake.

Bob Junior: Can I go now, Dad?

BobBob Junior: But Dad, that's not me.

Tom: It looks a little like Bob Junior, but it also looks a little like the Pope.

(Pause. To BobBob Junior.)

BobBob Junior. Are you sure?

Bob Junior: It looks like Dad too.

Eileen: BobBob Junior, it's a very vital concern of ours having to do with a national security matter.

Senator: Shut up, Bob Junior. Here's fifty bucks. Go buy a pair of shoes. Go and buy a pair of normal, American wing-tip shoes and go and throw those faggot shoes away, Bob Junior.

BobBob Junior: Eileen, it's not me.

Bob Junior: Thanks, Dad.

Eileen: I believe you, BobBob Junior. Good-bye, Bob Junior.

Senator: I don't believe you, BobBob Junior.

Bob Junior: Good-bye, Eileen.

BobBob Junior: I know you don't believe
me, Dad. You never believe
me, Dad.

Tom: Good-bye, Bob Junior.

(*Pause. To the Senator.*)

The boy's got a point, Bob.
This there, the thing in question
attached to the offending part
over here . . . the part you, Eileen . . .

Bob Junior: Good-bye, Reverend Tom.

Eileen: That's the part that decked Dot.

Senator: Good-bye, Bob Junior.

Tom: That part only looks that way
because it is not . . .
what it looks like.

Bob Junior: Good-bye, Dad.

Senator: What are you driving at, Tom?

Tom: That thing there is not a blowjob,
it's a borzoi.

Senator: Let me see.

(*Looks hard*)

Hot damn, you may be right. But
that does too look like the Pope.

BobBob Junior: Can I go now, Dad?

Tom: It looks a little like BobBob Junior, but
it also looks a little like the Pope.

BobBob Junior: It looks like Dad too.

Senator: Shut up, BobBob Junior. Here's fifty bucks.
Go buy a pair of shoes. Go and buy a pair
of normal, American wing-tip shoes and go
and throw those faggot shoes away, BobBob Junior.

BobBob Junior: Thanks, Dad.

Bob Junior: Wait a minute, who is this guy? I am Senator Bob's son, not this fraud.

Tom: Don't get all hot under the collar, son.

Senator: It'd take too long to explain, Bob, BobBob.

Eileen: An idea of surveillance, Bob, BobBob.

(*Pause*)

Good-bye, BobBob Junior.

(*An odd pause. BobBob Junior smiles and prepares to go.*)

Eileen: Good-bye, BobBob Junior.

BobBob Junior: Good-bye, Eileen.

Tom: Good-bye, BobBob Junior.

BobBob Junior: Good-bye, Reverend Tom.

Senator: Good-bye, BobBob Junior.

BobBob Junior: Good-bye, Dad.

(*Pause*)

Senator: Good-bye, BobBob.

Good-bye, Bob.

Bob Junior: Good-bye, Bob. Ah . . . Dad.

(*An awkward moment*)

BobBob Junior (*To Bob Junior*): Good-bye, Bob.

Bob Junior: Good-bye, BobBob.

(*Bob and BobBob Junior go out.*)

Senator: It *does* look kinda like the Pope.

Tom: It couldn't be the Pope. He's
still a Christian gentleman—
even if he is fullblown antichrist.

Eileen: Well, I think we can lay to rest
the idea of the thing being a smear.
If it is not Bob Junior it is not a smear.

Senator: Looks like the Pope. With no clothes.

(*Pause*)

That means its surveillance, but
is it his surveillance or ours? Dead
Senator Dick's surveillance, I mean.

Eileen: Maybe this is a matter of a sort
that his surveillance wanted to
let our surveillance know about.

Senator: What's that supposed to mean?
Eileen, please, talk ivy-league.
That kind of talk is not what
I expect of you. That kind of
talk is Bob Jones University
kind of talk and that kind of
talk sucks hind-titty and not
only does it suck hind-titty,
it gets itself fired, like that
fag, Bruce. You recall Bruce?

Eileen: I recall the case of Bruce, sir.
You recall that it was I, sir,
who first told Bruce to bag it, sir.

Tom: Calm down, everybody, let's
not get excited. Indeed,
not only should we all not
get excited but perhaps we
should all get down on
all fours and pray to the
Lord for illumination from
this case of sado-botomy.

(*They all get down.*)

Christ Jesus, hear us, in
our prayers and illumine
the sick pathways of desire
for bad things and cure us
of what we should not
think about if we want to
avoid being chained to the
wall of the State Home for
the Criminally Insane and

Lord Jesus, we have not
gotten excited but have,
as you can plainly see,
gotten down on all fours,
and are praying that you
will come into the foul
pismire that is the human
heart and cleanse it of
the odium of knowing far
too much about the rub,
that soft, seductive rub,
the rub the devil delights
in, and exploits for his
fun and games while we poor,
lost sinners turn upon the
spit and roast in the red-hot
flames of . . . of what . . .
of what has no good name . . .
but might possibly come to
mind, or may be invoked
with reference to these, vile
photos of unnatural acts,
photos of unnatural acts,
capable of rendering a
full-grown man *happy*.

(*Pause*)

Photos of unnatural acts
capable of rendering a
full-grown man happy
should not only not get
us all excited but perhaps . . .
we should stay down on
all fours and pray to the
Good Lord of Stone and Rubble,
the Lord God of Goose Fat,
the Savior of our Common
Dementia, and our need
to be nailed to the Death-Tree
like him, in the Son's agony
against the opaque Father, oh,
we should stay down on
all fours and pray to the

Lord for horripilation at the
mere thought of such an
act, even though, in these
photos the things are not
in actual contact with the
other things, and therefore
the 7 blowjobs are seven
unconsummated blowjobs
but they suggest the worst,
worse than the actual act
would have done did and
had you come up to that
act and said in the voice
of faith: "Blowjob, you
stand in the need of
prayer, so get up off of
your knees, and pull
yourself up by your
underpants like a man
should, and be saved."
That blowjob, being a
child of Satan still in
his or her heart would
leer, and say: "Tom,
GO TO HELL! MIND YOUR
OWN BEESWAX BECAUSE
I AM HAVING A GOOD TIME
THANK YOU!" Thus the fate
of that blowjob would be
sealed, in the full horror
and knowledge of sin, and
photos of unnatural acts,
photos of unnatural acts
capable of rendering a
full-grown man, *happy*!

(*He weeps.*)

Photos of homo-sado-mystical,
maso-sado-momo-dodo, beasto-
lesbo-sado-christmastree, eroto-
catamitical-beasty-phallic-momo-
centric, quasi-sodomitical-eroto-
maniacal-beasty-philo-pro-phallo-

centric, eroto-philo-beasty-centric-
momo-sado-ontological-proto-organistic-
hyper-pan-psycho-super-maniacal-dodo-
gomorrahmy . . .* christmastree . . .

(*Dot enters with beer and pizza.*)

Senator: As for that Bruce fuck
the dumb* fuck was no damn
fucking good at all. . .

Reverend Tom: Hallelujah! Praise the Lord!

(*Pause*)

Eileen: Dot, Dot is back.

Dot: Good lord, whatever has come
over the denizens of the hog
farm? All of you down on
all fours talking about
blowjobs and being happy!
You all are lucky I'm not
with the oppositional party!
This would look like: smear.

(*All get up.*)

Eileen: Bag it, Dot.

(*Pause*)

Dot: Beer and pizza.

Tom: We were consulting the will
of a higher authority, Dot.

Dot: I was chewing the fat with the
receptionist over at dead Senator
Dick's. Her name's Dot too. I'm
Dot White, she's Dot Black. So,
we're sisters under the tablecloth
of receptionist activities . . .

Eileen: Come to the point, Dot.

Dot: It seems dead Senator Dick was
under a surveillance for
his part in a car-park
deal in which his hands

were not clean. Our
surveillance, says the
other receptionist, Dot,
says the hands were
definitely in the till,
so to speak, at the time
of the apocalyptoplectic
attack which ended him.
Dead Senator Dick was no
dummy, he needed an
object of public outrage
for deflection of his own
car-park scam problem.
These photos are art, Dot
says, the other Dot that is,
art funded by a public
agency and performed by
artists in his own state.
Dot does not say how he
came upon these photos,
but only that they were a
contributory cause to his
fatal apocalyptoplectic
demise, God rest his soul.

Senator: Flowers to his widow, Eileen.
Remind me please. Go on, Dot,*
Go on.

Eileen (*Aside*): Dot is the secretary, I am the
Administrative Assistant, why
must I "flowers to his widow"?
him being dead from a picture!
It really, really bothers me . . .*
really, really, really, really . . .

Dot: Dead Senator Dick did not approve
of this art even before it did him
in, much as it did in Bruce—
only worse.* Bag it, Eileen.
Dead Senator Dick did not approve
of this kind of art on the grounds
of not being able to understand the
moral implications touching upon

its wiggly parts, the sheer
touchiness of this and that and
especially the ones that
goosed Bruce and beaned Eileen.

Eileen: One of them decked you too, Dot.

Dot: It did not deck me, Eileen, I
fell over on account of lunch
hour having come and gone and
no lunch—in the bread basket . . .

(*Pause*)

So: the public funding of immoral
art seemed a fine idea of
getting people not to think
of this car-park scam, on
account of how there are
more people in the car-park
scam than in the published
poet and funded immoral
art scam and they all vote.
So you see: it makes sense.
Even the car-park scam victims
hate immoral art more than
car-park scams, or so they
think when they are told how
to think by their moral betters.
That's where you come in,
Reverend Tom. You make the
people think religious thoughts
tending to the re-election of the
saved and eternal damnation
for the published poets, and the
non-elect immoral acts . . .
acts such as these . . .

Tom: You mean these
photos of unnatural acts,
photos of unnatural acts
capable of rendering a
full-grown man happy?

Dot: That is *precisely*
what I mean, Reverend Tom.

Acts such as these, funded
by the American people are
immoral. These acts are
immoral even though in these
photos themselves the things
are not in contact with
the other things, ever,
because they are clever,
the acts I mean and so have
honored the letter of the
law even though what they
suggest is the worst. It
is worse than the actual
act would have done did
had you come up to that
act and said: "Blowjob . . ."

Senator: You can skip that part,* Dot.

Tom: We have more than covered
that topic, Dot. In full.

Dot: So the fact that in these photos,
a thing does not touch any
other thing does not matter
because it's the thought that
counts, as the other Dot says.
And since the author of the
act in question is few and
a faggot, it means the logic
is a circle squared, a perfect
and indestructible argument.
Ipso facto. Carpe diem . . .

(*Pause*)

Only he keeled over dead, did
Senator Dick and left you, Senator
Bob, the legacy of his re-election bid.
He did this having curried your
favor, knowing your principled
dislike of anyone a bit unusual
in the American scheme of things.
You *too* have a re-election bid to
face, and your dislike of anyone

who is a bit unusual, the poor, the
queer, the colored, the women and
others who had their shanties torn
down by Eileen while at Dartmouth
is legend among many of them, the
unusual, I mean, and they are many.
These people do not like you,
Senator Bob, they want your hide.
Ipso facto. I would say
take up the burden of dead
Senator Dick's legacy and run
with it. Reverend Tom can
wrap it in the American flag
of God versus crypto-sado-momo.
And solve *his own* problem of
hands in the till—a matter the
other Dot apprised me of, the
dear. Simply put: it'd be as
easy as shooting whatever
it is you shoot, in the bucket.

(*Long pause.*
Applause.)

Tom: Christ in a tree, she's right.
Bob. She's right. Gee, Bob.

Eileen (*Aside*): Dot is the secretary, I am the
Administrative Assistant, it
really, really bothers me . . .
really, really, really, really . . .

(*They all look at her.*
She falls silent. She smiles.
Pause.)

Senator: I think we got us an agenda here.

Dot: The pizza will turn to plaster.
Eat, Bob eat. Eat, Tom.

Senator: Let's have us a drink. Eileen,
Get us the bourbon. The bourbon
bottle ought to be buried in the
ant farm, somewhere. Pour Dot
a drink, Eileen. We got us a

bona fide agenda here, hot damn.
Pour Dot a drink, Eileen.

(*Eileen does as she's told.*)

Dot you're gonna be my new
Legislative Assistant. I need
a mind like yours to draft all
my restrictive legislation.*
Dot, you got balls. Doesn't
Dot have balls, Tom?

Eileen (*Aside*): Dot is the secretary, I am the
Administrative Assistant, why
must Dot get to be Legislative Assistant?
It really,* really bothers me . . .
really, really, really, really . . .

Tom: Not only does Dot have
balls, she has faith, Bob.
Dot possesses the power
of faith that surpasseth
understanding, a faith
that surpasseth all that
wiggles and likes to be
touched, rubbed, as well as
photos of unnatural acts,
photos of unnatural acts
capable of rendering a
full-grown man *happy*!

Eileen: But Dot is not a lawyer,
Senator.

Senator: Eileen, it's like the good book
says: Ignorance of the law
is nine-tenths of the law.
Here's to Dot and the war
against International Faggotry.

(*All drink.*
A slow blackout begins.)

Betcha didn't know: George Bush?
Fag. Ronald Reagan: a faggot.
General Schwartzkopf: a fairy.

Senator Orrin Hatch: a damned
homosexual. Alphonse D'Amato:
a flagrant queen. Gerald Ford:
fag. Richard Nixon: faggot.
General Dwight David
Eisenhower: fag. Woodrow
Wilson: queer as a three-
dollar bill. Abraham Lincoln:
a faggot. George Washington:
a confirmed sodomite . . .
Napoleon Bonaparte: fag.
Frederick the Great: fag.
William the Silent: fag.
Norman Conquest: fag.
Julius Caesar: faggot.
Alexander the Great: you guess . . .
Cain and Abel? faggots.

(*Total darkness*)

END OF PLAY

Contributors

Allan Havis earned an M.F.A. from the Yale School of Drama and heads the M.F.A. playwriting program at the University of California at San Diego. His plays have been produced nationally by Seattle's ACT (A Contemporary Theatre), Mixed Blood Theatre, Long Wharf Theatre, L.A.'s Odyssey Theatre Ensemble, Hartford Stage, American Repertory Theatre, South Coast Repertory, Virginia Stage Company, The Philadelphia Theatre Company, Berkshire Theatre Festival, the Ohio Theatre, Ensemble Studio Theatre, and Home for the Contemporary Arts. He has also directed his plays at WPA, the West Bank Cafe, and BACA. Havis's *Morocco* received the 1985 Foundation of Dramatists Guild/CBS Award, the 1986 Playwrights USA Award from HBO, and a 1987 Kennedy Center/American Express Grant, and a number of his plays, including *Morocco, Hospitality, Mink Sonata, Haut Gout, Lilith, A Vow of Silence, Sainte Simone, The Ladies of Fisher Cove,* and *A Daring Bride* have been published in various anthologies. Play commissions have come from Ted Danson's Anasazi Productions, Mixed Blood Theatre, Sundance, England's Chichester Festival, South Coast Rep, and Classic Stage Company Repertory. In addition, Havis has received fellowships from the Guggenheim Foundation, the Rockefeller Foundation, the McKnight Foundation, and the National Endowment for the Arts and grants from California and New York State arts agencies. He is also the author of a children's novel, *Albert the Astronomer,* published by Harper and Row.

Velina Hasu Houston is an associate professor, resident playwright, and director of the playwriting program at the University of Southern California School of Theatre. She is also a member of the Writers Guild of

America West and the Dramatists Guild and is an artistic associate at the Sacramento Theatre Company. Her signature play *Tea* has been produced internationally to popular and critical acclaim. Houston's other plays include the PEN Center USA West–honored *Cultivated Lives, Ikebana, Necessities, Asa Ga Kimashita, As Sometimes in a Dead Man's Face, The Matsuyama Mirror, Hula Heart,* and *Sentimental Education.* Her plays have been commissioned by the Mark Taper Forum, the Manhattan Theatre Club, the Asia Society, the Honolulu Theatre for Youth, the Lila Wallace–Readers Digest Foundation New Generations Play Project, Dr. Juli Thompson Burk, the Kennedy Theatre, the State of Hawai'i Foundation on Culture and the Arts, and the Cornerstone Theatre Company. They have been presented by Pasedena Playhouse, Old Globe Theatre, Manhattan Theatre Club, Syracuse Stage, the Smithsonian Institution, the Whole Theatre (Olympia Dukakis, producer), Japan Society, National Public Radio, the NHK Nippon Hoso Kai, Negro Ensemble Company, Odyssey Theatre Ensemble, Lincoln Center Institute, and the Purple Rose Theatre (Jeff Daniels, producer). Houston has also written for Columbia Pictures, Sidney Poitier, the Public Broadcasting Service, Lancit Media, and several indie producers. Her critical essays and poetry have been published in various journals and anthologies, as have her plays, and she has edited two anthologies of Asian American drama, *The Politics of Life* (1993) and *But Still, Like Air, I'll Rise* (1997), both published by Temple University Press. Houston's awards include the Remy Martin New Vision Award in screenwriting from Sidney Poitier and the American Film Institute, a California Arts Council fellowship, the Japanese American Woman of Merit 1890–1990 by the National Japanese American Historical Society, and two Rockefeller Foundation fellowships.

Russell Lees is from Salt Lake City, where he acted and directed extensively with TheatreWorks/West. He studied playwriting at Boston University under the Nobel laureate Derek Walcott and served as director of ImprovBoston and as director-in-residence of the Boston Playwrights' Theatre. He has also worked with the 52nd Street Project in New York City. Lees's produced plays include *The Case of the Blue Narcissus, The Shepherds Play, The Foggiest Notion, Lost Scene from "Cyrano,"* and *The Fatwah Caprice.*

Suzan-Lori Parks, a two-time Obie Award winner, is an associate artist at the Yale School of Drama and a member of the theater program faculty at the California Institute of the Arts. She first gained national attention with *Imperceptible Mutabilities in the Third Kingdom* (1989), produced at Brooklyn's BACA Downtown. *The Death of the Last Black Man in the Whole Entire World* was also produced at BACA and was subsequently seen at Yale Repertory Theatre. A collection of Park's plays and essays, *The America Play and Other Works*, was published by the Theatre Communication Group, and her play *In the Blood* was a finalist for the Pulitzer Prize in 2000. Her other produced plays, several of which have premiered at Yale Repertory Theatre and the New York Shakespeare Festival, include *Betting on the Dust Commander, The Sinner's Place, Fishes, Devotees in the Garden of Love, Venus, Topdog/Underdog,* and *Fucking A.* Parks is also the author of screenplays for Spike Lee (*Girl 6*), Jodie Foster, and the novel *Telephone Game.* She is the recipient of a Whiting Foundation Writers Award, two National Endowment for the Arts fellowships, and grants from the Rockefeller Foundation, the Ford Foundation, the Kennedy Center Fund for New Plays, the New York State Council on the Arts, and the New York Foundation for the Arts.

José Rivera is the author of the Obie Award–winning play *Marisol*, as well as *Cloud Tectonics, Each Day Dies with Sleep, The Promise, The House of Ramon Iglesia, Giants Have Us in Their Books, The Street of the Sun, Sonnets for an Old Century, References to Salvador Dali Make Me Hot, Sueño,* and *Lovers of Long Red Hair.* His plays have been produced nationally by the La Jolla Playhouse, the Joseph Papp Public Theatre, Playwrights Horizons, Berkeley Repertory, Circle Repertory, Los Angeles Theatre Center, Ensemble Studio Theatre, the Magic Theatre, Mark Taper Forum, Greenway Arts Alliance, South Coast Repertory, Hartford Stage, Manhattan Class Company, and the Humana Festival. The Puerto Rican–born Rivera has studied with the Nobel Prize–winning writer Gabriel García Marquez at the Sundance Institute and has been a writer-in-residence at the Royal Court Theatre, London. His work has been generously supported by the Kennedy Center Fund for New American Plays, the National Arts Club, the National Endowment for the Arts, the Rockefeller Foundation, the New

York Foundation for the Arts, the Fulbright Commission, PEN West, and the Whiting Foundation. Television credits include co-creating and producing the critically acclaimed NBC series "Eerie, Indiana," and his play *The House of Ramon Iglesia* appeard on the PBS series "American Playhouse." Rivera's film credits include: *The Jungle Book: Mowgli's Story, Mr. Shadow,* and *Family Matters,* all for Disney, and the screenplay for the IMAX film *Riding the Comet* for Sony. Recent theater and film projects include *Brainpeople* (commissioned by South Coast Repertory), *Adoration of the Old Woman* (commissioned by La Jolla Playhouse), and the films *A Bolero for the Disenchanted* (Showtime), *Somewhere in Time, II* (Universal Home Video), *The Motorcycle Diaries* (Robert Redford's Wildwood Company), and *Lucky* (Interscope Pictures).

Naomi Wallace, who makes her home in Kentucky and England, is the award-winning playwright of *Slaughter City* (the 1995 Mobil Prize), *In the Heart of America* (the 1995 Susan Smith Blackburn Prize), *One Flea Spare* (the 1996 Susan Smith Blackburn Prize, the 1996 Fellowship of Southern Writers Drama Award, the 1996 Kesselring Prize, and the 1997 Obie Award for Best Play), and *Birdy,* a stage adaptation of William Wharton's novel that opened in 1997 on London's East End and simultaneously in Athens. Her plays have been produced by the Actors Theatre of Louisville, the New York Theatre Workshop, the Edinburg Theatre, London's Bush Theatre, the New York Shakespeare Festival, the Comedy Theatre (London), the Royal Shakespeare Company, and Long Wharf Theatre. Her most recent play, *Fugitive Cant,* will be produced by the Oxford Stage Company in 2002. Wallace's plays are published in Great Britain by Faber and Faber and in the United States by Broadway Play Publishing. She is also a published poet in both England (*To Dance a Stony Field,* 1995) and the United States and has received grants from the Kentucky Foundation for Women, the Kentucky Arts Council, and the National Endowment for the Arts. Her film *Lawn Dogs,* produced by Duncan Kenworthy, opened successfully in England, moved to the United States, and has won numerous awards. She and co-writer Bruce McLeod have adapted *The War Boys* for film, scheduled for production in 2001. She has also adapted for film Carolyn Haines's novel *Touched.* Wallace, who received a prestigious MacArthur Fellowship in 1999, is under commission by the Royal Shakespeare Company, the New York Shakespeare Festival, and the Actors Theatre of Louisville.

Mac Wellman is the Obie Award–winning playwright of *Bad Penny, Terminal Hip, Crowbar,* and *Sincerity Forever,* as well as *Cat's-Paw, Infrared, Fnu Lnu, The Sandalwood Box, Second-Hand Smoke, The Lesser Magoo,* and *Girl Gone.* He has also directed *I Don't Know Who He Was, and I Don't Know What He Said* as part of a four-month Mac Wellman Festival at New York's House of Candles and elsewhere. He has received numerous honors, including a Lila Wallace–Readers Digest Writer's Award, and is a recipient of both National Endowment for the Arts and Guggenheim fellowships. Three collections of Wellman's plays have been published: *The Bad Infinity* (Performing Arts Journal/Johns Hopkins University Press) and *Two Plays* and *The Land Beyond the Forest* (both from Sun & Moon Press). He is also the author of a collection of poetry, *A Shelf in Woop's Clothing,* and two novels, *The Fortuneteller* and *Annie Salem.*

The University of Illinois Press

is a founding member of the

Association of American University Presses.

———————————————————————

Composed in 10.5/12.5 Trump Mediaeval

with Meta display

by Jim Proefrock

at the University of Illinois Press

Designed by Copenhaver Cumpston

Manufactured by Thomson-Shore, Inc.

University of Illinois Press

1325 South Oak Street

Champaign, IL 61820-6903

www.press.uillinois.edu

5600